来往车辆（一、道路交通 7）

路口让行（一、道路交通 6）

机场包裹规定（二、机场航班 12）

咪表说明（三、停车指示 22）

博物馆停车说明（三、停车指示 38）

出租车价格（五、出租汽车1）

停车警示（三、停车指示29）

自行车停车标示（七、非机动车2）

自动扶梯说明（八、电梯安全4）

自动售货机说明（九、自动售货机5）

校园免费电话说明（十、电话说明9）　　投币电话说明（十、电话说明8）

恶意火警（十五、消防报警7）

露天咖啡厅（十三、餐饮服务36）　有辐射房间说明（十四、安全卫生10）

大楼入口说明（十七、大门管理16）

公园入口说明（十九、公德告示11） 大门说明（十七、大门管理33）

遛狗（十九、公德告示28） 华盛顿纪念碑安全（二十、旅游景点62）

新世纪美国公示语 1000 例

周一兵 编著

北京大学出版社
PEKING UNIVERSITY PRESS

图书在版编目(CIP)数据

新世纪美国公示语 1000 例/周一兵编著. —北京：北京大学出版社，2012.3
(英语好学系列)
ISBN 978-7-301-19934-3

Ⅰ. ①新… Ⅱ. ①周 Ⅲ. ①标志－英语 Ⅳ. ①H31

中国版本图书馆 CIP 数据核字(2011)第 265104 号

书　　　　名：	新世纪美国公示语 1000 例
著作责任者：	周一兵　编著
责 任 编 辑：	黄瑞明
标 准 书 号：	ISBN 978-7-301-19934-3/H · 2984
出 版 发 行：	北京大学出版社
地　　　　址：	北京市海淀区成府路 205 号　100871
网　　　　址：	http://www.pup.cn　电子信箱：zpup@pup.pku.edu.cn
电　　　　话：	邮购部 62752015　发行部 62750672　编辑部 62754382
	出版部 62754962
印　刷　者：	三河市博文印刷厂
经　销　者：	新华书店
	787 毫米×1092 毫米　16 开本　15.75 印张　233 千字
	2012 年 3 月第 1 版　2012 年 3 月第 1 次印刷
定　　　　价：	38.00 元

未经许可，不得以任何方式复制或抄袭本书之部分或全部内容。
版权所有，侵权必究
举报电话：(010)62752024　电子信箱：fd@pup.pku.edu.cn

前　言

　　几年前在美国短期学习期间，发现公共场合有很多标识语，于是信手拍下了4000多张相关资料，后来我又请前往北美的同事收集了一些，通过筛选归类，精选出了约1000个有代表性的标识语辑录成书。希望能够通过这些真实的材料比较全面地反映出美国日常生活中标识语的特点，同时也希望能够对国内标识语的翻译起到一个提示或者引导作用，为国内英语标识语的规范使用尽微薄之力。另外，也希望本书能够对即将赴美学习或旅游的中国人具有一定的实用价值。

　　本书中的标识语是广义上的，实际上这里出现的食品说明、门票等从严格意义上来说并不能归结为标识语。因此全书在分类上主要根据重点、数量、适切等方面进行归类，其中有些章节的内容是互相交叉的。根据类型，全书分为39个单元。书中的每个标识语一般通过其使用场所、大意以及有关文化背景方面进行阐述，内容简单的就相应减少说明。

　　由于篇幅、成本等原因，本书未使用所拍摄的相片，而是将所摄图片内容全文誊录下来。在誊录过程中，文字基本保持原来的内容，但字体的大小、对齐等方面不完全按原始格式出现。标识语中所使用的图形等基本不再使用。

　　在编写的过程中，本书总体构架和内容得到了周建中老师的支持，他长期为上海市政府法制办翻译法律文件，在百忙之中精心修改了全部书稿，并提出宝贵的意见和建议，在此表示诚挚的感谢。

　　美国标识语的内容宽泛庞杂，然而编者水平有限，错误与不当之处在所难免，敬请读者不吝指正。

编者

2011年3月26日于北洋园

目 录

一、道路交通 …………………………………………（1）
二、机场航班 …………………………………………（10）
三、停车指示 …………………………………………（15）
四、巴士站台 …………………………………………（25）
五、出租汽车 …………………………………………（30）
六、火车地铁 …………………………………………（32）
七、非机动车 …………………………………………（35）
八、电梯安全 …………………………………………（37）
九、自动售货机 ………………………………………（39）
十、电话说明 …………………………………………（42）
十一、厨房用具 ………………………………………（46）
十二、洗衣烘干 ………………………………………（48）
十三、餐饮服务 ………………………………………（50）
十四、安全卫生 ………………………………………（59）
十五、消防报警 ………………………………………（72）
十六、吸烟管理 ………………………………………（78）
十七、大门管理 ………………………………………（80）
十八、饮酒枪支 ………………………………………（86）
十九、公德告示 ………………………………………（90）
二十、旅游景点 ………………………………………（95）
二十一、纪念文字 ……………………………………（119）
二十二、购票说明 ……………………………………（133）
二十三、博物馆 ………………………………………（143）
二十四、超市商店 ……………………………………（155）
二十五、临时告示 ……………………………………（172）
二十六、办公场所 ……………………………………（177）

二十七、邮政服务 ………………………………（179）
二十八、图书馆 …………………………………（184）
二十九、医院诊所 ………………………………（193）
三十、体育场馆 …………………………………（201）
三十一、影院剧院 ………………………………（204）
三十二、学校 ……………………………………（209）
三十三、施工工地 ………………………………（215）
三十四、教堂墓地 ………………………………（217）
三十五、酒店旅馆 ………………………………（220）
三十六、奖励通告 ………………………………（226）
三十七、救助 ……………………………………（229）
三十八、幽默告示 ………………………………（232）
三十九、其他 ……………………………………（235）

一、道路交通

1
PUSH BUTTON
WAIT FOR WALK SIGNAL

按下按钮，等待过路信号。
（路口手动红绿灯提示说明）

2
NO PARKING OR STANDING
FIRE LANE

消防通道，不准停车或稍作停留。
（超市门口机动车有关通道使用的说明）

3
SIDEWALK CROSSED
→
CROSS HERE

人行道关闭
从这里通过
（路口告示牌）

4
CYCLING	WALKING
SKATING	RUNNING
←	→
BIKEWAY	WALKWAY

纽约道路说明。箭头和文字指明一边用于骑自行车和滑滚轴鞋，另一边用于步行和跑步。

5
TO CROSS STREET PUSH BUTTON
WAIT FOR WALK SIGNAL

过马路按信号灯
通行灯亮再通过
（路口手动红绿灯的提示说明）

6
STATE LAW
STOP
FOR PEDESTRIANS IN CROSSWALK

本州法律规定
十字路口避让行人
（交通告示牌）

7

CAUTION ON-COMING TRAFFIC

小心过往车辆
（人行道口文字提示）

8

This Fleet Is Equipped With
Global Tracking System

本车安装全球定位系统
（运货卡车上的说明。车载全球定位系统是为了保证司机安全。）

9

E/Z Pass
Can be Used in any
Toll Lane

高速公路简易通行证可以在任意一条通道上使用
（公路上接近收费站前的说明。E/Z表示easy，即在收费站的任何一条通道上使用easy pass（高速公路简易通行证）可以迅速通过。在美国，为了简易以及表达方式新颖，经常会在标识语中使用字母来代替一个词。）

10

Narrow Shoulder

路肩
（高速公路上表示车道变窄的说明。路肩，英文叫SHOULDER，一般指的是高速公路两边的比正常的行车道略窄的通道，就像人的肩膀一样。较老的道路有时只有一边才有SHOULDER（肩）或没有路肩。另外，沥青水泥铺的叫硬路肩（HARD SHOULDER），没有铺过的叫软路肩（SOFT SHOULDER）。）

11

Yield

让行

12

Slower Traffic Keep Right
Toll Booths
Caution Toll Plaza Ahead 1 Mile

慢行车辆靠右行驶，离收费站及停车区域还有1英里。
（高速公路上前方收费站的提示）

一、道路交通

13　Stop

路口停车标志牌。这是美国十字路口的一个交通规则：在没有任何红绿灯的路口，所有车辆到达之后一定要先停下来，先停下来的车辆，或者说先到达的车辆就先行，极少会发生在路口因为抢行而撞车的事故。

14　Fast Lane　Keep Right　No Turns

快速车道　靠右行驶　严禁转弯
（公路指示牌）

15　Left Shift Ahead

前方左转

16　Reduce Speed Ahead

前方减速

17　Truck Test Brakes

测试卡车刹车带
（公路上快要到陡坡路段时提示司机检测刹车，以免出现安全事故。）

18　Trucks Use Low Gear

卡车车道　低档速度
（行车道标志牌。在下滑的路面上提示卡车司机使用低速档。）

19　Buckle Up It's the Law

扣上安全带
这是法律规定
（公路上提示司机系安全带的标识。在美国高速公路上这样的标识很多，时时刻刻提醒司机要系安全带。）

3

新世纪美国公示语 1000 例

20

Utility Ahead

前方水电施工
（路面施工指示牌）

21

Household Moves

搬家用车
（箱式卡车身上的文字，表示该车是搬家公司的。美国各州规定搬家公司车辆必须使用箱式卡车。）

22

Business Rentals

商务租赁
（车身上的文字）

23

This is a Sidewalk
Pedestrians Yield To Traffic

这里是人行道
行人避让车辆
（道路提示牌）

24

CROSS TO HERE
ON THIS SIGNAL

请看到信号再从这里过马路
（路口的标识牌。为了醒目，使用了 TO HERE 这种不规范的语言。道路指示牌中常使用一些不太规范，但是又容易看懂的文字。）

25

WARNING
PHONOSCOPE BURIED FIBER
OPTIC CABLE
BEFORE DIGGING ANYWHERE
IN THIS AREA CALL 1-713-272-4600

注意！
地下埋设光缆，在本地区掘土之前要与有关部门联系。
（地下电缆警告）

一、道路交通

26

| Weigh Station
1 Mile | 磅站
距离1英里
（公路指示牌。在美国的高速公路上，走上一段路程就会看见牌子提示前方有称量卡车的磅站。） |

27

| Watch for Ramp Traffic | 请注意匝道上的车辆
（公路警示牌） |

28

| Right Lane
Must Turn Right | 右行车辆必须向右转
（公路上转弯提示牌。为了让司机以最快的速度看懂看清提示牌，交通指示经常使用不符合语法的文字来表达。如果使用比较正规的英语来表达，则应该是If you are driving on the right lane, you must turn right。） |

29

| Fallen Rock Zone | 落石区域
（高速公路上的指示文字） |

30

| NO THRU TRUCKS | 禁止卡车通行
（交通标志。thru代表through。） |

31

| ◆ RIGHT LANE
BUSSES AND RIGHT TURNS ONLY
7AM－6 PM MON－FRI | 右车道每周一至周五上午7点至下午6点只能通行公共汽车和右转弯
（车道提示） |

5

新世纪美国公示语1000例

32.
LANE ENDS
MERGE RIGHT

车道截止
向右并道
（道路指示）

33.
USE CROSS WALK

请走人行横道
（道路指示牌）

34.
NO BICYCLING SKATEBOARDING ROLLER SKATING ON SIDEWALK

请勿在人行横道上骑自行车、溜滑板和滑四轮冰鞋
（道路指示说明）

35.
EXCEPT VEHICLES WITH PERMIT
ACTIVE LOADING & UNLOADING
COMMERCIAL PASSENGER
MIDNIGHT TO 3:30 PM
FREIGHT 5:30 PM TO MIDNIGHT

除非有特许停车证，一切车辆停车后立即离开。
商务乘客午夜至下午3:30，货物车辆下午5:30至午夜。
（道路停车标志牌）

36.
CLEARANCE AT CENTER
13 FEET

中部净高13英尺
（道路桥梁净高说明。13英尺约等于3.96米。）

37.
NO RIDING ON WALKWAYS

人行道上禁止行车

38.
PEDESTRIANS
PROHIBITED THIS SIDE

桥栏杆以外禁止行人
（有人找刺激在桥栏杆外行走，故有如此告示。）

一、道路交通

39 | NO TURN ON RED | 红灯时请勿转弯

40 | TURNING VEHICLES YIELD TO PEDESTRIANS | 转弯车辆避让行人

41 | NO PARKING ON BRIDGE | 桥上禁停车辆

42 | NO FISHING FROM BRIDGE | 请勿在桥上钓鱼

43 | CAUTION WATER ON ROAD DURING RAIN | 小心，下雨路上积水。

44 | Seat Belts Must Be Worn | 必须系上安全带

45 | PARK UNDER BILLBOARD AT YOUR OWN RISK. (PIGEON DROPPINGS) | 广告牌下停车 鸽粪掉落自负

46 | TOLL PLAZA – 1.5 MILES
TOLL RATES
AXLE VEHICLES $2.50
EA. ADDITIONAL AXLE $2.50
| 收费站，前方1.5英里
收费标准
带斗车2.5美元
每增加一个斗加收2.5美元
（高速公路即将到达收费站的说明）

47

LAST EXIT BEFORE TOLL

收费站前的最后一个出口

（进入高速公路入口前路口说明。在美国高速公路收费的比较少，一般在网络上还会专门告知司机如何避让收费公路，所以在进入收费公路以前往往都会有一个人性化的提示。）

48

**NOTICE
ALL VEHICLES OVER 5T GVW
MUST USE 2 RIGHT LANES**

车辆总重量超过5吨必须使用两条右车道

（GVW全称为gross vehicle weight，表示"车辆总重量"。）

49

**GOLDEN GATE BRIDGE
MAIN SPAN: 4,200 FEET
LENGTH OF ONE CABLE: 7,650 FT. (2,331.7m)
DIAMETER OF ONE CABLE: 363/6IN. (92.4m)
WIRES IN EACH CABLE: 27,572
TOTAL WIRE USED: 80,000 MILES (128,748 km)
WEIGHT OF CABLE (SUSPENSERS & ACCESSORIES) 24,500 TONS
(22,226 m. tons)**

金门大桥

主跨度4,200英尺
单根缆绳长度：7,650英尺（2,331.72米）
单根缆绳直径：36 3/6英寸（92.4米）
每根缆绳中缆线：27,572条
所用缆线总长度：80,000英里（128,748公里）
缆绳和附件的重量（suspensors and accessories）：24,500吨（22,226公吨）。

（美国金门大桥说明。其中m. tons相当于metric tons，表示"公吨"。金门大桥建于1937年，耗资300万美元，是世界上最大的单孔吊桥之一。大桥两端有两座高达227米的桥塔，橘黄色的桥梁两端矗立着钢柱，用粗钢索相连，钢索中点下垂，几乎接近桥身，钢索和桥身用一根根细钢绳连接起来，使整座大桥显得朴素无华而又雄伟壮观。金门桥是世界上最繁忙的桥梁之一，每天约有10万辆汽车从桥上驶过。）

一、道路交通

50
CRISIS COUNSELING
THERE IS HOPE
MAKE THE CALL.
THE CONSEQUENCES
OF JUMPING FROM
THIS BRIDGE ARE
FATAL AND TRAGIC

危难咨询
希望尚有，请拨电话。
从这座桥上跳下的后果是致命的，悲惨的。
（美国金门大桥上对自杀者的劝说文字。自从1937年建成以来，金门大桥上已经有超过1,200人在此结束了自己宝贵的生命——旧金山金门大桥因此成为世界上"最要命的旅游景点"。大桥上的这块提示牌是为了在最后一刻挽救轻生者。）

51
STOP FOR ME IT'S THE LAW!

请为我停车，这是法律规定！
（斑马线附近的文字提示）

52
NO ENGINE IDLING
MAX FINE $2,000

禁止车辆引擎空转
最高罚款2,000美元
（纽约时代广场上的一个标志牌。车辆不熄火，引擎空转，除浪费汽油，还会排放更多废气，污染环境。）

53
SLOW AMPHIBIAN CROSSING
MARCH THRU JUNE

慢行！三月至六月之间，公路上会有爬行动物通过。
（公路上对司机的提示）

54
LOOK BOTH WAYS

请注意两边车辆
（人行道口的文字提示）

55
DON'T HONK
$350 PENALTY

请勿鸣笛
违者罚款350美元
（道路行车说明）

56
STAY IN LANE

请勿并道
（纽约荷兰隧道口入口电子牌说明）

新世纪美国公示语1000例

二 机场航班

1

To Baggage Claim
To Domestic Ticketing
To Ground Transportation

通往行李提取
通往国内航班购票
通往地面交通
（这类标志一般附有方向箭头）

2

CONTINENTAL AIRLINES
LEGEND

Concessions
Continental Airlines
Service Center
Defibrillator AED
Elevator to Restaurant
Emergency Exit Stairs

Men's Restroom
Women's Restroom
Family Restroom
Moving Sidewalk
Telephone

美国大陆航空公司图示上的内容。旅客可以通过图上所示找到办理机票的地方、航空公司的服务中心、旅客心脏急救、通往饭店的电梯、紧急出口楼梯、男女卫生间、家庭卫生间、自动走道、电话等内容。Legend表示"图示"。

3

Please check monitors for your flight, terminal and gate.

请核对显示屏上航班、终点站和登机口
（登机口提示文字）

4

WARNING RIDE SAFE
Refuse offers for transportation from "helpful strangers,"
they may be illegal operators.
Report all violators to the nearest uniformed officer or Airport employee.

安全搭乘警示
拒绝陌生人帮助提供运输，他们可能是非法运营者。就近向穿制服的警官或机场工作人员举报。
（机场安全提示）

二、机场航班

5

IMPORTANT
Many bags look alike.
Please claim your bag by the claim check number.
ATTENTION
You may claim golf clubs, sport equipment, and oversize items at slide #11.
PLEASE NOTE
In the course of handling, your baggage will have evidence of use, such as, minor cuts, scratches, scuffs, dents and soil. Continental Airlines is not responsible for conditions that result from normal wear and tear or the following:
- Damage to wheels, feet, extending handles, over packed bags and items of a fragile or perishable nature
- Loss of external locks, pull straps and security straps
- Manufacturer's defects

重要提示
旅行包多数相似，
请按行李号码认领行李。
注意
高尔夫球杆、运动器材或超大的行李可在11号行李滑道上领取。
请注意
行李托运过程中可能会出现小口子、划痕、磨损、凹痕和弄脏。大陆航空公司对正常磨损情况，箱轮、箱脚、箱杆、塞得过满的包裹损坏、易碎易烂物品损坏变质、外锁、拖带、扣带等脱落以及产品缺陷概不负责。
（机场对包裹托运的提示）

6

CREDIT AND DEBIT CARDS ACCEPTED

本机接受信用卡和借记卡
（信用卡可以透支，而借记卡不可透支。在美国超市，柜台结账可直接办理借记卡。）

7

| COINS | CREDIT CARDS | Change given for amount over purchase BILLS |

$ 3.00　1. Insert payment
　　　　2. Pull cart out
For customer service call
　1-800-328-9006
Please refer to unit number

美国机场手推车租用说明。在美国机场使用行李手推车需支付3美元的费用。这里机器上一共显示三种支付方式：投入硬币(COINS)；刷信用卡(CREDIT CARDS)；塞入纸币(BILLS)，纸币找零。但是不管哪一种方式，旅客都要先付款，然后再将手推车拉出。在下方还提供了免费电话号码，一旦有问题，要报告机器的号码，这样服务人员可以根据号码知道具体位置以尽快处理问题。

8

SHOE SHINE	
MEN-WOMEN	
SHOES	$4.00
BOOTS	$5.00
BELT	$4.00
BRIEFCASE	$5.00
FREE SHOE SHINE IF WE FAIL TO SIGN YOU IN	
PHONE (281)443-2742	

擦皮鞋
男士—女士
擦皮鞋、靴子、皮带和皮箱的标价
（小费不在内）
免费擦鞋
如未示意进入，拨打电话
（281）443-2742。
（机场内擦鞋子等的标志）

9

Baggage Claim

行李提取处

10

Domestic Baggage Claim
Elevator to Ticketing/ Gates
Car Rentals   Restrooms

国内航班行李提取处
电梯通往购票处、大门、租车处和洗手间

11

Lost Baggage Retrieval
1-800-699-2005
www.laovernight.com

取回丢失行李，联系电话1-800-699-2005。
（据美国官方统计，美国国内航班，每天旅客在机场丢失的行李达一万件左右。）

12

Baggage Weight Allowances
Checked baggage to/ from/ between all Continental Domestic and International Destinations, and flights departing Guam and Saipan.
COACH CLASS DOMESTIC AND INTERNATIONAL WEIGHT LIMITATIONS AND CHARGES

Up to 50lbs.(23kgs.)   —FREE
Over 50lbs.(23kgs.) up to 70lbs. (32kgs.)   —$25.00 USD
Over 70lbs. (32kgs.) up to 100lbs.(45.5kgs.)   —applicable overweight fee
Items over 100 lbs. are not accepted as checked baggage.
If you think your bag may weigh over 50lbs., please use the scale to verify.

允许携带包裹重量
本入口所检包裹包括前往/来自/往来国内国际的大陆航空公司目的地航班，包括前往关岛和塞班岛航班。
普通舱国内和国际航班行李重量规定和收费标准
50磅（23公斤）以下免费，50-70磅（23-32公斤）收费25美元，

70–100磅（32-45.5公斤），按相应超重收取费用。100磅以上物件不作托运行李。如行李可能超过50磅，请使用磅秤核实。
（机场有关行李重量的规定。coach class相当于economy class；头等舱(first class)和商务舱(business class) 对行李重量的规定相应放宽一些。）

13
Property of the U. S. Government
DO NOT REMOVE OR DEFACE
VIOLATORS ARE SUBJECT TO PENALTIES UNDER FEDERAL LAW

美国政府财产
请勿移动或损毁
违者按联邦法惩处
（机场财产标签说明）

14
ATTENTION
NO LIGHTERS are permitted beyond the Security Checkpoint. Hazardous materials, including lighters with fuel and matches, are prohibited in checked baggage.

注意
禁止打火机带过安检点
危险材料包括带汽油的打火机和火柴禁止放入检查过的行李中
（安检提示）

15
Passengers or Authorized Persons Only
Passengers must present a BOARDING PASS and PHOTO IDENTIFICATION
Your bags may be searched at any time.

乘客或经授权的人进入
乘客需出示登机卡和带相片身份证明
包裹随时会被检查

16
↑ Gates 60 62 thru 69 Restrooms
↙ Gift Shop Newsstand Snack Bar Cocktails

通往60号、62号到69号登机口
洗手间 礼品店 报刊亭 小吃店 鸡尾酒店
（机场通往各处的指示牌上的文字）

17
RESTRICTED AREA
TRESPASSING/ LOITERING PROHIBITED BY LAW
ALL AUTHORIZED PERSONNEL MUST DISPLAY ID BADGE BEYOND THIS POINT

限制区
法律禁止侵入/徘徊
经授权的人员必须出示身份识别卡
方可进入

新世纪美国公示语 **1000** 例

18

| RESTRICTED AREA UNAUTHORIZED PERSONS NOT PERMITTED BEYOND THIS POINT L.A. CITY ORDINANCE NO 95-789 | 限制区 未经授权的人员不得超越此点 洛杉矶市第95-789号条例 （美国是法治国家，很多标志语会提供法律依据。） |

19

| Newspapers on Sale | 机场内自动售报处的文字说明。 |

20

| Classic Shoe Shine Valet Shoes $5.00 Boots $7.00 Hours: Sun – Fri: 6am to 7pm; Sat: 6am to 1pm | 一流擦鞋服务 皮鞋5美元；皮靴7美元。 时间：周日至周五早6点至晚7点 周六早6点至下午1点 （机场擦鞋广告牌） |

21

| Diaper Changing Station | 尿布更换处 （美国机场都有给孩子换尿布的房间） |

22

| New FAA Regulation Limits Carry-On Baggage To 1 Piece. It Must Be Of A Size To Fit Under Your Seat Or In The Overhead Compartment. Excess Pieces Must Be Checked. | 联邦航空局新规定：随身行李为一件。必须能放入座位下或头顶上的行李箱内，超额物件须经检查。 （登机前告示） |

23

| This portion of the boarding pass should be retained as evidence of your journey. | 登机牌的这部分要留作旅行证据 （飞机登机牌上说明） |

24

| NO REENTRY BEYOND THIS POINT | 禁止回返 （机场海关告示旅客入关检查后） |

25

| NOTICE ALL PERSONS VEHICLES PACKAGES BAGGAGE ARE SUBJECT TO SEARCH | 人员、车辆、包裹、行李均需检查 (package指装食品的纸袋或塑料袋；baggage指旅客的大件行李) |

14

三、停车指示

1

| Taxis Only
No Parking/Tow Away Zone
Unattended Vehicles Will Be Towed | 出租车专用
禁止停车/拖曳区；无人车辆将被拖走
（机场禁止停车标志牌） |

2

| NO STANDING
ACTIVE LOADING
AND UNLOADING
ONLY
← | NO STOPPING
ANY TIME
→ | （左边）禁止暂时停车，仅可即时装卸
（右边）任何时候禁止停车
（立在道牙上的告示牌） |

3

FOUR POINTS SHERATON HOTEL
901 SPRING STREET, ELIZABETH, N.J. 07201

HOURLY PARKING RATES
0 MIN. --------- 15 MIN. = FREE
15 MIN .... 2 HRS. = $3.00
2 HRS. .... 5 HRS. = $5.00
5 HRS. .... 8 HRS. = $7.00
8 HRS. .... 24 HRS. = $9.00

DAILY PARKING RATES
# OF DAYS	AMT.
1	$ 9.00
2	$ 18.00
3	$ 27.00
4	$ 36.00
5	$ 45.00
6	$ 54.00

这是喜来登酒店的停车收费说明。

小时停车计费：
0–15分钟　　　免费
15分钟–2小时　3美元
2–5小时　　　5美元
5–8小时　　　7美元
8至24小时　　9美元

每天停车收费：
1天9美元，依次累计。住店客人停车每晚7美元，离店时需持有效票据或通行证。

新世纪美国公示语1000例

```
7        $ 63.00
8        $ 72.00
9        $ 81.00
10       $ 90.00
```
ALL HOTEL GUEST PAY PER-NIGHT $7.00
ALL HOTEL GUEST MUST HAVE THEIR TICKET VALIDATED, OR HAVE A PASS WHEN THEY LEAVE THE HOTEL.
THANK YOU,
MANAGEMENT

4

No Parking No Waiting
Immediate Loading and Unloading Only
All Unattended Vehicles Will Be Towed Away
Minimum Towing and Impound Charge $86.00

禁止停车 禁止等客
仅可即刻装卸
所有无人车辆将被拖走
最低托运费和扣押费为86美元
（机场停车说明）

5

**NO STANDING EXCEPT TRUCKS
LOADING & UNOADING**
9AM-7PM EXCEPT SUNDAY

除卡车装卸，禁止暂时停车。
9点（上午）-7点（下午）星期日例外

6

SNOW ROUTE
NO STANDING DURING EMERGENCY
VEHICLES TOWED

运雪通道
紧急情况下禁止临时停车
否则车辆被拖走

7

1 HOUR PARKING 9AM-7 PM
EXCEPT SUNDAY

1小时停车：9点（上午）-7点(下午)
星期日例外

三、停车指示

8

Monday-Friday Rates	Saturday-Sunday Rates	Feast/Special Rates
Up to 1 hr 12.67	Up to 1 hr 16.90	Up to 1 hr 16.90
Up to 2 hrs 16.05	Up to 2 hrs 18.59	Up to 6 hr 22.81
Up to 3 hrs 19.43	Up to 3 hrs 20.27	Each Addl hr after 8 hrs 3.38
Up to 8 hrs 21.12	Up to 8 hrs 21.94	SUV-Vans-Oversized Addl 4.22
Each Addl hr after 8 hrs 3.38	Each Addl hr after 8 hrs 3.38	
SUV-Vans-Oversized Addl 4.22	SUV-Vans-Oversized Addl 4.22	
SUV-Vans-Oversized Addl 4.22		
Monthly Inquire Within		
SUV-Vans-Oversized Addl 42.24	18.375% Parking Tax Extra	18.375% Parking Tax Extra
Park & Lock Addl 42.24		
18.375% Parking Tax Extra		

停车场收费说明。收费标准分为三个时段：周一至周五的费用；周六至周日的费用；参加宴会或特殊场合的费用。停车第一个小时的费用往往较高，但随着停放时间增加费用反而降低。八小时后每增加一小时的费用在任何时段都是3.38美元。如需整月停放需内部咨询。但是轻型跑车、箱式货车以及超大型车辆，需要加收4.22美元，每月42.24美元；加锁停放每月42.24美元。另外，停车场还要收取18.375%的停车税。Addl是additional；hr是hour；SUV是Sports Utility Vehicle 运动型多功能车；Vans旅行轿车。

9

NOTICE

Pursuant to law operator's liability for loss or damage of vehicle by fire, theft or explosion limited to $25,000 unless add'l fee paid when vehicle was first parked and receipt issued for same.

通知

根据法律，经营者对因火灾、盗窃或爆炸造成车辆丢失或损毁的责任限额为25,000美元，车辆初次停放时交付附加费并获取相应票据者除外。

（停车场说明）

10

PLEASE LOCK YOUR VEHICLE. MANAGEMENT NOT RESPONSIBLE FOR VEHICLE OR ITS CONTENTS

请锁好车辆
酒店对车辆及车内物品丢失不负责
（酒店停车场告示）

11

NO PARKING ANY TIME
CARS WILL BE TOWED AWAY AT OWNERS EXPENSE

任何时间禁止停车
随意停放车辆会被拖走，车主支付拖车费。
（OWNERS即OWNER'S省略'）

12

Cars Parked Illegally Will Be Towed By George Smith Inc.
Charge: $175 Towing Fee $25.00 Per-Day Storage

违法停放车辆将由乔治·斯密斯公司拖走
拖车费175美元，保管费每天25美元

13

RESERVED PARKING

专用停车位

14

NO PARKING
MAIL LOADING ZONE

禁止停车
邮件装载区

15

PENALTY $100-500 FINE TOW-AWAY ZONE
FOR FAILURE TO DISPLAY VALID PERMIT
VIOLATIONS CALL 228-7141

本区车辆无有效许可证将被拖走
罚金100-500美元
违章联系电话228-7141

16

NO PARKING 5AM-8AM SATURDAYS

禁止停车
周六上午5点至8点

17

| RESERVED SPECIAL PERMIT HOLDERS ONLY 6AM-3PM | 保留车位
特许证持有者停车位
上午6点至下午3点 |

18

| NO PARKING EXCEPT OFFICIAL SIGHTSEEING VEHICLES ONLY | 禁止停车
官方认可的观光车辆例外 |

19

| NO PARKING 10:00 A.M. – 5:00P.M. TUESDAY TOW AWAY ZONE EXCEPT HOLIDAYS STREET CLEANING | 禁止停车
周二上午10点至下午5点拖曳区，假日清扫大街除外。 |

20

| TWO HOUR TOUR BUS PARKING 7AM-6PM DAILY | 2小时旅游车辆停放
每天上午7点至下午6点
（白宫南草坪路边停车标志。为了给一些旅游车辆提供方便，白宫的道路边上可以短暂停留车辆，供游人从远处参观白宫。） |

21

| NO BUS PARKED IDLING $500 FINE BY ORDER OF METROPOLITAN POLICE DEPARTMENT | 禁止大巴车空闲停放
市警局责令罚款500美元
（白宫南草坪旁路上的禁止停车标志） |

新世纪美国公示语 1000 例

22.

| Pay Meter At Booth When No Attendant On Duty Valid Until 6AM Only | 无值班人员时，请用亭内付费表。有效至上午6点 |

23.

| CYBERCAMP Drop OFF/Pick UP | 电脑夏令营在此上下车
（麻省理工学院班车停靠点标志） |

24.

| NO PARKING
LOADING DOCK 24 HR ACCESS | 禁止停车 24小时装载码头
（码头上禁止车辆停靠的指示牌） |

25.

| Lovett Lot Permit Required | 凭许可证停放车辆
（大楼前的停车场说明） |

26.

| Visitor Parking
North Lot
Central Garage
West Lots
Performance and Athletic Venues | 访客停车
北停车场、中心停车库和西停车场为演出和运动员停车区
（校园内一个指示来访者停车的牌子） |

27.

PULL $250 PENALTY
UH DISABLED PARKING PERMIT ALSO REQUIRED
MON-FRI 7:30AM-8:00 PM
AVAILABLE AT INFORMATION BOOTH ON UNIVERSITY DRIVE
VIOLATORS TOWED AT OWNER'S/ OPERATOR'S EXPENSE
TOWED VEHICLES CALL (731)743-0600

三、停车指示

车辆拖走，罚款250美元

周一至周五上午7点30分至晚上8点，休斯敦大学残疾人也需要停车证 大学车道上问讯亭可获得　违规拖车费用由车主或驾驶者支付 车辆被拖 联系电话(731)743-0600

（休斯敦大学内停车说明。UH为University of Houston。）

28

PARKING IS STRICTLY PROHIBITED FOR BUFFALO WILD WINGS CUSTOMERS

严禁停车，限本店顾客。

（BUFFALO WILD WINGS为美国一家著名的快餐厅，又被称为B-Dubs, BWW, B2W 或 BW3。餐厅成立于1982年，以出售buffalo wings出名，实际就是鸡腿。）

29

TOWING ENFORCED CUSTOMERS ONLY UNAUTHORIZED VEHICLES WILL BE TOWED AT OWNER'S OR OPERATOR'S EXPENSE TOWING ENFORCED AT ALL TIMES: CALL 713-228-2221

顾客专用，擅自停车随时拖走，费用由车主或驾驶员支付。

联系电话713-228-2221

（违章拖车说明）

30

VAN ACCESSIBLE

面包车可通行

（van指旅行轿车，一般可以乘坐7人左右。）

31

Resident Parking

住校生停车处

（校园内各类人员停车都有具体规定）

新世纪美国公示语 1000 例

32

| STUDENT PATIENTS ONLY | 学生就诊专用车位
（校诊所门口的停车告示牌） |

33

| CATHEDRAL PARKING ONLY | 教堂专用停车位 |

34

| RESERVED MUSEUM VEHICLES | RESERVED CHAIRMAN EMERITUS | RESERVED CHAIRMAN of the BOARD | 博物馆保留车位
名誉主席专用车位
董事长专用车位
（博物馆停车位上的标识） |

35

| STAIR TO PARKING GARAGE | 楼梯通往停车库 |

36

| Visitor Parking
North Lot
Weekdays after 6:00pm and Weekends
Best Parking for: Hamman Hall
Credit Card Required | 游客停车
北部停车场，工作日6点以后及周末主要用于哈曼楼停车。需用信用卡。
（停车场说明） |

37

| GARAGE FULL | 停车库已满 |

38

| MUSEUM GARAGE
MEMBER $5.00
MUSEUM VISITORS $8.00
(WITH MUSEUM TICKET STUB)
ALL OTHERS $10.00 | 博物馆停车库
会员5美元，博物馆参观者8美元
（需凭博物馆票根）
其他人员10美元 |

39

For after-hours retrieval of vehicles, please contact Museum Security via the intercom. Please note that only the gate to the right will open for after-hours access.

超时取车，请通过内部对讲机与博物馆保卫部门联系，注意只有通往右边的大门为过时车辆开门。
（博物馆停车场说明）

40

Visitor Parking
Credit Card Required
Insert credit card face up
Use same credit card when exiting
No receipt issued
Only one car can enter per card
Hourly Rate
$1 Per 20 Minutes, Daily Maximum $9
No Overnight Parking: This parking lot is for Rice Business or events only. Violators are subject to ticketing, booting, and towing at owner's expense.

游客停车处
需要信用卡：
1. 面向上插入信用卡
2. 退出停车场使用同一张信用卡
3. 无收据提供
4. 每张卡只可进入一辆车
按小时收费
每20分钟1美元，一日最高9美元。
禁止停放过夜：本停车场只供莱斯大学公务或活动使用。违者罚款、车辆被固定或拖走，拖费自负。
（校园内停车说明）

41

Please Insert Same Credit Card Used at Entry

请插入进入时使用的同一张信用卡
（停车场出口说明）

42

ADDITIONAL VISITOR PARKING AND EXIT

附加访客停车位及出口
（校园内停车说明）

43

TENANT PARKING ONLY
UNAUTHORIZED VEHICLES WILL BE TOWED AT
OWNERS OR OPERATORS EXPENSE.
TOWING ENFORCED AT ALL TIMES.

仅限租客停车
未经许可车辆将随时被拖走
费用由车主或驾驶员支付

44
DO NOT PARK IN STRIP CENTER
YOU WILL BE TOWED

请勿在中心位置停车
否则将被拖走

45
PAID PARKING
Parking HERE
Display Ticket ON Dashboard

收费停车
此处停车，请将票据放在汽车仪表盘上。

46
Special Needs Parking

特殊需要停车

47
RESERVED PARKING
$50–200 FINE WITHOUT VEHICLE PERMIT

专用停车位
无停车许可证，罚款50至200美元。

48
3 HR PARKING 7 AM TO 5 PM
Except by Permit

3小时停车 上午7点至下午5点
有许可证除外

49
20 MINUTE PARKING
ADMISSIONS & DISCHARGE PATIENTS ONLY

限时停车20分钟
仅限入院和出院病人

四、巴士站台

1 Passenger Pick Up At Red Tram Stops Only

仅在红色通勤车站接客
（机场通勤车上的标识语）

2 PLEASE ALLOW ELDERLY AND PERSONS WITH DISABILITIES TO USE THESE SEATS

请给老人和残疾人让座

3 CAUTION
KEEP HANDS CLEAR OF DOOR MECHANISM

警示
勿碰车门机械装置

4 Shuttle Bus To Gates
44A – 44L

穿梭车通往44A–44L
（机场往返穿梭车说明。由于机场面积很大，乘客可能会通过不同的航站楼登机，所以机场往往会安排往返车运送乘客于不同的航站楼或登机口。）

5 EMERGENCY EXIT
BREAK WINDOW FLIP RED HANDLE PUSH DOOR TO OPEN

紧急出口
打破窗户 急拉红把 把门推开
（公共汽车上紧急情况处置说明）

6 PASSENGERS ARE NOT PERMITTED TO STAND FORWARD OF WHITE LINE WHILE BUS IS IN MOTION

车行途中 乘客不准超越白线站立
（公共汽车上的安全提示）

7

| Kneeling Bus | 这是一种专门方便公共汽车乘客,可调低前轴与地距的巴士。当这类公共汽车在停下来的时候,车头会向下倾,就像跪下来一样,以方便乘客上下车,尤其是为了方便老人、推婴儿车或者坐轮椅的人。 |

8

| Travel Time
APPROXIMATELY 80 MINUTES
from Harlem to Union Square | 从哈莱姆到联合广场
行车时间 约80分钟
(纽约市环城旅游车上的广告) |

9

| FREE WALKING TOURS
MEET HERE… 11:00AM – 2:00PM | 免费导游步行游览
此处集合 上午11点至下午2点 |

10

| WELCOME TO THE ROBINSON ROSE
VISITOR CENTER
PLEASE NO FOOD, DRINK, OR SMOKING
HOURS OF OPERATION
DAILY 10:00 AM–5:00 PM | 欢迎来到罗宾森·罗斯游客中心
请不吃零食 不喝饮料 不吸香烟
营业时间 每日10AM—5:00 PM |

11

| as a courtesy to children and non-smokers, please do not smoke within waiting area. | 为了儿童和非吸烟人士,请勿在等候区内吸烟
(标识语中常用as a courtesy to短语,表示"承蒙"、"鉴于"等意。) |

12

| ONLY BUS | 公共汽车专用车道
(路面车道上的文字说明) |

四、巴士站台

13

WARNING
CCTV SYSTEM ONBOARD
FOR THE PROTECTION OF
PASSENGERS AND DRIVER
AUDIO & VIDEO ARE BEING
RECORDED

警告
车上闭路监视系统为保护乘客和司机正在录制音像
（美国"灰狗"长途车上的告示。美国在很多公共场所安装监视系统并贴有告示。）

14

★-Freq. in mins: all trips not shown

班次间隔以分钟：不含所有路线
（美国城市中公共汽车告示牌上的最后一行说明）

15

DOT　ARRIVAL TIMES AT THIS STOP ARE STARTING TIMES PLUS TRAVEL TIMES to the DOT. All times approximate.
Schedules subject to change. Detailed printed schedules available upon request or at mbta.com.

本公共汽车站的到达时间为出发时间加运行时间，所有时间均为近似数；班次可变化；详细运行时刻表可索取或查阅mbta.com网站。
（美国城市中公共汽车告示牌上的说明）

16

BUS LOADING AND UNLOADING ONLY

仅供公共汽车上下乘客

17

Where's my bus?
You are at the
HARVARD/HOLYOKE GATE bus stop.
The following routes serve this stop:
　1　to Dudley Station
　68　to Kendall/MIT Station
　69　to Lechmere Station
— Buses stop where traffic permits.
— Please check bus headsigns and be alert for your bus, which may be to your left OR right.

哈佛大学校门口公共汽车站牌上的说明。从内容上可以看出：本站有三路车经过，1路（通往Dudley站），68路（通往Kendall/MIT站）和69路（通往Lechmere站）。公交车在车辆允许停靠的地方进站；请核对公交车车头标示，注意等待的车，可能停靠在左边或右边。

18

METROPOLITAN TRANSIT AUTHORITY
OF HARRIS COUNTY, TEXAS
Effective May 30, 2004 Printed May 30, 2004
Route Operating Hours and Average Frequencies
Weekday Hours: 4:56a.m. to 12:11a.m.
AM Rush (first trip–9a.m.): 15 minutes
Midday (9a.m.–3 p.m.): 18 minutes
PM Rush (3–7 p.m.):15 minutes
Late Evening (7 p.m. until last trip): 30 minutes
Saturday Hours: 5:23 a.m. to 12:26 a.m.
AM Rush (first trip–9 a.m.): 30 minutes
Midday (9 a.m.–3 p.m.): 30 minutes
PM Rush (3–7 p.m.): 30 minutes
Late Evening (7 p.m.–until last trip): 45 minutes
Sunday Hours: 5: 18 a.m. to 12:19 a.m.
AM Rush (first trip–9 a.m.): 30 minutes
Midday (9 a.m.–3 p.m.): 30 minutes
PM Rush (3–7 p.m.): 30 minutes
Late Evening (7 p.m.–until last trip): 50 minutes
Actual times and frequencies may vary slightly from scheduled times because of changing traffic conditions, construction detours and/ or bad weather.

德克萨斯州哈里斯县交通管理局公告
2004年5月30日生效，2004年5月30日印发
线路运营时间和通常班次：
周一至周五：上午4:56至凌晨12:11。
早高峰（头班车至上午9点）：间隔15分钟；正午（上午9点至下午3点）：间隔18分钟；晚高峰（下午3点至晚7点）：间隔15分钟；晚上（晚上7点至末班车）：间隔30分钟。
周六：上午5:23至凌晨12:26。
早高峰（头班车车至上午9点）：30分钟间隔；正午（上午9点至下午3点）：间隔30分钟；晚高峰（下午3点至晚7点）：间隔30分钟；晚上（晚上7点至末班车）：45分钟间隔。
星期日：上午5:18至凌晨12:19。
早高峰（头班车至上午9点）：间隔30分钟；正午（上午9点至下午3点）：间隔30分钟；晚高峰（下午3点至晚7点）：间隔30分钟；晚上（晚上7点至末班车）：间隔50分钟。实际运营时间和班次可能因交通状况变化、施工绕行或天气恶劣而稍有变动。
（公共汽车运营信息）

19

WHEELCHAIR SEATING AREA SECUREMENTS ARE LOCATED BELOW THESE SEATS

轮椅座位区，座位下面有固定轮椅的装置。
（有些公交车辆有提供摆放轮椅的专门区域）

四、巴士站台

20
| PLEASE ALLOW SENIORS AND PERSONS WITH DISABILITIES TO USE THESE SEATS | 请让老年人和残疾人使用这些座位
（在美国一般在称呼老人的时候都会使用senior，elderly之类词语以示尊重。） |

21
| Yield these PRIORITY SEATS to elderly and disabled passengers. | 老人和残疾乘客优先座位，请让座。 |

22
| CAUTION
DO NOT STAND IN DOORWAY WHILE BUS IS IN MOTION | 注意
汽车运行时请勿站在车门前。 |

23
| WAIT FOR GREEN LIGHT TOUCH BARS TO OPEN DOORS | 等待绿灯亮，按门栅开门。
（公共汽车上有关停车开门的说明） |

24
| THESE SEATS MUST BE VACATED FOR SENIORS AND DISABLED PERSONS | 这些座位必须留给老人和残疾人
（这里告示语的语气要强硬一些） |

25
| WHEELCHAIR SEATING AREA. SECUREMENTS ARE LOCATED BELOW THESE SEATS | 轮椅座位区域
固定装置在座位下面
（公共汽车上轮椅座位位置说明。为了给残疾人提供方便，公共汽车上还为残疾人提供专门固定轮椅的地方，也提供轮椅使用。） |

26
| PRIORITY SEATING:
Please give up this seat to seniors or persons with disabilities, upon request. | 优先座位
请在需要的时候将此座位让给老人或残疾人。
（公共汽车座位说明） |

出租汽车

1

	TAXI FARE	出租车收费
$2.50	INITIAL CHARGE	起步价为$2.50；每1/5英里增加40¢；停车等待或慢速行驶每1/5英里增加40¢；工作日下午4点到晚8点加收$1.00；晚8点到凌晨6点加收50¢。
40¢	Per 1/5 Mile	
40¢	Per 2 Minutes Stopped/Slow Traffic	
$1.00	Weekday Surcharge 4pm–8pm	（这是纽约市出租车上印的收费标准。纽约的出租车和中国的一样，可以招手要车，但在其他城市很少有招手停的出租车，一般都是电话预约。）
50¢	Night Surcharge 8pm–6am	

2

Truck Rental
Household Moves
Business Rentals

卡车出租
搬家或者商务租用

3

License for year 2006
TAXICAB LICENSE

2006年执照
出租车执照

4

RATES – MILEAGE & WAITING
HOURLY – $24.00 PER HOUR FOR ONE OR MORE PASSENGERS
MILEAGE – $2.30 FOR FIRST 1/6 MILE & $.40 FOR EVERY 1/6 MILE THEREOF
WAITING – $.40 EACH MINUTE WAITING TIME (INCLUDING TRAFFIC DELAYS)

费用收取为里程加等待时间
小时计费：一个或多个乘客每小时24美元
里程计费：初1/6英里为2.3美元，之后每1/6英里0.40美元
等待计费：每分钟0.40美元（包括堵车耽搁）

（美国纽约州水牛城出租车上印的收费说明）

五、出租汽车

5

006080
City of Houston
TAXICAB LICENSE
BEREKET TEKLEAB
DOB: 9/11/60
HT: 5'6   WT: 145
ISSUED: 10/21/04
EXPIRES: 10/21/06

休斯敦出租车执照上的内容。上面不仅有司机的姓名，而且还有司机的身高、体重、生日、发证日期和失效日期等信息。

6

Meter Rates First 1/6 mile or less $2.50
Each add'l. 1/6 .30¢
Waiting time $20.00 Hr.
Surcharge $1.00 add'l per trip 8:00pm to 6:00am
NO CHARGE FOR ADD'L PASSENGERS
City ordinance allows $2.75 per trip service charge at Bush International Airport on all metered fares. This charge does not apply to zone rates.

计程费：初1/6英里(或以下)2.5美元，每增加1/6英里为.30美分；等待时间每小时20美元；晚8点至凌晨6点每次行程加收1美元。增加乘客不另收费
城市法令容许在布什国际机场所有计程费上每次行程收取2.75美元服务费。本收费规定不适用于按区收费。
（休斯敦市出租车的收费标准和说明）

7

Refueling Options		
Fuel Purchase Option (FPO) Purchase a tank of gas from Hertz at time of rental. No need for you to refill prior to return. No refunds for unused fuel.	Fuel and Service (FSC) Allow Hertz to refill the tank for you. Pay for the fuel required to fill the tank and for service to refuel.	Self-Refueling Refill the tank yourself prior to returning the car.

汽车租赁处汽车加油的选择。在美国租赁汽车的业务非常发达，这里向需要租赁汽车的顾客提供了三项选择：第一选择是在租赁期间从租赁处购买一罐汽油，归还前无需灌满，剩余汽油也不退款；第二选择请租赁汽车的公司灌满油箱，支付油费和服务费；第三是归还汽车前自己加满油箱。

新世纪美国公示语1000例

六

火车地铁

1

AMTRAK WAITING ROOM

AMTRAK候车室
（火车站告示牌。美国铁路不发达，货运主要靠集装箱拖车，短途客运主要靠自驾汽车，长途客运主要靠飞机，大城市之间的机票相对便宜，机场附近都有汽车租赁服务，所以大部分美国人都不坐火车。Amtrak是美国国家铁路客运公司(National Railroad Passenger Corporation)的商标，简称美国国铁或美铁，是一家长途和城际铁路客运公司，创立于1971年5月1日。Amtrak是由American train track缩略合成。该公司有雇员1.9万，线路总长3.5万公里，每天经营1250班列车。）

2

Train Approaching
STAND BACK

火车进站，请靠后站。

3

THIS VEHICLE STOPS AT
ALL RAILROAD CROSSINGS

本车辆在所有铁路道口停车
（火车铁轨维修车车体上的说明）

4

WARNING!
Danger
Do Not Cross Tracks

警示
危险，请勿跨越铁轨。

5

This Vehicle Is A No Smoking Area

本车辆为禁烟区

6

        Priority Seating   优先座位
- Senior Citizens   ● 老人
- Handicapped Persons   ● 残疾人

（火车车厢内座位说明）

7

Control Panel
ON-BOARD TRAIN EMERGENCY INSTRUCTIONS

ALWAYS Contact a Train Crew Member
           Listen for Announcements
Fire   Move to an unaffected car
      Remain inside- tracks are electrified
      Follow instructions of emergency workers
      Train crews can access fire extinguishers
      Do not activate emergency cord
Medical   If a passenger is in distress, notify a crew member immediately
          If you are medically qualified and able to assist, identify yourself to the crew
POLICE   Notify the crew of any unlawful or suspicious activity on board your train
         Train crews can contact the police en route
EVACUATION
Listen for directions from authorized personnel
Open this panel
Follow instructions inside
Exit the train only when directed

控制面板
地铁紧急情况说明
例行 听从列车乘务人员指挥 注意广播通知
火警 去无火情车厢 留在车厢内（铁轨带电）
     听从应急人员指示 乘务人员可使用灭火器
     请勿触动紧急线缆
医警 乘客有危难，立即通知乘务人员
     有医疗资格且能协助者，请向乘务员说明身份
匪警 车上有违法或可疑行动，告知列车乘务员，列车员会联系乘警
疏散 听从指定人员的指令 打开面板 遵照内部指示 听指挥撤出车厢

（地铁紧急情况操作指令）

新世纪美国**公示语**1000例

8

NOTICE

You must have a ticket or other proof-of-payment before entering the "Fare Paid" area of an underground rail station.

On the Buffalo Place Mall section, you may ride free of charge between stations. However, if your ride takes you into the subway (past theater station) you must buy a ticket or have other proof-of-payment before you board the train.

FINES OF PENALTIES FOR FARE EVASION

1. Initial fine $ 50.00
2. After 10 days $ 100.00
3. After 45 days $ 180.00
4. After 90 days $ 280.00
5. After 120 days a judgment will be filed where any assets in New York State can be attached.

IMPORTANT

Persons cited for fare evasion are subject to arrest if fines are not paid.

公 告

在进入地铁车站"车费已付"区之前,必须持有车票或其他付费证据。在布法罗市伯蕾丝卖场地段,各站之间免费乘坐。但如果进入地铁(超过剧院站)乘客需购票或持有其他付费证明方可乘座。

逃票罚款

1. 初犯罚款50美金;
2. 10天后罚款100美金;
3. 45天后罚款180美金;
4. 90天后罚款280美金;
5. 120天后判决查封当事人在纽约州的财产。

注 意

逃票拒付罚款者将遭逮捕。

(纽约州布法罗市乘坐地铁的说明)

9

SPITTING
On the Platforms or other Parts of this Station is
UNLAWFUL
Offenders are Liable to Arrest

在站台上或车站的任何位置吐痰
为违法行为
违者可能会遭逮捕
(纽约地铁告示)

七、非机动车

1 PLEASE WALK YOUR BIKE 请下车推行（校园内自行车提示牌）

2 BIKE RACK 自行车架
（在美国，有为数不多存放自行车的地方，通常采用支架来存放。一旦设置新的自行车存车架，还会作为新闻报道。）

3 CITY OF CORONADO BICYCLE ROUTES LEGEND:
· Bicycle / Bus Stop
— Bicycle Path
⋯ Bicycle/ Pedestrian Path
— Bike Route

洛杉矶科罗拉多岛上的自行车路线图图示。legend表示"图标"，这里指示了自行车和公共汽车停靠站、自行车路线、自行车兼人行道路线、自行车(bike)路线。其中bicycle指岛上三个轮子的旅游自行车。

4 BICYCLES MUST PARK IN BIKE RACKS 自行车必须停放车架内
（在美国几乎看不到自带支架的自行车，自行车一般都停放在车架内，或横放在草地上或靠在墙上。）

5 RIDE YOUR BIKE ON THE STREET WITH TRAFFIC FLOW 街上骑单车，随车流而行。

6

| WALK YOUR BIKE ON THE SIDEWALK POLICE BIKES EXEMPT | 人行道上，下车推行 警察自行车除外 |

7

| Bicycles or other property attached to the railings will be removed and delivered to The Lost Property Unit Located at St & 8 AV | 栏杆上的自行车或其他物件将被移除，送到第八大街和第八大道交口的失物认领处 （铁栏杆上禁止锁停自行车的告示） |

8

| NO MOTOR VEHICLES | 禁止机动车 （车道上的提示文字） |

9

| SCOOTERS AND SKATEBOARDS PROHIBITED | 禁止单脚滑行车和滑板车 （道路上禁行告示） |

10

| YIELD TO BIKES | 给自行车让道 （小道上要求给主路上自行车让道的告示） |

八、电梯安全

电梯安全

1 Stand Right Walk Left
No Wheelchairs No Strollers No Carts

右立左行
禁止轮椅、童车和行李推车
（机场自动扶梯上说明）

2 PLEASE HOLD HANDRAIL

请握住扶栏（自动扶梯说明）

3 No Carriages or Strollers on Escalator

自动扶梯上禁止手推车或童车
（自动扶梯说明）

4 CAUTION
Hold Handrail Hold Child's Hand
Keep Feet Away From Side Panel
Face Forward No Baby Strollers No
Riding Barefoot

警示
握住扶手 牵住孩子手
脚离侧壁面向前 禁止婴儿推车
禁止赤脚
（自动扶梯说明）

5 FIREFIGHTERS' OPERATION
When flashing , exit elevator

To operate car	Insert fire key and turn to "ON"
To cancel floor selection	Press desired floor button
To close power-operated door	Press "CALL CANCEL" button
To open power-operated door	Press and hold "DOOR CLOSE" button
To hold car at floor	Press and hold "DOOR OPEN" button
To automatically send car to recall floor	With doors open, turn key to "HOLD"
	With doors open, turn key to "OFF"

消防员操作 灯闪亮，出电梯。
操作电梯： 插入防火钥匙，转向"开"，按所去楼层的按钮。
取消楼层：按"呼叫取消"按钮。
关电动门： 按住"关门"按钮。
开电动门： 按住"开门"按钮。
电梯停某楼层：门开着时，将钥匙转向"停驻"键。
电梯自动到呼叫层：门开着时，将钥匙转向"关闭"键。
（电梯内给消防人员的电梯使用提示，其中car指电梯的轿厢。）

6

Elevator to N Q R W only.
For elevator to A C E enter at 8 AV

电梯仅通往N，Q，R和W线地铁
通往A，C，E线地铁电梯从第八大街进入
（纽约大街上电梯通往各线路地铁的指示。纽约的地铁线路为世界上最长，全市约有20多条线路，每条线路用英文大写字母来表示，整个网络有600多个车站。）

7

FOR YOUR SAFETY
Tennis Shoes, Bare Feet & Strollers
ARE PROHIBITED

为了你的安全
禁止穿网球鞋、赤脚或者推童车
（商场内扶梯上的安全提示）

8

Caution
Passengers Only
Hold Handrail Attend Children
Avoid Sides

小心
乘客专用
握住扶手,看好孩子,避开两侧。
（机场电梯告示）

9

NO FREIGHT CARTS, DOLLIES,
HAND TRUCKS OR ANY
ROLLING UNITS IN THE LOBBY!
USE THE FREIGHT CAR LOCATED AT
69 NEW STREET.

禁止货运车、独轮台车、手推货运车或任何带轮的车进入厅堂电梯。
货梯位于新街69号。
（客梯使用说明）

九、自动售货机

1

AT&t PrePaid Phone Card	Flat rates per minute	AT&T 预付电话卡　每分钟统一话费
No monthly fees	No hidden	无月费　无隐含附加费　无失效期
surcharges	No expiration date	购卡不找零
DOES NOT GIVE CHANGE		（自动售货机上预售电话卡的部分说明）

2

VENDING
Ice Available On Floors 2, 4, 6, 8 & 10

自动售货机
第二、四、六、八和十层有冰供应
（大楼内自动售货机上的说明。在美国，快餐店的制冰机都放在自助区，加不加、加多少都自选，即使外卖饮料也是自己决定是否加冰。）

3

NOTICE ALL MONEY REMOVED FROM THIS MACHINE DAILY

注意
机内的钱每天全部取走
（自动售货机上的特别提示，以防有人有非分之想。）

4

75¢ PER COPY
USE ANY COIN COMBINATION
(Nickels, Dimes, Quarters)

TO OPERATE
① Insert proper coins
② Wait for coins to drop
③ Pull door & remove paper

报纸每份75美分
可用5美分、10美分和25美分组合支付
操作：1. 投入适量硬币
2. 等待硬币落下
3. 拉门，取报纸
（街头购买报纸的投币指令）

5

INSERT $1 BILL for purchase only
Receive Change Below
INSERT BILL FACE UP

限插入1美元的纸币购物
下方接零找
纸币面向上插入
（自动售货机上纸币购物说明）

6

OPERATING INSTRUCTIONS
1. TO CHECK VEND PRICE, PUSH SELECTION BUTTONS. PRICE WILL APPEAR IN DISPLAY.
2. DEPOSIT APPROPRIATE MONEY.
3. AMOUNT DEPOSITED WILL APPEAR IN DISPLAY.
4. PUSH BUTTONS MATCHING ITEM SELECTED.
5. RECEIVE ITEM BELOW.
6. RECEIVE CHANGE BELOW.

操作说明
1. 查看售价，按选购钮，价格即显示
2. 投入适量的钱
3. 显示投入的钱数
4. 按相应的选购扭
5. 下方取物品
6. 下方接找零

7

Deposit nickels, dimes or quarters
Change returned below 45¢.
When light appears in push button, make another selection.

请投入5美分、10美分或25美分硬币，找零45美分以下
按钮亮灯，再选购
（自动售货机上硬币购物说明）

8

⊙ SOLD OUT
⊙ CORRECT CHANGE ONLY WHEN LIT
⊙ PRESS FOR COIN RETURN

已经售出
亮灯显示准确找头
按钮退回硬币
（售货机说明）

九、自动售货机

9

INSERT DOLLAR BILL FOR
PURCHASE ONLY
INSERT BILL FACE UP AND MAKE
SELECTION
CHANGE RECEIVED IN CHANGE
OPENING BELOW

限插入纸币购物
纸币面向上插入，然后选购
找零在下面槽口取
（售货机有关纸币使用的说明）

10

50¢ Daily
$1.75 Sunday

Use any coin combination.
Do not use Pennies.
Accepts $1.00 Coin

日报每份50美分
请用硬币组合，一分币除外。
周日1.75美元
本机接受1美元硬币
（自动售报机说明）

新世纪美国公示语1000例

电话说明

1

WARNING
Telephone is for Crisis Emergency Hotline Calls Only
Misuse of Phone Will Result in Prosecution

警示
紧急热线电话
滥用将被起诉
（墙面电话箱上的告示语）

2

50C
LOCAL CALLS NO TIME LIMIT
CHANGE NOT PROVIDED

50美分
拨打本市电话无时间限制，不找零。
（公用电话说明）

3

No Coins?? Call COLLECT!
Or Use Your Credit Card

没有硬币？？拨打对方付费电话！或者用信用卡
（collect是指对方付费电话，往往是通过接线员来实现的。公用电话上的文字说明。）

4

CREDIT CARDS
INSERT FACE-UP AND REMOVE
DIAL 0+ AREA CODE+ NUMBER
INSERT CALLING OR CREDIT CARD

信用卡
面向上插入后移除，拨0+区号+号码
插入电话卡或信用卡
（机场电话亭内说明。在美国许多公用电话可以用信用卡。）

5

Call Anywhere in the USA!
Only 50C
Domestic:
Dial: 1 – area code – number

打电话至美国任何地方！只需50美分
国内电话：拨1-区号-电话号码

十、电话说明

Call Anywhere Else in the World Only $1		打电话至世界上任何地方只需1美元。
INTERNATIONAL:		国际电话：拨011-国家号码-电话号码
Dial: 011-country code-number		
Mexico-Mexico City	10 min	墨西哥墨西哥市10分钟、墨西哥7分钟、萨尔瓦多4分钟、危地马拉4分钟、香港10分钟、哥伦比亚5分钟、印度尼西亚5分钟、意大利10分钟、日本5分钟、菲律宾4分钟、韩国5分钟、泰国4分钟、中国8分钟。（机场投币电话说明。在美国，很多电话卡的优惠程度比较高。）
Mexico	7 min	
El Salvador	4 min	
Guatemala	4 min	
Hong Kong	10 min	
Colombia	5 min	
Indonesia	5 min	
Italy	10 min	
Japan	5 min	
Philippines	4 min	
South Korea	5 min	
Thailand	4 min	
China	8 min	

6

Four Points
Sheraton

GUEST SERVICES	51
EMERGENCIES	0
FRONT DESK/MAIL/CASHIER	51
VOICE MAIL/MESSAGES	52
CAFÉ/ROOM SERVICE	54

DIALING INSTRUCTIONS

GUEST ROOMS	
Floors 1-9	7+Room Number
Floors 10 and up	Dial Room Number
LOCAL CALLS	9+ Number
LONG DISTANCE	9+1+ Area Code + Number
OPERATOR ASSISTED CALLS, CALLING CARD, COLLECT OR THIRD PARTY	9+0+Area code + Number
INTERNATIONAL CALLS	9+011+Country Code + City Code + Number
800/888 NUMBERS	9+1+800/888 + Number

喜来登饭店客房内在电话机上提供的数字服务，包括客户服务、紧急呼叫、前台/邮件/银台、语音邮件/留言、咖啡/房间服务。拨号说明，1-9楼客房，拨7加房间号码，10层和以上客房 拨打房间号码，本市电话拨9加号码；长途拨9+1+区号+电话号码；接线员辅助电话、电话卡、对方付费电话或加入第三方电话拨9+0+区号+电话号码；国际长途拨打9+011+国家区号+城市区号+电话号码；拨打800/888号码，则拨9+1+800/888+电话号码。

（800号码在美国几乎所有电话都可以拨打，拨打人不需付费，你申请一个真实的美国800电话号码，可以将这个号码开通设置为呼叫转移到全球任何一个电话上。由于800电话已经几乎用完，所以现在又开通了888，其功能和800电话号码功能相同。）

7

Telephone surcharge information is located in your telephone guide
WAKE-UP CALL: Touch "0"
CONCIERGE
FRONT DESK
EXCEPTIONAL STAY
LAUNDRY/VALET
MESSAGES
ROOM SERVICE
SPINNAKER
VALET PARKING
EMERGENCY

电话附加费信息在电话指南中
叫醒服务按0键
管理人员键
前台键
特殊逗留键
洗衣房/服务生键
留言键
客房服务键
预定大三角帆
代客停车服务键
紧急呼叫键
（酒店室内电话说明）

8

NO COIN FOR EMERGENCY AND TOLL FREE CALLS
FOR DIALING INSTRUCTIONS SEE BELOW.
Call LONG DISTANCE Anywhere in the U. S. A. for 25¢/ Min.
THIS TELEPHONE WILL NOT RECEIVE INCOMING CALLS
Collect Calls Dial *11

紧急和免费电话勿需投币
拨打指令见说明；美国国内长途电话每分钟25美分；
本机不可接来电；
对方付费电话拨打*11
（公用电话上的指令）

十、电话说明

1. PHONE USE IS LIMITED TO PARTICIPANTS ENROLLED IN CONTINUING STUDIES COURSES ONLY.
2. PLEASE LIMIT ALL PHONE CALLS TO 3 MINUTES.
3. THESE PHONES CAN BE USED FOR LOCAL CALLS ONLY. PLEASE DIAL "9" AND THEN THE 7-DIGIT LOCAL NUMBER.

1. 本机仅限进修课程人员使用。
2. 请将电话使用时间限定在3分钟以内。
3. 本机只能用于拨打本地电话,请先拨9,然后再拨本地7位数电话。
(校园大楼内免费座机使用说明)

 厨房用具

1

ELEMENT ON

开启。
（微波炉上的标识。微波炉上有一个指示灯表示是否处于开启状态。在国内我们经常看到使用的都是on/off。）

2

Quick Touch		
POPCORN	BEVERAGE	POTATO
CLOCK	AUTO DEFROST	KITCHEN TIMER
1	2	3
4	5	6
7	8	9
COOK TIME	0	POWER
STOP	START	QUICK ON
CLEAR		

烤箱上的说明。第一行文字是提供快速操作的按键信息，包括爆米花、饮料和土豆，下面包括时钟、自动除霜和厨房计时器，其他的还有烹调时间、开关按钮、停止/清除、启动、电源、快速操作按钮等。

3

REDDI BAGS
LARGE TRASH BAGS
WARNING:
To avoid danger of suffocation, keep this bag away from babies and children. Do not use this bag in cribs, beds, carriages or playpens.
Not recommended for food storage.
Made in U.S.A.

大型垃圾袋
注意：为避免窒息危险，请将此垃圾袋远离婴儿和儿童。不要在婴儿床、床、童车、婴儿用围栏上使用这种垃圾袋。建议不要用来储存食品。美国制造。
（垃圾袋上的说明）

十一、厨房用具

4

BAKE	CANCEL		CLOCK SET	COOK TIME
BROIL	CLEAN	OVEN PREHEAT DOOR LOCKED	TIMER ON/OFF	STOP TIME

烤箱上的说明。说明文字包括烘焙、炖煮、取消操作、清除设定、微波炉预热、微波炉门锁定、时钟设定、计时器开启/关闭、烹调时间、停止时间等功能。

5

WARNING:
TO AVOID DANGER OF SUFFOCATION, KEEP THIS PLASTIC BAG AWAY FROM BABIES AND CHILDREN. THIS BAG OR ANY OF ITS COMPONENTS MAY CLING TO NOSE AND MOUTH AND PREVENT BREATHING. PROTECTED BY ONE OR MORE OF THE FOLLOWING U. S. PATENTS. MADE IN THE UNITED STATES OF AMERICA

注意：
为防止发生窒息危险，请将塑料袋远离婴幼儿。本塑料袋或其任何部分可能会粘附在鼻子和嘴上而阻挡呼吸。本产品受到以下美国专利（略）的保护，美国制造。

（塑料袋上警告文字）

新世纪美国公示语 1000 例

十二

洗衣烘干

1

PERSONAL SAFETY RULES
- NEVER REACH INTO THE WASHER UNTIL THE TUB HAS COMPLETELY STOPPED SPINNING.
- NEVER WASH ARTICLES CONTAINING FLAMMABLE FUMES.
- NEVER ALLOW CHILDREN TO OPERATE OR TO PLAY IN, WITH OR AROUND THE WASHER.

个人安全准则
- 洗衣桶停转之前切勿将手伸入洗衣桶内
- 切勿洗涤含有易燃烟气的物件
- 切勿让孩子操作或在洗衣桶内外周围玩耍。

（洗衣机安全提示语）

2

DELICATES AND KNITS	⊙ MACHINE IN USE
WHITES	⊙ SOAK
COLORS	⊙ RINSE
BRIGHT COLORS	⊙ FINAL SPIN
PERMANENT PRESS	⊙ NBALANCE
WOOLENS	

左边一栏表示所需要洗涤物品的按钮位置：精细织物和编织物、白色衣物、彩色衣物、鲜艳色彩衣物、免烫衣物、羊毛织物；右边一栏则是通过二极管提示洗衣机的状态：使用中、浸泡、漂洗、最后甩干、不平衡。

（洗衣机上的说明）

3

COMMERCIAL WASHER INSTRUCITONS
1. ADD DETERGENT TO RUB
2. LOAD TO TOP ROW OF HOLES
3. CLOSE LID
4. INSERT CARD AND/ OR SELECT SETTING
UNBALANCE: DISTRIBUTE CLOTHES EVENLY-CLOSE
BLEACH: MAY BE ADDED AFTER TUB IS FILLED WITH WATER

商用洗衣机操作说明
1. 向桶内加入洗衣粉
2. 将水加到最上排水孔
3. 关上洗衣机盖子
4. 插入洗衣卡/或选择设定
不平衡：将衣物放置均衡然后关闭盖子
漂白粉：可在桶内注水后加入漂白粉

（洗衣机操作说明）

十二、洗衣烘干

4

TEMPERATURE	SETTING	CYCLE
HOT	WHITES	REGULAR
WARM	COLORS	REGULAR
	PERMANENT PRESS	COOL-DOWN
	DELICATES	SHORT WASH/SOAK
COLD	BRIGHT COLORS	REGULAR
	WOOLENS	SHORT WASH/SOAK

COLD WATER RINSE ON ALL CYCLES

该洗衣机的温度设定共分三个大档：热水、温水和冷水。设定热水洗涤白色织物，使用普通转速；温水用于洗涤彩色衣物，使用普通转速；用于免烫衣物，使用逐渐冷却；洗涤精细织物，使用短水洗/浸泡；冷水用于洗涤鲜艳色彩衣物，使用普通转速；洗涤羊毛衫，使用短水洗/浸泡。漂洗都用冷水。
（洗衣机洗涤温度指示）

5

OPEN DRYER HERE

请从这里打开烘干机（的门）。
（烘干机说明）

6

FOR BEST DRYING, LINT SCREEN MUST BE CLEANED AND REPLACED

为了取得最佳烘干效果，纤维屑滤网务必要清洗并更换。
（烘干机提示文字）

7

SEE UPPER UNIT DATA LABEL FOR ADDITIONAL INFORMATION

更多信息，请看上面的单位数据标签。
（烘干机提示文字）

8

Dryers help protect the environment.
They save trees from being used for paper towels.
They eliminate paper towel waste.
They are more sanitary to use than paper and help maintain cleaner facilities.

干手机有利于环境保护
节省用于做纸巾的树木
消除纸巾废物
比用纸更卫生，保持设施更清洁。
（干手机说明）

新世纪美国公示语1000例

十三 餐饮服务

1

```
MENU
REGULAR POPCORN BOX $2.95
YARD BAG OF POPCORN $3.75
PRETZELS $2.28
PLAIN, SALTER OR CINNAMON
CHEESE $1.00
SODAS $2.00
SMALL WATER $2.00
LARGE WATER 2.40
JUICE'S $2.40
SPORT DRINK $2.40
ALL PRICES INCLUDE TAXES
```

机场售货摊上公示的食品饮料价格。普通盒装的爆米花和大袋(yard bag)的爆米花、（普通型、加盐型和桂皮型）脆椒盐卷饼、奶酪。饮料有汽水、小瓶水(small water)和大瓶水(large water)、果汁、运动型饮料。所有价格包括购物税。

2

BREAKFAST SERVED 5:00 AM TO 10:00 AM		
Biscuits	Combo	Sandwich Only
BACON, EGG 'N CHEESE	3.59	2.09
SAUSAGE 'N EGG	3.59	2.09
BREADFAST PLATTERS		
BUTTERMILK PANCAKES	W/SAUSAGE OR BACON	2.59
SCRAMBLED EGGS	W/SAUSAGE OR BACON	3.89
SIDE DISHES		
BISCUITS 'N GRAVY		1.99
HASH BROWNS		.89

汉堡快餐店内上午5点至10点提供的早餐价格。早餐有软烤小圆饼(biscuits)套餐（培根、鸡蛋加奶酪或香肠加鸡蛋）或者只要价格更便宜的三明治；还有一种大盘(platters)早餐（香肠或培根加黄油牛奶饼、香肠或培根炒鸡蛋）、附餐(side dishes)，有肉汁饼(biscuits 'n gravy)/土豆饼(hash browns)。

3

DO THE RIGHT SIZE COMBO FOR YOU.					自选套餐
SMALL COMBO	MEDIUM COMBO	JUST ADD49¢	LARGE COMBO	JUST ADD89¢	（汉堡快餐店内的套餐(COMBO)价格 分大中小三个类型，中型和大型汉堡只需分别增加49美分和89美分。）

4

Place Orders Here	请在此点餐

5

Food Court Near Gate D	机场就餐处标示语。告知旅客在D号大门附近有就餐的地方。court经常用来指球场，但也可指室内外有特殊用途的大场地。

6

KID'S MEAL 1/4 Old Fashioned Sub (your choice) Apple Slices or Organic Carrots with Dip 16.9 oz. Wegmans Bottled Water All in an Activity Bag with Crayons!!! $ 4.29	儿童餐 1/4老式汉堡包（任选） 苹果片或无化肥的胡萝卜带调料 16盎司威哥曼超市瓶装水 活动袋盛装，画笔赠送！！！ 4.29美元。 （超市餐厅儿童套餐说明。sub 是submarine（sandwich）的简称，可称"潜艇（三明治）"。这种汉堡包长达一尺，故有此名。）

7

Toddler Toys Available Upon Request	顾客可索取儿童玩具 （美国快餐店中的告示牌子上内容）

8

Picture Menus Available Upon Request	顾客可索取有图片的菜单 （美国快餐店中告示牌子上的内容）

新世纪美国公示语1000例

9
PAY IT YOUR WAY　　　　　支付方式自选
（美国快餐店中告示牌上内容。在美国，购物后有多种支付方式，包括现金、信用卡、借记卡、旅行支票等。）

10
NOW HIRING ALL SHIFTS　　　　招聘各班次人员
（快餐店招聘广告）

11
DRINK RECIPES Concoct a new drink. Or stick with the usual.
HALF & HALF　　BLACK & WHITE　　FOUR WAY　　BLACK GOLD

饮料配方；调制新饮料或固有原味饮料。
半伴（两种饮料混合在一起）
黑加白（可乐加雪碧）
四式配方（四种饮料混合在一起）
黑金（可乐加橙汁）
（快餐店内提示顾客将饮料进行搭配的说明）

12
DO NOT USE WATER OUT OF USE!　　不要将饮料机内的饮料用光
（快餐店饮料添加说明。在美国的快餐店，饮料基本都是随意享用的，不以一杯为限，但自添饮料。这里的标示语是为了提示就餐顾客不要将饮料机内的饮料倒光，以免损坏机器。）

13
TOSS IT IN. DROP IT IN. SLIDE IT IN OFF THE TRAY. JUST GET YOUR TRASH IN HERE SOME WAY.　　投、扔或从餐盘上滑进去，总之将垃圾倒在这里。
（快餐店内垃圾箱说明）

十三、餐饮服务

14

Restaurant Hours

	OPEN	Dining Room Open Until	Drive Thru Open Until
SUN.	7:00AM	11:00PM	12:00AM
MON.	6:00AM	11:00PM	12:00AM
TUES.	6:00AM	11:00PM	12:00AM
WED.	6:00AM	11:00PM	12:00AM
THURS.	6:00AM	11:00PM	12:00AM
FRI.	6:00AM	11:00PM	1:00AM
SAT.	7:00AM	11:00PM	1:00AM

No solicitation
Only medically necessary pets allowed
Shirt and shoes required

快餐店营业时间。从表中可以看出这家快餐店一般早晨6点就开门（周六、周日会在7点开门），餐厅会一直开放到晚间11点。另外，外卖窗口一直开到夜间12点，顾客不用下车就可买到自己需要的快餐。最后提示这里严禁乞讨、需要医护的宠物可进入、衣冠要整齐。

15

BUSES WELCOME!!!

欢迎大巴车！！！
（快餐店窗户玻璃上的告示语。因为大型客车能够一下子带来很多食客，也就给快餐店带来更多的利润。）

16

Consistent Low Prices
Fresh Rotisserie Chickens
Bigger and Better Price Best Value!
WITH SHOPPERS CLUB CARD
$4.99

永远低价位
新鲜转炉烤鸡
价位实惠，物超所值！
使用购物会员卡4.99美元。
（超市烹制好的成品菜说明。rotisserie可以用来指"电热轮转烤肉器"，也可以用来指"烤肉馆"。）

17

Hot Dog Sausage Pretzel
Hot Knish Shish Kebab Chestnuts
COLD SODA, WATER & SNAPPLE

大街上一个快餐车的招牌。快餐车上有热狗、香肠、扭结饼或热夹馅烤饼、烤羊肉串、栗子，另外还供应冷苏打水、水和snapple（一种玻璃瓶装的品牌冰茶或果汁饮料）。

18

MENU

FOOD		ICE CREAM	
Hot Dog Hebrew National	$3.75	Ice Cream Sandwich	$1.60
Hot Dog 1/4lb	$3.45	Patriot Rocket Pop	$1.95
Turkey & Cheese	$5.10	Italian Ice	$2.75
Ham & Cheese	$5.25	Häagen-Dazs	$2.95
Cheese Sandwich	$4.20	**BEVERAGES**	
Vegetable Sandwich	$5.10	Bottle Water	
Deli Meal	$7.75		$1.85
Any Sandwich with 20oz Drink & Chips		BRISK ICED TEA & JUICE	$1.95
Kids Meal HOT DOG	$5.50	Pepsi	$1.85
With any Small Fountain Drink & Chips		Diet Pepsi	$1.85
SNACKS		Dr. Pepper	
Candy	$.95		$1.85
Pop Corn	$.95	Mountain Dew	$1.85
Chips	$.80	Pink Lemonade	$1.85
Muffins	$1.65	Unsweetened Iced Tea	$1.85
Cookies	$1.75	Coffee	$1.35
Bagel & Cream Cheese	$1.65	Hot Chocolate	$.80
Extra Cream Cheese	$.35	Hot Tea	$1.35
Yogurt	$1.65	Milk	$.80
		GATORADE	$2.00
		Souvenir Cup	$3.25
		With Fountain Drink	

博物馆内餐饮区的一个菜单说明。菜单中有食品、小吃、冰淇淋、饮料等，其中食品有热狗、火鸡芝士、汉堡芝士、芝士三明治、蔬菜三明治、餐厅餐，任何一种三明治还带有20盎司的饮料加薯条，还有儿童热狗外加小杯泉饮加薯条；小吃包括糖、爆米花、薯条和松饼、小饼干、

倍果奶酪芝士、特大奶酪芝士、酸奶、冰淇淋三明治、爱国者火箭汽水、意大利冰、哈根达斯冰淇凌；饮料包括瓶装水、清凉冰茶和果汁、百氏可乐、低糖可乐、无糖可乐、乐倍、山露、柠檬水、无糖冰茶、咖啡、热巧克力、热茶、奶、佳得乐；还有专门的纪念品杯子（杯中装泉水）。deli原来的形式为delicatessen（熟食店），但是全拼的形式已基本不用，而代之以deli；佳得乐是一种非碳酸性运动饮料，由桂格公司销售，属于百事公司旗下产品；Dr Pepper的中文名称常译作：乐倍、澎泉、胡椒博士、派珀博士等，是美国Dr Pepper/ Seven Up（七喜）公司生产的一种焦糖碳酸饮料；bagel的中文意思为"倍果"，形状像甜甜圈，中间有一个洞，质地很硬，有嚼劲，因为它的高筋面团先在水里煮过，再拿去烤箱烘烤，倍果可以有许多种，如小蓝莓、巧克力、芝士等。

19

WE STILL WANT YOU TO EAT.
Due to Sammy's being closed, we now offer the following alternate eating options:

13th Street, located across from Sammy's, offers goumet deli sandwiches and houses a Smoothie King.

WILL RICE COLLEGE SERVERY：
On-campus hot lunch line and deli sandwiches.
Open from 11a.m. until 2 p.m.
Lunches start at $5; also offers a one-time through, put-all-you-want-on-your-plate option for only $7.50.
GRAD STUDENTS: Bring your ID, get a discount!
Daily menu accessible from the Student Center Web site:
www.rice.edu/sc.

Please pick up a map from the Coffeehouse counter for directions to the servery.

暑期就餐信息
由于萨米餐厅关闭，我们现在提供就餐选择。
13大街餐厅位于萨米餐厅对面，供应三明治，内有Smoothie King快餐厅。
威尔·莱斯学院餐厅：提供校园午餐热线和熟食三明治，营业时间上午11点至下午2点；午餐起价5美元，还提供7.5美元一次性供餐服务。毕业生：请出示ID，可以享受减价！学生中心网站上可以获取每日菜单。请从咖啡屋柜台上自取地图了解前往餐厅路线。
（校园餐厅暑期供餐告示。在西方文化中，13是个不吉利的数字，但并不是所有的人都忌讳。）

20

| WILLY'S PUB RESERVES THE RIGHT TO REFUSE SERVICE TO ANYONE. | 威力酒吧保留拒绝提供服务的权力。（酒吧说明。本说明是为了防止违反公共场所行为的人员进入而发出的一个告示。） |

21

New Summer Housing Meal Schedule
Will Rice Servery is now open for the Summer Rice student population.
You can purchase meals through Housing and Dining in the H&D office during normal office hours.
Sunday:　 Dinner – 5:30 to 7:30
Monday:　Lunch – 11:30-1:30　Dinner – 5:30-7:30
Tuesday:　Lunch – 11:30-1:30　Dinner – 5:30-7:30
Wednesday: Lunch–11:30-1:30　Dinner – 5:30-7:30
Thursday: Lunch–11:30-1:30　Dinner – 5:30-7:30
Friday:　 Lunch – 11:30-1:30　Dinner – 5:30-7:30
Saturday: None

暑期餐厅就餐新安排
威尔·莱斯餐厅暑期向莱斯大学学生开放，可在正常营业时间前往住房餐饮办公室购餐。周日正餐5点30分至7点30分；周一至周五的午餐均为11点30分至1点30分，正餐5点30分至7点30分；周六不供餐。
（学校暑期就餐告示）

22

NO SEPARATE ORDERS, PLEASE

请勿分开点餐
（餐厅点餐要求。这里只允许顾客按照配置的套餐来点。）

23

NO PERSONAL CHECKS

此处不接受个人支票
（餐厅付费说明）

24

NO SHOES NO SHIRT NO SERVICE

不穿鞋，不穿衬衣就得不到服务
（餐厅就餐要求）

十三、餐饮服务

25

NO SMOKING INSIDE	餐厅内禁止吸烟 （餐厅告示）

26

WOOD FOR SMOKING AND GRILLING WOOD CHUNKS: (FOR GRILLING) MESQUITE 20 LB BAGS $20.00 PECAN $20.00 OAK $20.00 LOGS: (FOR SMOKING) MESQUITE 50LB BAGS $14.00 PECAN $14.00 OAK $14.00 PLEASE ASK CASHIER FOR ASSISTANCE	熏烤和烧烤木块 木块：（用于烧烤） 20磅包的牧豆树木、山胡桃木、橡木各20美元； 圆木：（用于熏烤） 50磅包的牧豆树木、山胡桃木、橡木各14美元。 请向收银台咨询 （烧烤餐厅出售烧烤材料说明）

27

NO RUNNING ON THE DECK	请勿在台上奔跑。 （酒吧外说明。酒吧分为室内和室外两个部分，外面的桌椅安放在有围栏的平台上。）

28

COLD BEER	HOT COFFEE	冰啤酒　热咖啡 （酒吧墙上说明）

29

Happy Hour 4 pm to 7 pm Mon thru Fri	周一至周五，每天下4点至7点为欢乐时光。 （酒吧优惠时段告示。餐厅等地方的happy hour就意味着"优惠时段"。）

30

Bag Lunches, Salads and Baked Potatoes Available at Sammy's All this Week	本周在萨米店内供应袋装午餐、沙拉和烤土豆 （一家快餐店的临时告示）

新世纪美国公示语1000例

31
| Order Here | 点餐处
（餐厅指示牌） |

32
| Pick Up Here | 取餐处
（餐厅指示牌） |

33
| PLEASE ENTER HERE
NO OUTSIDE FOOD
OR DRINKS PERMITTED | 请勿外带食品或饮料进入本店
（餐厅外带食品说明） |

34
| ICE COLD WATER | 冰水
（餐厅内所提供的饮料。在西方的餐馆内，在进食以前往往会有一杯冰水提供，其他可能的饮料还有可口可乐、啤酒、冰水、矿泉水、威士忌、白兰地等。） |

35
| Please do not throw plastic trays away. | 请勿丢弃塑料餐碟。
（餐厅说明） |

36
| Please see hostess for outside seating. | 如果需室外就餐，请联系女服务员。
（咖啡厅告示） |

37
| NOW HIRING LOSERS
$6 AN HOUR | 雇用失主，每小时6美元。
（一家快餐店贴出的幽默告示。由于快餐店内人们经常丢失东西，于是快餐店出此计策提醒顾客不要忘记自己的东西。） |

十四、安全卫生

1

Know what you're getting into…
It is unsafe to accept a ride from drivers who approach you. Follow signs to the Ground Transportation Center for authorized transportation providers.

当心黑车载客
搭乘拉客的车辆是不安全的；按照路标前往地面交通中心乘坐正规车辆。
（机场安全提示）

2

SAFETY ALERT
Our number one goal is for you to have a safe visit with us.
PLEASE
1. No running.
2. Watch your step.
3. Parents & guardians keep control of your children. Their safety is your #1 priority and responsibility
Welcome Aboard

安全警示
安全参观为第一目标。
敬请
1. 不要奔跑
2. 注意脚下
3. 父母或监护人管好孩子，保证孩子的安全是首要责任。
欢迎上船参观。
（美国中途岛号航空母舰上的安全告示）

3

DO NOT PARK
NO HAZARDOUS WASTES ACCEPTED

CAUTION
DO NOT PLAY IN, ON OR AROUND OR OCCUPY THIS CONTAINER FOR ANY PURPOSE

CAUTION
CONTAINER MUST BE PLACED ON HARD LEVEL SURFACE AND LOADED UNIFORMLY

请勿在附近停车
请勿倾倒危险垃圾
小心！
请勿在垃圾箱内外或周围玩耍，勿将垃圾箱占为其他用途。
小心！
垃圾箱必须置于坚硬的平面上，且装载均匀。
（大型垃圾箱上的提示文字。所有提示都是从安全的角度来考虑的。最后一条是为了防止垃圾箱内的垃圾因重量不平衡而发生倾倒危险。）

新世纪美国公示语1000例

4

WARNING
FALLING HAZARD
TIPPING HAZARD
LOAD EVENLY
Container must be placed on hard level surface. Tilted or unevenly loaded container could result in serious injury or death

注意！
会有坠落或者倾斜的危险。
小心平放！
垃圾箱必须置于平稳的坚硬地面上
垃圾箱倾斜或装载不均匀可能会导致严重的伤亡
（室外垃圾箱安全提示。美国很多产品的警示把有可能产生的最坏结果都考虑得非常周到。）

5

EMERGENCY
DIAL 9-1-1 FIRE
POLICE
MEDICAL

警车上的说明。遭遇火灾、需要警察或医疗救助等紧急情况下，请拨打911寻求帮助。美国警察不仅要管火灾警，还要管医疗救助。据说美国警察还要学会在紧急情况下为产妇接生。

6

ATTENTION:
72 PASSENGERS MAXIMUM CAPACITY ON SECOND DECK

注意：
二层（顶层）甲板上最大容量72名乘客
（船上限定乘客人数的警示牌）

7

ROOM CAPACITY 325

本室容量325人
（学校礼堂最大人数使用说明）

8

U. S. COAST GUARD
INSPECTED SMALL
PASSENGER VESSEL
CERTIFICATE EXPIRES:
YEAR 07 MONTH 5 DAY 13
PREVIOUS EDITION MAY BE USED

美国海岸警卫队对小型船只检查证失效日期为2007年5月13日。前版本可使用
（美国海岸警卫队对船只的安检告示）

60

十四、安全卫生

9

WARNING
To avoid serious injury from fallen or shifting cargo, be cautious when opening this door.

开门小心,以防货物掉落移动而受重伤。
(货车车身上的警示说明)

10

DANGER
DO NOT ENTER
WITHOUT WEARING
PROTECTIVE CLOTHING

危险!
未穿防护服请勿进入。
(房屋门上说明文字。一般这类房间内有辐射。)

11

<u>In Case of Emergency:</u>
In the event of emergency inside the building please report to your companies designated meeting area in the field north of the building. Do not return to the building until the situation has been deemed "All Clear".

如大楼内发生紧急情况请往大楼北边公司指定会合区报到。警报解除以前,请不要返回大楼内。
(紧急情况告示)

12

FOR YOUR SAFETY
REMAIN SEATED WITH HANDS, ARMS, FEET AND LEGS INSIDE THE VEHICLE.

SUPERVISE CHILDREN.

为了您的安全
请留在座位上
勿将手、臂、脚和腿伸出车外
监管孩子
(迪斯尼乐园内一些速度较快的娱乐项目的安全提示。一般提示中都会特别提示儿童的安全。)

13

INDIAN JONES
ADVENTURE
Temple of the Forbidden Eye
This off-road journey is a high speed, turbulent ride adventure over rough and rugged terrain that include sharp turns and sudden drops… it's unlike any ride you've ever experienced.
WARNING!

新世纪美国公示语1000例

For safety, you should be in good health and free from high blood pressure, heart, back or neck problems, motion sickness, or other conditions could be aggravated by this adventure.
Expectant mothers should not ride.
Supervise children at all times.
Persons who do not meet the minimum height requirement may not ride.
Must transfer.

印第安纳·琼斯历险记
禁眼神殿

这是一段在崎岖不平的地形上高速湍流历险,有急转弯和突然下落等,不同于任何乘坐体验。

警告!

为了安全,乘客必需身体健康,没有高血压、心脏、颈背问题、晕动症或本历险项目可能会加重的其他病况。孕妇不得乘坐;要随时监管儿童;没有达到最低身高的人不得乘坐;中间要更换交通工具。

(迪斯尼乐园中印第安的琼斯历险项目的说明。横跨上世纪80年代10年间的《夺宝奇兵》三部曲在1981年推出首部《法柜奇兵》,这个系列电影由斯皮尔伯格导演,乔治·卢卡斯监制并编剧,哈里森·福特主演。影片展现了一个观众从未见过的新型银幕英雄:印第安纳·琼斯博士是一个考古学家,但并不是书呆子,他在各地冒险探宝时身手矫健、思维敏捷,是智慧与力量结合的英雄。之后《夺宝奇兵》第二部和第三部分别于1984年和1989年拍摄完成并上映。在此后的几十年中,琼斯始终保持着极高的知名度及银幕经典地位。迪斯尼乐园正是根据电影的场景于1995年设计推出了类似的游乐项目。)

14

You May Get Wet!
Join the Swashbuckling adventures of pirates as
They invade a Caribbean Seaport. Your boat will drop down short waterfalls into dark, mysterious caverns where "dead men tell no tales."
Supervise children at all times.
Must transfer
Enter through Exit

你可能会浑身湿透!
请参与到恃强凌弱的海盗历险项目中来。因为他们侵入一个加勒比海海港,你乘坐的船会从一个瀑布跌入一个漆黑、神秘的大洞穴中,那里"死人不会说话的"。
随时监管儿童。
必须中转
从出口处进入。

(迪斯尼乐园内一刺激性水上项目的文字说明。Dead Men Tell No Tales(死人不会说话)是根据美国1971年拍摄的同名电影中的类似场景而设计的一个娱乐场所。)

十四、安全卫生

15

| The number of the people Permitted in this room Shall not exceed 49 by Order of the State Fire Marshal | 根据本州消防长官指令 本室人数限额不得超过49人 （公共场所内有关房间人数限制的标识牌） |

16

| Authorized Vehicles Only C.M.C. 11.18.040 No Alcoholic Beverages C.M.C. 10.28.010 No Overnight Sleeping Camping C.M.C. 10.48.010 No Dogs Off Sidewalk C.M.C. 7.16.020 C.P.D. 522-7353 | 仅限获准车辆C.M.C. 11.18.040 严禁酒精饮料C.M.C. 10.28.010 严禁野外夜宿C.M.C. 10.48.010 严禁在人行道以外溜狗C.M.C. 7.16.020 （有相关法律依据的告示牌。在美国很多告示很正规，往往会给公众提供法律条款出处，以显示其严肃性。） |

17

| RESTRICTED AREA ENTER ON OFFICIAL BUSINESS ONLY | 禁区 非公莫入（闲人免进） （禁区说明） |

18

| RESTRICTED AREA NO UNAUTHORIZED PERSONNEL BEYOND THIS POINT NO TRESPASSING VIOLATORS WILL BE PROSECUTED | 禁区 未经许可不得超越此点 不得穿行 违者必究 （禁区说明） |

19

| THE FOLLOWING ARE PROHIBITED: ALCOHOLIC BEVERAGES ANIMALS | 严禁以下行为 饮酒 溜动物 露营 |

新世纪美国公示语 1000 例

CAMPING
VEHICLES ON GRASS
GOLFING
LITTERING
OPEN FIRES
SOLICITATION
VIOLATORS ARE SUBJECT TO
A FINE, IMPRISONMENT OR BOTH.

草地上停车
打高尔夫
随地乱扔杂物
明火
乞讨
违者处以罚款、监禁或两项兼罚
（公共场合行为规定）

20

WARNING
HAZARDOUS
CLIFFS
STAY BEHIND
RAILINGS

警告
悬崖危险
勿越围栏
（旅游点悬崖边的安全警告）

21

WARNING
NO LITTERING NO ALCOHOL NO
EXCESS NOISE
HIKE ONLY ON IMPROVED TRAIL

警示
请勿随地乱扔、请勿饮酒、请勿
大声喧哗、请走修缮的小道。
（森林公园警示）

22

DO NOT CLIMB ON OR GO OVER WALL

请勿攀登翻越围墙。

23

No Hiking
KEEP OUT
Area Closed to Hiking
No Public Access

禁止徒步旅行
请勿靠近
本区关闭徒步旅行
非公共区域
（禁止徒步旅行的标志牌）

24

EMERGENCY ACCESS TO STREET
LEVEL THROUGH THIS DOOR

此门为通向街面的紧急出口
（紧急通道说明）

十四、安全卫生

25

| EMERGENCY VEHICLE PARKING ONLY | 限紧急车辆停放
（限制停车位说明） |

26

| NO SWIMMING IN THIS AREA | 请勿在此游泳
（池塘边上的安全提示） |

27

| Please be aware that oversized bags and backpacks cannot be brought into the theatre. Thank you for your cooperation. | 注意，请勿将超大包裹或背包带入剧场，谢谢合作。
（剧院门口的携物告示） |

28

| For Emergencies in the Park Call (Crime/Medical/Fire/Rescue) 951-443-2909 Or 911 Lost and Found in the Park? Park Visitor Center 619-220-5422 | 洛杉矶圣地亚哥公园内的有关紧急情况或物品丢失的电话告示。如园内发生紧急情况（比如罪案、疾病、火灾或救援）可拨打951–443–2909 或 911；物品丢失可拨打游客中心的电话619–220–5422。 |

29

| NO JUMPING OR DIVING | 请勿跳下或潜入水中
（一座木桥上的告示牌） |

30

| Please Be Safe
Do not stand, sit, climb or lean on zoo fences.
If you fall, animals could eat you and that might make them sick.
Thank you. | 注意安全
请勿站、坐、爬或靠在动物园栏杆上。如果落下，会被动物吃，而可能会喷使它们咬人。谢谢。
（动物园安全提示；sick 有喷使动物咬人的意思。） |

31

| NO TRESPASSING
VIOLATORS WILL BE ARRESTED | 请勿穿行，违者将被逮捕。
（禁止穿行警示） |

新世纪美国公示语 1000 例

32

| WARNING
THE FOUNTAIN AREA CONTAINS
EQUIPMENT THAT CAN CAUSE INJURY
AND SERIOUS BODILY HARM
DO NOT ENTER | 小心！
喷泉区域内有设备，
可能会造成伤害和身体重伤。
请勿入内
（喷泉附近警示语） |

33

| NO DIVING | 请勿跳入水中
（湖边告示牌） |

34

| WARNING
BUILDING UNDER
SURVEILLANCE
24 HOUR SECURITY CAMERAS
NO GRAFFITI
NO DUMPING
VIOLATORS WILL BE
PROSECUTED | 注意！
大楼监控，24小时安保摄像。
禁止涂鸦
禁倒垃圾
违者必究
（大楼外的警示牌） |

35

| Emergency
Break Glass
Pull Handle Down
Push Door to Open | 紧急情况
打碎玻璃
拉下把手
把门推开
（公共汽车上安全警示牌） |

36

| PLACEMENT OF GRAFFITI IN THIS AREA IS ILLEGAL
OFFENDERS WILL BE PROSECUTED | 本区涂鸦违法，
违者必究。 |

十四、安全卫生

37

CANS & BOTTLES
Cans, bottles & jars made of metal, glass or plastic. No caps or lids; no visible food or beverage residue; food, beverage and laundry containers only. Thanks for reducing, reusing and recycling!

瓶罐垃圾箱
金属、玻璃或塑料制作的瓶罐,不可带盖子,无可见残留食品或饮料;限食品、饮料和洗衣的容器。感谢废物减量、再生及循环使用!
(垃圾箱上说明文字。利用英语中的头韵修辞手法号召人们废物利用。要求不带盖子丢弃为了防止瓶子内部产生气体而发生爆炸等问题。)

38

$25.00 FINE FOR DISPOSAL OF HOUSEHOLD OR COMMERCIAL RUBBISH

丢弃生活垃圾或商务垃圾罚款25美元
(墙壁上有关乱扔垃圾的处罚说明)

39

NO DUMPING VIOLATORS WILL BE PROSECUTED

禁止倾倒垃圾　违者必究
(随意倾倒垃圾会严重到诉诸法律的程度)

40

Integrated Waste Management Services
Aluminum Cans and Clean Foil only

综合废物管理服务公司
铝材废物
限罐头盒和干净铝箔
(垃圾桶上的文字)

41

We want ALL your:
Newspaper
Magazines
Office & School Papers
Shopping Catalogs
Mail

Please do NOT include:
Plastic
Glass
Metals
Trash

我们需要所有的:
报纸、杂志、办公文件、学校试卷、购物目录和信件;
请勿投入塑料、玻璃、金属、垃圾。
(垃圾箱上的文字)

42

Baby Changing Station

婴儿尿布更换站

（卫生间旁边给孩子换尿布的房间门上标识。室内提供简易而实用的设施，方便父母更换孩子的尿裤等。）

43

TO THE LIST OF PLACES YOU MIGHT FIND SEXUAL PREDATORS

Each year 1 in 5 children is sexually solicited over the internet. To learn more or report an incident, call 1-800-THE LOST or visit cybertiploine.com

Help Delete Online Predators

以下所列之处可能会有色狼

每年，五个孩子中就有一个孩子被网络色情勾引。欲知详情或举报，请拨打1-800-THE LOST或访问cybertiploine.com网站。

协助消灭网上色狼

（招贴画中关于防止性攻击者的文字说明）

44

As a Courtesy To The Next Passenger May We Suggest That You Use Your Towel To Wipe Off Water Basin. Thank You!

为了下一位乘客，建议您使用纸巾擦干水盆。谢谢！

（飞机上卫生间内的文字提示。短语as a courtesy经常在公开场合下的文字中使用，相当于"请"，表示客气、礼貌等。）

45

Pull Door Open for Towels

门拉开取纸巾

（飞机上卫生间内的提示牌。这里提示如何取出纸来。towel即paper towel，通常较厚，用于擦干手上的水。）

46

Federal Law Provides for a Penalty of up to $2,200 for Tampering with the Smoke Detector Installed in this Lavatory.

联邦法律规定，损毁安装在卫生间内部的烟雾探测器最高罚款可达2,200美元。

（飞机上卫生间内对损毁内部安装的烟雾探测器的罚款警示。根据美国联邦法律规定，飞机上吸烟罚款额度为2,200美元，在飞机上的卫生间内吸烟罚款额度为3,300美元。）

十四、安全卫生

47

| MENS RESTROOM OCCUPIED WHEN DOOR IS LOCKED | 男卫生间锁闭即为有人使用（餐厅内男卫生间的说明） |

48

| If you sprinkle while you tinkle, please be neat and wipe the seat! | 如小便淋滴坐圈，请擦干保持清洁。（卫生间内的顺口溜） |

49

| CLOSED FOR CLEANING | 卫生间关闭清洁（卫生间门上提示） |

50

| NOTICE SEXUAL HARASSMENT IN THIS AREA WILL NOT BE REPORTED. HOWEVER, IT WILL BE "GRADED." | 注意！本地区性骚扰不会被报道，但是会被"划定等级"。（卫生间内有关性骚扰的文字提示。一般美国法律中只有在谋杀罪中会划分等级，比如"一级谋杀罪"等，这里使用be "graded" 来表达问题的严重性。） |

51

| OUR AIM IS TO KEEP THIS BATHROOM CLEAN GENTLEMEN Your aim will help. Stand closer LADIES Please remain seated for the entire performance | 我们的目标是保持卫生间清洁。先生，请协助我们实现目标。请再上前一步。女士，请自始至终保持坐姿。（卫生间内提示） |

新世纪美国公示语 1000 例

52

| Did you wash your hands? Use soap & water. Rub hands for 20 seconds. Rinse. Dry with paper towel. Use towel to turn off faucet. Your health is in your hands. | 你洗手了吗？使用肥皂和水；搓手20秒钟；用水冲洗；用纸巾擦干；用纸巾关闭水龙头。你的健康就在你的手中。（这是麻省理工学院公共卫生系张贴的一张洗手告示，可见其无微不至的专业程度。） |

53

| DANGER DEMOLITION AHEAD | 危险！前方拆迁（警示语） |

54

| Please Do Not Put Sanitary Napkins In the Commode STOP Thank you. | 请勿将卫生巾放入便桶内（卫生间卫生提示） |

55

THE DISCHARGE OF PLASTIC OR GARBAGE MIXED WITH PLASTIC INTO ANY WATERS IS PROHIBITED. THE DISCHARGE OF ALL GARBAGE IS PROHIBITED IN THE NAVIGABLE WATERS OF THE UNITED STATES AND, IN ALL OTHER WATERS, WITHIN THREE NAUTICAL MILES OF THE NEAREST LAND.

| THE DISCHARGE OF DUNNAGE, LINING, AND PACKING MATERIALS THAT FLOAT IS PROHIBITED WITHIN 25 NAUTICAL MILES FROM THE NEAREST LAND. | OTHER UNGROUND GARBAGE MAY BE DISCHARGED BEYOND 12 NAUTICAL MILES FROM THE NEAREST LAND. | OTHER GARBAGE GROUND TO LESS THAN ONE INCH MAY BE DISCHARGED BEYOND THREE NAUTICAL MILES OF THE NEAREST LAND. |

A PERSON WHO VIOLATES THE ABOVE REQUIREMENTS IS LIABLE FOR A CIVIL PENALTY OF UP TO $25,000, A FINE OF UP TO $50,000, AND IMPRISONMENT FOR UP TO FIVE YEARS FOR EACH VIOLATION. REGIONAL, STATE, AND LOCAL RESTRICTIONS ON GARBAGE DISCHARGES ALSO MAY APPLY.

十四、安全卫生

船上有关禁止倾倒垃圾的告示。严禁将塑料或塑料和垃圾混在一起倾入任何水域；在美国航海水域内、所有其他水域内以及近海距离陆地最近的3英里内禁止倾倒垃圾。距离海岸25海里以内禁止倾倒漂浮的衬垫物、织物和包装材料；其他未被粉碎的垃圾可以在距离最近海岸12英里以外的范围内倾倒；其他已经粉碎的小于1英寸的垃圾可以在3海里以外的地方倾倒。违规者依次处以民事罚款25,000美元、50,000美元和5年以下监禁。各区、各州和各地方对垃圾倾倒的限制也同样适用。

（nautical mile为英制单位，表示"海里"，大约合1.853公里。）

56

CITY OF BOSTON
INSPECTIONAL SERVICES
DEPARTMENT
HEALTH DIVISION
1010 MASSACHUSETTS AVENUE
BOSTON, MA 02118
THIS PERMIT MUST BE POSTED
IN A CONSPICUOUS PLACE
COMPLAINTS REGARDING THE
SANITARY CONDITIONS OF
THIS ESTABLISHMENT MAY BE
REFERRED TO INSPECTIONAL
SERVICES DEPARTMENT,
HEALTH DIVISION
(omitted)

波士顿市监查服务部卫生处颁发的游船许可证内容。许可证必须张贴在显要位置；有关本设施的卫生健康状况可以咨询监查服务部卫生处。另外许可证上还提供了拥有人名字(owner name)、场所名称(establishment name)、许可证号(permit number)、许可证类型(permit type)、许可证说明(permit description)、发证日期(date issue)、失效日期(expiration date)、办证金额(amount)、市长签字(mayor)等内容。

57

BE ADVISED
POWER LINES OVERHEAD

注意！
架空电源线
（露天告示）

58

CAUTION
Low Tree Limbs
Ahead

小心前方低矮树枝
（道路上对低矮树枝警示）

71

新世纪美国公示语1000例

十五 消防报警

1
False Alarm is a violation of Texas Penal Code Sec. 42.06

恶意火警是违反得克萨斯州相关法规的。
（火警装置边上的提示。最后还明示法规的具体条目，而通过这些条目的名称和代码均可以在网络上搜寻到具体的内容。）

2
PUSH/PULL TO RELEASE DOOR IN AN EMERGENCY

紧急情况下把门推开或者拉开。
（火警警示牌边上的另外一块告示。这里可以看出，该门的设计是通过两种方式紧急逃生，因为人们在紧急情况下往往无法迅速反应，双重开门方式无疑给逃生者最大化的人性呵护。）

3
GARAGE SPRINKLER SYSTEM ONLY

车库专用喷淋系统
（车库内防火喷头附近张贴的文字）

4
IN CASE OF FIRE USE STAIRS UNLESS OTHERWISE INSTRUCTED

发生火灾 请用楼梯，除非另有指示。
（电梯内预防火灾指示牌上的内容）

5
In Case Of Fire, Use Stairway For Exit Do Not Use Elevators

发生火灾，使用楼梯，勿用电梯。
（楼道内的火灾逃生提示）

十五、消防报警

6

SPRINKLER	喷水设备
FIRE ALARM	火警铃响,打电话给消防部门或警方。
WHEN BELL RINGS CALL	(路边墙上火灾报警说明)
FIRE DEPT OR POLICE	

7

| MALICIOUS FIRE ALARM PULLS INCUR $600 FINE AND POSSIBLE SUSPENSION | 恶意拉火警,罚款600美元,还可能被拘留。(大楼内有关恶意火警的告示) |

8

Fire Extinguisher Inspection
Building:
Location:
Make:
Type:
Size:
Serial Number:
Serviced:
Due:
  Environmental Health & Safety X4444

灭火器上的安全标签检查说明文字。需要填入的内容包括楼号、位置、型号、类型、大小、序列号、维修日及到期日。

9

DO NOT REMOVE BY ORDER OF THE STATE FIRE MARSHAL Fire Equipment Co.

ECR 1410
Certification of Registration Number
Name of Licensee
Signature
License Number
  TYPE of WORK
  MAINTENANCE   ☐
  NEW EXTINGUISHER   ☐
  SERVICE (List on back) ☐
DATE OF LAST SERVICE

本州消防长官令,本标签不得揭除。
消防设备公司
(灭火器上的安全检查文字说明,另外标签上还有登记证号码、注册单位名称、签字、许可证号。还有该灭火器的使用情况:维修状态、新灭火器或维护(列在背面),以及最近一次维护时间等。)

新世纪美国公示语 1000 例

10

| EXTINGUISHER TYPE, SIZE and LOCATION:
OWNER'S NAME and ADDRESS:
LIST SERVICE PERFORMED:
(Monthly Inspection–Initial and date below) | 灭火器另一张标签说明文字。所列信息包括灭火器类型、大小和存放位置；拥有者名称和地址；列出所进行的维护；每月检查（最初的检查和日期列在下面）。 |

11

| IN CASE OF FIRE USE STAIRS UNLESS OTHERWISE INSTRUCTED
IN CASE OF FIRE DO NOT USE ELEVATORS USE EXIT STAIRS | 发生火灾，使用楼梯，除非另有指示。发生火灾，不要使用电梯，使用消防楼梯。
（楼梯和电梯在火警中的两个使用说明） |

12

| In case of emergency please call:
(713)348-6000
Do Not Call 911 | 紧急情况，请拨打(713)348-6000，不要拨打911。
（学校一部门报警提示） |

13

| FIRE DEPARTMENT CONNECTION | 商场内消防栓接口提示。摘下牌子即是消防龙头接口。 |

14

| Do Not Hang Items From Sprinkler Head This Will Cause Flooding | 请勿在喷头上悬挂物件，悬挂物件会导致水大量涌出。
（消防栓说明） |

15

| FIRE HOSE | 消防栓（超市等火警告示） |

16

| SPRINKLER SHUT OFF VALVE | 喷淋系统关闭阀（超市等火警告示） |

十五、消防报警

17 ALARM SOUNDS WHEN DOOR OPENS — 门打开警铃响。（超市等火警告示）

18 FIRE DOOR DO NOT BLOCK — 消防通道，请勿堵塞。（超市等火警告示）

19 FIRE ESCAPE — 防火通道（超市等火警告示）

20 FIRE DOOR KEEP CLOSED — 防火门，请勿打开。（商场火警告示）

21 BY ORDER OF FIRE DEPARTMENT THIS DOOR MUST REMAIN CLOSED AT ALL TIMES FAILURE TO COMPLY WILL RESULT IN INDIVIDUAL LEGAL ACTION — 消防部门令 此门必须一直关闭 不遵守者会导致法律诉讼（机场大门上的告示）

22 SPRINKLER CONTROL VALVE — 喷水设备控制阀（超市等火警告示）

23 SPRINKLER FIRE ALARM WHEN BELL RINGS —CALL— FIRE DEPT. OR POLICE — 喷水设备 火警 警铃响 电话通知消防部门或警方（超市等火警告示）

24

FIRE BLANKET　　防火毯（超市等火警用具告示）

25

FIRE HOSE REEL　　消防水管盘（超市等火警用具告示）

26

THIS EXTINGUISHER
WATER
TO BE USED FOR WOOD,
PAPER, RUBISH FIRES
NOT FOR ELECTRICAL OR
FLAMMABLE LIQUIDS FIRES

本灭火器
水型
用于木材、纸张和垃圾引起的火灾，不适用于电或可燃液体引起的火灾。
（超市等火警用具告示）

27

THIS COLOURED EXTINGUISHER
FOAM
TO BE USED FOR OIL AND
FLAMMABLE LIQUID FIRES
NOT FOR ELECTRICAL FIRES

本彩色灭火器
泡沫型
用于油、易燃液体引起的火灾，不适用于电引发的火灾。
（灭火器说明）

28

THIS EXTINGUISHER
CO_2
TO BE USED FOR PAINT,
OIL, ELECTRICAL AND
OTHER LIQUID FIRES

本灭火器为
二氧化碳灭火器
用于因漆、油、电以及其他液体引起的火灾
（灭火器说明）

29

THIS COLOURED EXTINGUISHER
A:B(E) POWDER
TO BE USED FOR PAPER,
WOOD, TEXTILE, OIL,
LIQUID, AND ELECTRICAL
FIRES

本彩色灭火器
A:B(E)粉末型
用于纸张、木材、织物、油、液体以及电引发的火灾
（灭火器说明）

十五、消防报警

30

| THIS COLOURED EXTINGUISHER B(E) POWDER TO BE USED FOR OIL, LIQUID AND ELECTRICAL FIRES | 本彩色灭火器 B(E)粉末型 用于油、液体以及电引发的火灾 （灭火器说明） |

31

| FIRE HAZARD AREA NO SMOKING Beyond this Point | 火灾危险区域 此点以外禁止吸烟 （森林火警警示） |

新世纪美国公示语1000例

十六 吸烟管理

1
This Is A Smoke Free Floor. Thank You For Not Smoking.
这里是非吸烟区，谢谢您的合作。
（酒店大堂内禁止吸烟的标识）

2
Cigarette Butt Disposal Only
烟头处置专用
（酒店外专门处理吸剩烟头设施的说明。英语中除了使用tobacco，cigar和cigarette表示"香烟"以外，还经常使用butt，fag和weed等俚语来表达。）

3
NO SMOKING PLEASE THE INTREPID MUSEUM COMPLEX, INCLUDING THE SHIPS AND THE PIER, IS A DESIGNATED NON-SMOKING AREA
请勿吸烟！
整个航空母舰参观区域包括船和船坞为指定的非吸烟区域。
（航空母舰博物馆上禁止吸烟的标识。该博物馆不仅有航空母舰，还有一架早期的"协和"空客和一艘潜水艇等可以参观。）

4
SMOKING AT CURBSIDE DESIGNATED AREAS ONLY
只可在道边指定区域内吸烟

5
SMOKE FREE ZONE
无烟区

6
No Smoking. Use designated outdoor areas only.
严禁吸烟，只可到户外指定区域吸烟。

十六、吸烟管理

7 | Park Plaza Hospital is smokefree. Please Don't Smoke. | Park Plaza医院为无烟区 请勿吸烟

8 | NO SMOKING Permitted in This Area | 本区域内禁止吸烟

9 | PLEASE DON'T THROW YOUR CIGARETTE ENDS ON THE FLOOR THE COCKROACHES ARE GETTING CANCER | 请勿将烟蒂扔到地板上 蟑螂会患癌症的
（动物园内有关吸烟的告示。据说蟑螂是不会患癌症的，而使用了这样危言耸听的语言是为了告诫吸烟者吸烟的危害性有多大。）

10 | NO SMOKING UNLESS YOU A LOCOMOTIVE | 禁止吸烟，除非你是一个火车头。
（一种比较幽默的方式劝告不要吸烟）

新世纪美国公示语1000例

十七 大门管理

1

CAUTION
Please Keep Clear
Of Automatic Doors

小心!
请远离自动门
(机场内自动门口的提示)

2

PULL
You can have things
your way and push if
you want, but this door
is pretty stubborn.

拉!
你可自行其是,想推则推,但这个门不听调动。
(这是一家快餐店大门上一个带点幽默色彩的开门提示。幽默的语言有利于创造和谐轻松的环境。)

3

CAUTION
AUTOMATIC
DOOR

小心!
自动门
(机场大门说明文字)

4

THIS DOOR TO REMAIN
UNLOCKED DURING
BUSINESS HOURS

该扇大门营业时间内开启
(机场大门文字说明)

5

THIS DOOR WILL
ALARM
PLEASE WAIT
BEHIND THE
ROPES
THE BUS DRIVER WILL
OPEN THE DOOR AND
ESCORT YOU TO THE BUS

此门会发出警报
请在警戒绳的后面等待
大巴司机会开门,护送你到大巴。
(机场内大门上的说明文字。机场内有的时候会用一辆大巴将乘客运送到飞机前,然后乘客再登机。)

十七、大门管理

6

Emergency Exit Only
Alarm Will Ring If Door Is Opened

紧急出口
门打开,警铃会响。
(机场大门上的警示)

7

ALARM LOCK DOOR
FAILURE TO SECURE THIS DOOR
IS A VIOLATION OF
FEDERAL AVIATION
REGULATIONS

应急大门
不关紧此门是违反联邦航空条例的行为
(机场大门上警示说明。一般在紧急出口附近都会有这样的文字提示,告诫人们不要随意打开大门,否则会发出报警声。)

8

ATTENTION
THIS ENTRANCE IS FOR USE BY THE GENERAL
PUBLIC AND THOSE DOING BUSINESS WITH
OR VISITING TENANTS OF THIS BUILDING
OR ANY OTHER COMPANY IN THE
BUILDING EXCEPT FOR COPSTAT SECURITY.
THIS ENTRANCE IS NOT FOR USE BY
EMPLOYEES OF, OR ANY OTHER PERSONS
SEEKING TO DO BUSINESS WITH, COPSTAT
SECURITY. ALL SUCH PERSONS
ARE DIRECTED TO USE THE MOST
WESTERLY
ENTRANCE ON 33RD STREET LOCATED AT
17 WEST 33RD STREET, THANK YOU FOR
YOUR COOPERATION.

注意
此入口为大众使用,包括大楼租户或楼内其他公司的办事人员人或游客,但不包括COPSTAT安保人员。楼内工作人员或者其他推销员不得使用本口进出,这些人员使用33号大街最西边的入口,位于33号大街17号。谢谢合作!
(纽约帝国大厦入口说明。COPSTAT为美国一家安保公司。)

9

ENTRANCE ON 45TH STREET

入口在45号大街上
(纽约一栋大楼外的指示牌)

10.

DOORS REMAIN LOCKED
MIDNIGHT THRU 6:00A.M.
PLEASE
USE MAIN ENTRANCE DURING
THESE HOURS.

这些门在午夜至凌晨6点关闭，请从正门出入。
（酒店大门开关信息）

11.

THIS GATE IS ERECTED TO THE
MEMORY OF
JOSEPH McKEAN
BY THE MEMBERS OF THE
PORCELLIAN CLUB
OF WHICH HE WAS THE HONORED
FOUNDER

此门是坡斯廉俱乐部成员为纪念俱乐部荣誉创始人约瑟夫·麦金而建立
（牛津大学麦金门的说明文字。坡斯廉俱乐部是1791年牛津大学成立的一个男性成员组成的俱乐部。）

12.

THE McKEAN GATE
THE REVEREND JOSEPH
MCKEAN STD LLD
BORN AT IPSWICH
MASSACHUSETTS 19 APRIL 1776
DIED AT HAVANA CUBA 17
MARCH 1818
A GRADUATE OF THIS COLLEGE
1794
TEACHER OF YOUTH MINISTER
OF THE GOSPEL
BOYLSTON PROFESSOR OF
RHETORIC AND ORATORY 1809-
1818

麦金门
尊敬的神学博士兼法学博士约瑟夫·麦金于1776年4月19日出生于马萨诸塞州的伊普斯魏奇，1818年3月17日卒于古巴哈瓦那，是本校1794届毕业生；1808年至1818年任青年导师、福音传道师、博伊尔斯顿修辞与演讲教授。
（哈佛大学麦金门的说明文字。STD为"神学博士"(Doctor of Sacred Theology)，来源于拉丁文Sacrae Theologiae Doctor; LLD为"法学博士"(Doctor of Laws)，来源于拉丁文Legum Doctor。）

13.

Access at North West Entry →

西北门进入本楼
（哈佛大学校园内大楼门上标示）

十七、大门管理

14

University Library
DIRECTOR'S OFFICE

大学图书馆馆长办公室
（哈佛大学一座名叫大学图书馆的门上的说明。哈佛大学有图书馆分馆100座，共计藏书1500万册。）

15

PHILANTHROPIC ADVISORS

慈善咨询处（大门上的一个说明牌）

16

Brown College
Is Locked Twenty Four Hours Daily.
Entry by ID Card Only.
For Deliveries Between
8:30am –12:00pm and 1:00pm–4:pm
Call Extension 4662.
For an outside line, dial 9.

布朗学院
大门24小时关闭
凭ID卡进入
8:30am –12:00pm 和 1:00pm–4:pm
以上时段送外卖拨分机4662；外线先拨9。
（这是美国莱斯大学布郎学院门口一块不锈钢牌子上写的说明。）

17

Inaccessible Entrance
Entrance For The Physically Challenged Located At Elevator
No Smoking
City of Houston Ordinance

有障碍通道
残障人士通道在电梯
严禁吸烟（休斯敦市法令）
（大楼入口说明）

18

Authorized Personnel Only
Police Visitors Use Front Entrance

闲人免进
报警请走前门
（警察局门上的说明文字）

19

RICE UNIVERSITY
Delivery Services & Transportation Staff Only

莱斯大学
汽车接送服务人员专用
（门上说明文字。这里staff only相当于汉语中的"闲人免进"。）

新世纪美国公示语1000例

20
This door is locked.
Please use exterior door to exit conference room.
To enter Dean's office, please use lobby entrance to room 116.

此门锁闭
请从外门出会议室
通过大厅进入116室（系主任办公室）
（会议室大门上的临时说明）

21
Please Ring Bell

请按门铃

22
Please use this door

请开这扇门
（门上的说明。门为两扇开的时候，其中一扇无必要使用，因此就会出现这样的文字。）

23
The entrance to the Multicultural Affairs and Student Activities Offices is located 2 doors down. ←

多元文化事务办公室和学生活动办公室向前走过两个门
（地点指示牌）

24
Nearest Accessible Building Entrance is located at Building West Side

最近入口位于大楼西侧
（进入大楼的说明）

25
Door Locked from 9:00PM – 5:00 AM
Check in at North Tower Lobby
← Ewing Street

晚9点至凌晨5点之间此门关闭
请从东翼大街进入北塔楼大厅
（医院大门管理说明。Ewing等于East Wing。）

26
PUSH/ PULL
TO RELEASE DOOR
IN AN EMERGENCY

紧急情况下推开或拉开大门
（大门使用说明）

27
PUSH BUTTON TO OPEN DOOR

按钮开门（医院侧门说明）

十七、大门管理

28

| NO VENDORS | 禁止商贩进入（大楼门口告示） |

29

| PLEASE CHECK IN AT ADMITTING RECEPTION | 请在入院处登记
（进入医院的登记要求） |

30

| WHEN CLOSED GO TO ER ADMITTING IN NORTH TOWER OR DIAL 0 AT LOBBY PHONE | 大门关闭时，请往北楼ER入口或在大厅拨电话号码0。
（进入医院内部的说明） |

31

| You must present a Harvard ID to enter the building. | 凭哈佛证件出入本楼
（哈佛一大楼门口的提示） |

32

| DOORS TO REMAIN UNLOCKED WHENEVER PUBLIC IS PRESENT | 来人参观，大门敞开。
（参观地点开放状态告示牌） |

33

| WARNING
Moving Gate Can Cause Serious Injury or Death
KEEP CLEAR! Gate may move at any time without prior warning.
Do not let children operate the gate or play in the gate area.
This entrance is for vehicles only.
Pedestrians must use separate entrance. | 警告
移动门可能会造成严重伤害或死亡请避开此门！大门会随时开闭，无提前预警。
不要让孩子触动大门或在大门附近玩耍。此入口只用于车辆。
行人必须使用其他入口。 |

新世纪美国公示语1000例

十八 饮酒枪支

1

All alcohol must be consumed here in this facility. THANK YOU!

含酒精饮料必须在本酒吧中饮用。谢谢！
（酒吧中的告示。美国对酒类出售管理非常严格，不仅要控制购买者的年龄，还要限制饮酒的地方。）

2

ALCOHOLIC BEVERAGES PROHIBITED

禁止含酒精的饮料。
（禁酒标志）

3

The consumption of any alcoholic beverages at this location is prohibited. Violation of this law is a Class C misdemeanor & carries a fine up to $500.

此地严禁饮用含酒精的饮料，违者属C类轻罪罚款500美元。
（汽车和地铁公司在车站上的公示语）

4

No Smoking Allowed.

休斯敦轻轨车站上禁止吸烟提示文字。站台是露天的，但是在这里等车仍然禁止吸烟。

5

WARNING
State law prohibits anyone under 21 from entering this business unless accompanied by a parent, court-appointed guardian or adult spouse.

注意
本州法律禁止21岁以下的人进入本商业区，除非有父母、法庭指定监护人或成年配偶陪同。
（一家俱乐部门口的警示语）

十八、饮酒枪支

6

FELONY NOTICE
THE LICENSED OR UNLICENSED POSSESSION OF A WEAPON ON THESE PREMISES IS A FELONY WITH A MIXIMUM PENALTY OF 10 YEARS IMPRISONMENT AND A FINE NOT TO EXCEED $10,000.

重罪提示
本区域携带无论注册或未注册的武器均为重罪行为，最高处罚10年监禁合并1万美元以下罚款。
（公共场所内有关携带枪支的警示）

7

If you have a complaint about the sale or service of alcoholic beverages in this establishment, please contact the Texas Alcoholic Beverage Commission.

如对本场所含酒饮料的出售或服务有投诉，请联系得克萨斯州含酒饮料委员会。
（有关售卖酒饮料的提示文字）

8

ABSOLUTELY NO BEER CAN BE SOLD TO ANYONE UNDER THE AGE OF 21
NO BEER CAN BE SOLD ON SUNDAY BEFORE 12:00 NOON

严禁啤酒出售给21岁以下的人
周日中午12点前不得出售啤酒
（禁酒告示。美国政府对出售啤酒也会有严格的规定。）

9

NO ALCOHOLIC BEVERAGES

禁止含酒精的饮料
（公共场所的告示）

10

NOTICE
The unlicensed possession of a weapon on these premises is a felony with a maximum penalty of 10 years imprisonment and a fine not to exceed $10,000.

注意
本场所内非法持有枪支为重罪，最高处罚10年监禁合并1万美元以下罚款。
（商店内有关携带枪支的警告）

新世纪美国公示语 1000 例

11

WARNING:
IT IS A CRIME (MISDEAMEANOR)
TO CONSUME LIQUOR OR BEER ON
THESE PREMISES.

警示：
本场所内饮用烈酒或啤酒为犯罪
（禁酒标志）

12

BUYING CIGARETTES
FOR MINORS COULD COST YOU.
IT'S NOT JUST WRONG, IT'S ILLEGAL.

向未成年人出售香烟要付出代价
不仅犯错，是违法。
（商店售卖香烟告示）

13

Under 18 No Tobacco
Please Have ID Ready

18岁以下不得购买香烟
请备好证件
（商店售卖香烟告示）

14

UNDER 21
WARNING
Police Officer May be
Posing As An Employee
"Cops in Shops"
Texas Alcoholic Beverage Commission
Texas Department of Transportation

21岁以下未成年人请注意！
警察可能会扮成顾客
得克萨斯州含酒饮料管理委员会
得克萨斯州交通部
（商店售卖香烟告示。Cops in Shops是美国的一个全国性的禁止青少年购酒项目。）

15

—21—
Anything less and you can't purchase Alcoholic
beverages in Texas.

IT'S A CRIME
- To purchase alcoholic beverages if you're under 21.
- To attempt to purchase alcoholic beverages if you're under 21.
- To present false ID.
- To misrepresent your age so you can buy alcoholic beverages.
- To provide alcoholic beverages to someone under 21 who is not your child or spouse.

BE PREPARED TO SHOW ID!

21岁
年龄低于21岁者不能在得克萨斯州
购买含酒饮料
以下均为犯罪行为
- 21岁以下购买含酒饮料
- 21岁以下企图购买含酒饮料
- 出示假证件
- 谎报年龄而购买含酒饮料
- 给21岁以下的人，不是你的孩子或配偶提供含酒饮料
请随时出示证件
（商店售卖香烟告示）

十八、饮酒枪支

16

| WARNING
CONSUMPTION AND/OR DISPLAY
OF ALCOHOLIC BEVERAGES
PROHIBITED IN VEHICLE
PARKING AREAS OF THIS PARK |

禁止
公园停车区内禁止饮用和/或展示含酒饮料
（禁酒警告。美国公共场所禁酒法令非常严格，因此有些流浪汉就会把啤酒瓶子放在纸袋里面喝，这样不容易看出是在喝酒。）

17

IT IS UNLAWFUL TO CARRY A HANDGUN ON HOSPITAL PROPERTY. VIOLATORS WILL BE PROSECUTED.

在医院范围内携带手枪是非法的，违者将受到起诉。
（医院禁止携带枪支说明）

18

DRUG FREE
GUN FREE
SCHOOL ZONE
VIOLATORS WILL FACE SEVERE
FEDERAL STATE AND LOCAL
CRIMINAL PENALTIES

校区无毒品 无枪支
违反者将遭到联邦法、州法和地方法规的严厉惩处
（学校有关禁毒禁枪的告示）

新世纪美国公示语1000例

十九

公德告示

1

DOGS NOT PERMITTED IN BUILDINGS
EXCEPTIONS
LICENSED GUIDE DOGS
DOGS FOR SHIPMENT

犬类不准进入大楼
有证照的导盲犬以及将被托运的犬类除外
（机场关于携带宠物狗的说明。导盲犬是一种经过培训的工作犬，主要给视障人员领路。美国的第一家导盲犬训练中心，于1929年在田纳西州的首府纳什维尔成立，目前使用导盲犬最多的国家为美国，大约有6万条。）

2

WE LIKE DOGS BUT THE CITY DON'T

我们喜欢狗，但是城市不喜欢。
（酒吧内关于宠物的告示）

3

NO DOGS ALLOWED

请勿带狗进入
（酒吧内关于宠物的告示）

4

NO PETS ALLOWED IN BUILDINGS

大楼内请勿带入宠物
（店家有关宠物的告示）

5

KEEP PETS ON LEASH

请牵着宠物
（电梯内有关宠物的告示）

6

NO DOGS OR PETS

禁止携带狗或宠物进入
（公共场合关于宠物的告示）

十九、公德告示

7 NO GLASS CONTAINERS

请勿携带玻璃容器
（露天剧场告示。由于很多人都是席地而坐，因此一旦玻璃破碎会伤及他人。）

8 NO LITTERING

请勿乱扔杂物（公共场合告示）

9 NO TRESPASSING
VIOLATORS WILL BE PROSECUTED

不准入内
违者必究

10 Secure Area
Access Restricted

警戒区域
严禁进入
（安全区域警示牌）

11 PLEASE
NO SKATEBOARDING
NO ROLLERBLADING
PARK CLOSES AT DARK
VIOLATORS WILL BE TREATED
AS TRESPASSERS PURSUANT TO
VA CODE SECTION 18.2-119

请勿溜滑板
勿溜滑四轮旱冰鞋
黄昏时刻 公园关闭
根据弗吉尼亚州相关法律，违者将被视为侵犯领地。
（公园门口告示牌。其中的VA是Virginia（弗吉尼亚州）的缩写。）

12 Private Property　No Soliciting
No Trespassing　No Smoking
Massachusetts Institute of Technology
Access to and presence in this building are limited to residents and other authorized persons. Violators will be prosecuted.

私人领地　禁止拉客
不准入内　禁止吸烟
麻省理工学院规定，只有居民和特许人员可以进入本大楼。违者将被起诉。
（麻省理工学院中工学院大楼侧门上的说明）

新世纪美国公示语 1000 例

13

| STAIR A
NO ROOF ACCESS | A号楼梯，不通顶层
（楼梯通行文字） |

14

| AUTHORIZED ACCESS ONLY
VIOLATIONS WILL
CONSTITUTE TRESPASS
Must See Mall Office or Security
Officer for Access Information | 闲人免进
违者构成非法入侵罪
通行咨询，找商场办公室或安保人员。
（大楼禁行告示） |

15

| Restricted Area Beyond This Point | 此点以外为限制区 |

16

| NO OPEN FIRES | 禁止篝火（野外告示） |

17

| NO CAMPING | 禁止露营（野外告示） |

18

| THE SOLICITATION OR DISTRIBUTION OF LITERATURE BY NON-EMPLOYEES IS STRICTLY PROHIBITED ON THESE PREMISES. | 本场所严禁拉客或
非雇员散发广告
（公共场所告示） |

19

| IN CONSIDERATION OF THE BUILDING TENANTS PLEASE TALK IN MODERATE TONES | 大楼内有住户，
请小声说话。
（大楼内告示） |

20

| No public postings permitted.
Please use public bulletin boards in the main computer lab. | 禁止张贴海报
请使用计算机主实验室内的公告栏
（张贴海报说明） |

十九、公德告示

21

HOUSTON CODE of ORDINANCES
sec. 46-93
Unlawful To Deface, Remove,
Knockdown or Alter
Any Traffic-Control Device.
Maximum Fine $200.00
City of Houston Traffic and
Transportation Department

休斯敦法令规定：非法污损、移动、推倒或者改变任何一个交通管理设施，最高罚款200美元。
休斯敦市车辆交通部
（休斯敦道路告示）

22

NO CELL ZONE

本区域请勿使用手机
（大楼内限制使用手机的文字。有些教学楼内专设一个小房间供手机使用者打电话。）

23

Graffiti
It's a Crime!

涂鸦违法（公共场合禁止涂鸦的告示）

24

NEWLY SEEDED
LAWN
PLEASE KEEP OFF

草坪上新播种
请勿踩踏
（草坪说明）

25

PLEASE HELP
US PROTECT THIS NEW
PLANTING BY
RESPECTING THE FENCES

请协助我们保护这些新植被
不要跨越栅栏
（公园新栽植被围栏外说明）

26

PLEASE DO NOT DUCK UNDER THE ROPE

请勿从绳下穿过
（排队警示，防止有人从拉起的排队绳子下弯身过去。）

27

PETS SHALL BE ON
A LEASH NOT OVER
6 FEET IN LENGTH
HANDLERS SHALL IMMEDIATELY PICK
UP PET EXCREMENT AND DISPOSE OF
IT IN TRASH CONTAINERS PENALTY
FOR VIOLATION OF REGULATIONS:
FINE UP TO $500.00 AND /OR
IMPRISONMENT
UP TO 6 MONTHS

宠物须用不超过6英尺长的绳子牵着。
遛狗者应立即将狗的粪便拾起并投入垃圾箱内，违者罚款高达500美元和/或监禁6个月以内。
（公园遛狗规定）

二十、旅游景点

1

NY SKYRIDE
OFFERS THE FOLLOWING
DISCOUNTS
TO OBSERVATORY VISITORS:
Observatory Ticket Holders
Save $5.50 on Adult/Senior
Save $4.50 on Child/Youth
Observatory Express Pass Holders
Save $13.50 on Adult
Save $8.50 on Senior/ Youth
Save $7.50 on Child
City Pass
Save $16.50 on Adult
Save $11.50 on Youth
NY Pass FREE
Visit our 2nd floor ticket window to receive your discount.
Use the escalator next to the US Post Office

这是竖立在帝国大厦内的环城游广告。在纽约市中心有双层公共汽车提供环城游(skyride)。为了吸引更多的顾客观光，环城游便推出了参观帝国大厦游旋转餐厅的优惠政策。针对不同的旋转餐厅票的持有人会有不同的优惠项目。持票者成人优惠5.5美元；儿童4.5美元。持有旋转餐厅快速通行票，成人优惠13.5美元，老人或青少年优惠8.5美元，儿童优惠7.5美元。拥有城市通行卡可免费搭乘环城游公共汽车。告示最后还告诉游客可以前往2层购票窗口领取优惠卷，同时还告知使用美国邮政局边上的电梯前往。

2

The Midway will remain open during Pier construction.

船坞建设期间中途岛号航空母舰将一直开放。（美国中途岛号航空母舰上的告示）

3

POWER PORTAL COMMITTEE
GRATEFULLY ACKNOWLEDGES
CONTRIBUTIONS FROM THE
FOLLOWING
（Omitted）

尼亚加利瀑布靠近美国边境的一个水电站的大门纪念文字。上面记载着水电站委员会对捐赠人员或机构的感激（省略捐赠人员或机构名单）。

新世纪美国公示语 1000 例

4

TO THE ENGINEERS FINANCIERS
SCIENTISTS
WHOSE GENIUS COURAGE AND
INDUSTRY
MADE POSSIBLE HERE THE BIRTH
OF HYDRO ELECTRIC POWER
AND CREATED THE FIRST FIVE
THOUSAND HORSE POWER WATER
TURBINES DIRECTLY CONNECTED TO
ALTERNATING CURRENT GENERATORS
AND INAUGURATED IN AMERICA LONG
DISTANCE TRANSMISSION OF POWER BY
ELECTRICITY

为纪念工程师、金融家和科学家,他们的天才、勇气和勤劳使水力发电能在此诞生,创造了第一批5000马力水轮机直接连接交流发电机,并在美国开创了电力长途输送的新纪元。
(美国尼亚加拉公园内一块纪念碑上的文字)

5

THIS IS THE ORIGINAL ARCH ENTRANCE
TO THE ADAMS STATION
THE WORLD'S FIRST HYDROELECTRIC
POWER PLANT.
Electric Power, its generation by water turbines, its
transmission in commercial quantities
to remote distances, the design and building of the
first large electrical equipment- all started with the
completion of the
Adams Station in 1895 at Niagara Falls.
Its entrance was re-erected on this site in 1966
to commemorate the tremendous impact
which the generation of electric power at the
Adams Station gave to civilization
throughout the world.
THIS ARCH DEDICATED 1967 BY
NELSON A.ROCKEFELLER, GOVERNOR

这是世界上第一座水电站——亚当斯水电站的原始拱门入口。水轮机发电在商业上大量远距输送,第一台大型电力设备的设计和建造均始于1895年尼亚加拉瀑布亚当斯水电站的落成。这里的大门是1966年原址重建,为纪念亚当斯水电站发电给全世界文明的巨大影响。这座拱门是当时的州长内尔森·A.洛克菲勒于1967年捐赠的。
(尼亚加拉瀑布美国一边公园内的一座古迹的说明。)

6

PLEASE KEEP OFF WALL

请勿靠近石碑
（阿灵顿国家公墓中石碑旁的文字说明。石碑是斜着放置的，被称为wall。）

7

NIAGARA FALLS STATE PARK
Terrapin Point
Horseshoe Falls
Crestline 2,500 ft. 762 M
Height 167ft. 51M
Summer daytime flow:
675,000gal/sec.
2.554.857L/sec.

尼亚加拉瀑布国家公园水龟点马蹄型瀑布：脊长为2,500英尺/762米；高度为167英尺/51米；每秒流量为675,000加仑/2,554,857升。

（尼亚加拉瀑布国家公园内竖立一块牌子上对马蹄瀑布的说明。为了表达清晰，公园内这块牌子上所有的数字都使用英制和公制两种方式。美国还在坚持使用美式英制单位的国家，任何其他国家，几乎都已经转向公制（世界上只有三个国家不法定使用公制：美国、利比里亚和缅甸）。英国早就通过法律强制使用公制，但是在美国几乎看不到"千克"、"摄氏度"、"千米"、"毫升"等公制单位，代之以"磅"、"华氏"、"迈"、"盎司"。然而更让人意想不到的是，这些单位之间的换算极其不方便，比如1oz = 29.57353ml, 1mile=1.609347km, 1华氏度=1.8摄氏度+32。）

8

THE EIGHTH WONDER OF THE WORLD

You are now in the most famous building in the world. This triumph of architectural and engineering genius, the Empire State Building—the Eighth Wonder of the World—soars 1,472 feet into the sky—as high as all the original Seven Wonders

世界第八大奇迹
现在你正在世界上最著名的建筑中，帝国大厦——世界第八大奇迹——是建筑和工程智慧的胜利。大厦高达1,472英尺，比原七大奇迹堆在一起还要高。帝国大厦本身就是一座奇迹城市，有

新世纪美国公示语1000例

stacked together. A city in itself—virtually a city of marvels—the Empire State Building has a population of 16,000 persons working in the building plus 35,000 visitors daily—totaling more visitors in a single year than the combined totals of all who visited the originnal Seven Wonders of the World throughout recorded history.

16,000人在里面工作,每天还有35,000名观光客,一年内游客总人数超过有记录以来参观七大奇迹的总人数。
(美国纽约帝国大厦入口说明。英语中the Eighth Wonder of the World并非实数,而是表示"一个超乎寻常的事物",比如全世界有几十个地方都被称为"第八大奇迹"。)

9

FEDERAL COMMUNICATIONS COMMISSION
ANTENNA STRUCTURE
REGISTRATION NUMBER 1007048
Latitude Overall Height Longitude
N40-44-54 443.0 Meters W73-59-10
Empire State Building
350 Fifth Avenue
New York, NY 10118

联邦通讯委员会
天线结构登记号1007048
总高度443米
纬度40-44-54
经度73-59-10
纽约州纽约市第五大街350号
(纽约市帝国大厦的指示牌)

10

EXIT Through Turnstiles

十字转门出口
(博物馆出口对游客的说明)

11

Growler Submarine
GUIDED TOURS:
15-20 Minutes
LAST TOUR OF THE DAY:
15 Minutes prior to closing
Children Under 6 Not Permitted

"黑鲈号"潜艇
随导游参观:15-20分钟
每天最后一次参观:闭馆前15分钟
6岁以下儿童不允许参观
("勇猛号"航空母舰博物馆区域内"黑鲈号"潜艇的参观须知。"黑鲈号"潜艇是美国第一艘战略飞弹潜舰。)

二十、旅游景点

12

WE ARE NOT RESPONSIBLE FOR ITEMS LEFT OVER 30 DAYS

物品丢失超过30天本景点概不负责
（旅游景点失物提示）

13

GRAY LINE | New York Sightseeing

纽约市区环城观光的一家旅游车上的公司名称，全名为GRAY LINE NEWYORK SIGHTSEEING。

14

Department of the Treasury
UNITED STATES MINT
VISITORS WELCOME
Monday to Friday
9:00 a.m. to 3:00 p.m.
CLOSED FEDERAL HOLIDAYS
Photo identification needed to enter.
For everyone's protection, no weapons of any type are permitted in the building.
No cameras, camera phones or packages are permitted in the building.
All persons entering consent to a search of their person and objects in their possession.
Thank You!

财政部美国造币厂
欢迎参观
周一到周五上午9点到下午3点
联邦假日关闭
凭照片身份证进入
为了大家的安全，不得携带任何类型的武器
不准带入相机、有摄像功能的手机或包裹
所有进入的人员同意对本人和所拥有的物品进行搜查
谢谢

（美国一共有四家造币厂，分别在费城、纽约、旧金山和丹佛，在华盛顿有一家纸币厂。）
（1971年生效的美国统一假期法案（Uniform Monday Holiday Act）对美国联邦节假日有了比较一致的规定。美国联邦政府的工作人员在联邦法定假日无需上班。美国一些州或地方政府、公立学校大多将联邦假日作为雇员休息日。私人企业、公司则往往有选择地将某些联邦假日作为休息日。这些节日包括元旦（1月

新世纪美国公示语1000例

1日)、马丁·路德·金纪念日(1月的第三个星期一)、总统节(2月的第三个星期一)、阵亡将士纪念日(5月的最后一个星期一)、独立纪念日(7月4日)、劳动节(9月的第一个星期一)、哥伦布日(10月的第二个星期一)、退伍军人节(11月11日)、感恩节(11月的第四个星期四)和圣诞节(12月25日)。)

15

1783
FREE QUAKER MEETING HOUSE
Owned by Independence
National Historical Park
Operated by Historic Philadelphia, Inc.

1783年自由教友会教徒集会场所产权归独立国家历史公园所有费城历史公司运作
(费城独立宫附近一座房屋说明。教友会为基督教的一个教派,既无任何正式仪式也无固定教义,其信条强烈反对暴力和战争。)

16

FREEDOM PARK
OWNED AND MAINTAINED BY
WESTFIELD REALTY, INC.

自由公园所属单位和管理单位的标示牌。

17

Freedom Park is dedicated to the spirit of freedom and brings that spirit to life with symbols of the worldwide struggle for liberty.
Thirty-minute guided tours of Freedom Park are available by reservation. To schedule a tour, call
703/284-3710
Freedom Park is made possible by the Freedom Forum, the Newseum, Westfield Realty Co., the Rosslyn community and Arlington County.

位于弗吉尼亚境内自由公园门口说明。文字指出该公园目的是为了献给自由精神,也是为了唤起世界范围内为自由而斗争的精神。公园可以预订30分钟的导游讲解,同时提供了联系导游的电话。最后一段内容显示该公园的建设是通过哪些部门来实现的。

18

| TICKETS SOLD HERE | 此处购票
（旅游车上售票的告示牌。美国有些旅游车上没有导游，司机兼任导游并承担售票等职责。） |

19

	Adult	Child (3-11)
Washington and Arlington Cemetery Tour INCLUDES 21 STOPS AT MAJOR MONUMENTS, MEMORIALS, SMITHSONIAN MUSEUMS, GOVERNMENT BUILDINGS, AND 4 STOPS IN ARLINGTON CEMETERY	$20.00	$10.00
Two-day Washington - Arlington Cemetery Tour AVAILABLE DAILY AFTER 9:30 A.M. GOOD ALL DAY OF PURCHASE AND NEXT CONSECUTIVE DAY	$30.00	$15.00
MOUNT VERNON TOUR INCLUDES NARRATED SERVICE TO GEORGE WASHINGTON'S ESTATE THROUGH HISTORIC OLD TOWN ALEXANDRIA, VA. AND ADMISSION TO ESTATE.	$25.00 Operates Seasonably	$12.00

美国首都华盛顿地区游览告示。华盛顿市区和阿林顿公墓游览，包括主要纪念碑和纪念堂、史密森尼博物馆、政府大楼以及阿林顿公墓等21个停靠点，成人20美元，儿童（3-11岁）10美元。。华盛顿市区和阿林顿公墓两日游，每天上午9点30分以后全天和第二天，成人30美元，儿童15美元。佛农山旅游包括前往乔治·华盛顿的庄园，并穿越具有历史意义的老镇——弗吉尼亚的亚历山大小镇，导游讲解，参观庄园，成人25美元，儿童12美元。参观分季节。

20

| Tourist Information Center | 旅游信息中心
（在美国的高速公路上，每隔上一段路程就会有一个旅游信息中心提供餐饮等服务项目。） |

21

DRAGON TREE
Native to the Canary Islands this unusual
tree was planted at The Del prior to the
turn of the century where it thrives
in our temperate Southern California
coastal climate.

The Dragon Tree was used as a backdrop
In the Marilyn Monroe movie
Some Like It Hot, which was filmed
at The Del in 1958.

龙血树
原产地为西班牙的加那利群岛，这棵树栽种于本世纪（19世纪）之前，在南加州温和的海岸气候下茁壮生长。此树在玛丽莲·梦露1958年拍摄的电影《热情似火》中用作背景。
（科罗纳多旅馆附近一棵龙血树的说明牌。当地人亲切地将科罗纳多这所旅馆称为The Del，现在已经成为这所旅馆的昵称。）

22

Some Fantasyland Attractions will
close early this evening
So you may enjoy the fireworks
spectacular Disneyland
Remember Dreams Come True

某些"梦幻世界"内的游乐项目将在今天傍晚早些时候结束，这样大家可以欣赏壮观的焰火。迪斯尼的梦幻将得以实现。
（迪斯尼"梦幻世界"游乐区的告示。提前告知游园内重大活动，让更多的人欣赏到精彩表演。）

23

LAFITTE'S ANCHOR
SAID TO BE FROM A PIRATE SHIP COMMANDED BY JEAN LAFITTE IN THE BATTLE OF NEW ORLEANS JANUARY 8, 1815. IT IS SAID THAT LAFITTE'S PRIVATEERING SHIPS LEFT A WAKE OF BLOOD FROM THE MAINLAND TO THE BARATARIA BAY. BUT DON'T BELIEVE EVERYTHING YOU READ.

拉菲特船锚
据说是1815年1月8日新奥尔良之战中拉菲特为首的一艘海盗船上的锚。据说拉菲特的私掠船尾从大陆到巴拉塔丽娅湾留下了血迹。但不要全信你所读到的。
（迪斯尼公园内的一个船锚的说明。最后一句话告知观众这里所提供的信息只是传说。）

二十、旅游景点

24

PETRIFIED TREE
FROM THE
PIKE PETRIFIED FOREST, COLORADO
THIS SECTION WEIGHS FIVE TONS AND MEASURES 7½ FEET
IN DIAMETER. THE ORIGINAL TREE, ESTIMATED TO HAVE
BEEN 200 FEET TALL, WAS PART OF A SUB-TROPICAL FOREST
55 TO 70 MILLION YEARS AGO IN WHAT IS NOW COLORADO. SCIENTISTS BELIEVE IT TO BE OF THE REDWOOD OF SEQUOIA SPECIES. DURING SOME PREHITORIC ERA A CATACLYSMIC UPHEAVAL CAUSED SILICA LADEN WATER TO OVERSPREAD THE
LIVING FOREST. WOOD CELLS WERE CHANGED DURING THE COURSE OF TIME TO SANDSTONE. OPALS WERE FORMED WITHIN THE TREE TRUNK ITSELF PRESENTED TO DISNEYLAND BY MRS. WALT DISNEY SEPTEMBER, 1957

石化树
源自于科罗拉多州派克石化森林这一段石化树重达5吨,直径71.2英尺(21.7米)。原树估计200英尺(61米)高,这里只是5500万年至7000万年前现科罗拉多州所在的部分亚热带森林,科学家认为属于杉树中的红木。在某个史前时期,一次巨大的自然灾难使混有大量硅土的水将一片生机勃勃的森林覆盖,木细胞慢慢变成砂岩,树干形成了蛋白石。1957年沃特·迪斯尼夫妇将这棵石化树献给了迪斯尼乐园。

(这是迪斯尼乐园中一棵石化树的说明。迪斯尼先生曾于1956年参观过科罗拉多州的派克石化林。)

25

LA CASA DE ESTUDILLO
THIS 170 YEAR OLD ADOBE HACIENDA IS A MUSEUM WHICH WAS BUILT BY JOSE MARIA DE ESTUDILLO, THE COMMANDANT OF THE PRESIDIO IN 1827. IT REPRESENTS HOW AN IMPORTANT FAMILY IN THE MID-NINETEENTH CENTURY WOULD HAVE LIVED AND WORKED.
MUSEUM IS FREE HOURS 10AM – 5 PM
THANK YOU FOR NOT SMOKING, DRINKING OR EATING INSIDE.

耶督迪奥住宅
这座具有170年历史的老宅现在是博物馆,由要塞指挥官耶督迪奥1827年建造。馆内再现19世纪中叶一个显要家庭如何生活和工作。上午10点到下午5点免费参观
室内请勿吸烟、喝饮料或吃零食,谢谢。

(圣地亚哥小镇内一栋古老房屋耶督迪奥房舍的说明牌)

26

CENTENNIAL PARK
ORIGINAL SITE OF THE CORONADO
FERRY LANDING 1886–1969
DEDICATED NOVEMBER 13, 1986

世纪公园
1886年至1969年期间渡口原址
1986年11月13日立此纪念牌
（纪念科罗纳多渡口原址的世纪公园）

27

CORONADO
1886 FERRY 1969
TICKET BOOTH

科罗纳多1886年至1969年渡口售票亭的纪念牌。

28

CORONADO FERRYBOAT TERMINAL
Original site of the Coronado Ferryboat Terminal which operated ferries between San Diego and Coronado from 1886 until the opening of the bridge in 1969. Equipped to accommodate passengers, horses and buggies, and later automobiles, the ferry system was a way of life for Coronadans. Upon cessation of the service the land was sold to private developers. Through the efforts of three residents, Parry Schmidt, Sally Krummenacher, and Wendy Longley-Cook, this park was created. Opening in 1986, the 100th anniversary of Coronado's founding, it was named Centennial Park.

科罗纳多渡口
1886年至1969年建桥开通之间，这里曾经是往来于圣地亚哥小镇和科罗纳多岛之间的渡船口岸。这个码头用来运送乘客、马车，以及后来的汽车，渡口是当时科罗纳多人的生活方式之一。渡口服务终止后，这块土地卖给了私人开发商。经过三个当地居民的努力，建起公园，并于1986年渡口成立100周年之际开放，命名为世纪公园。
（科罗纳多渡口说明牌）

29

ON THIS SPOT THE UNITED STATES FLAG
WAS FIRST RAISED IN SOUTHERN CALIFORNIA BY LT. STEPHEN C. ROWAK U.S. N. COMMANDING SAILORS AND MARINES JULY 29, 1846

1846年7月29日，就是在这里美国海军中尉斯蒂芬·C.罗沃克指挥水手和海军陆战队员升起了南加州的第一面美国国旗。
（加州圣地亚哥广场中心旗杆下的说明）

30

INQUIRE ABOUT FACILITIES
FOR
Private Parties Meetings & Catering

如果需要举办私人宴会、会议和餐饮，请咨询相关部门。
（旅游点租赁场地的告示）

31

GHOST TOURS
HAUNTED TOURS
At OLD TOWN SAN DIEGO
With THE GHOST HUNTER MICHAEL BROWN
THE ONLY GHOST TOUR ALLOWED IN OLD TOWN SAN DIEGO
STATE HISTORIC PARK
JOIN ME ON MY WALKING TOUR AND I WILL SHOW YOU WHERE
OVER 20 DIFFERENT PARANORMAL AND SUPERNATURAL
OCCURENCES HAVE HAPPENED TO ME
BRING YOUR CAMERA
TOURS ARE EVERY THURSDAY THRU SUNDAY
AT 9pm AND 11pm
TOUR LASTS ABOUT $1^{1/2}$ HOURS
AFTER THE TOUR PLEASE JOIN ME AS WE TAKE
A LOOK AT SOME OF MY PHOTOS
And LISTEN TO SOME AUDIO CLIPS (EVP's)
FOR MORE INFORMATION CALL ME OR VISIT MY
WEB SITE FOR MORE INFORMATION
619-972-3900 www.tghmb.com
TICKETS CAN BE PICKED UP AT TIENDA NUEVA
And TIENDA DEL PASADO
INSIDE PLAZA DELPASADO
IN THE OLD TOWN SAN DIEGO
STATE HISTORIC PARK
4 FOR THE PRICE OF 3 (save $19)
BUY 3 TICKETS AND BRING THIS FLYER
FOR THE 4TH PERSON TO GO FREE
ALL FOUR GUESTS MUST DO AT THE SAME DATE
KIDS 12 AND UNDER $ 10.00
WE WILL BE WALKING THROUGH TWO OF THE MOST HAUNTED AND
CURRENTLY ACTIVE BUILDINGS IN OLD TOWN STATE HISTORIC PARK
MAP AND SCHEDULE ON OTHER SIDE

新世纪美国公示语1000例

鬼魂漫游

老镇圣地亚哥猎鬼人麦克·布朗陪同"鬼魂漫游"。

老镇圣地亚哥州立历史公园内独家特许"鬼魂漫游"。

请随我徒步漫游，见识20多个发生超自然现象的不同场所，请带上相机。

游览时间为每个周四至周日晚上9点到11点，游程90分钟。

完毕后，请随我观看我的一些照片，然后再听录音片断。

欲知详情，请来电或访问我的网站。

购票地点（略）

三张票价，四人漫游（省19美元），购三张票再带上本广告传单，第四人即可免费漫游，四人必须在同一天游览。

12岁以下儿童每人10美元。

我们将带领大家走过镇上两座过去和目前仍在闹鬼的老房子。

本广告传单背面有地图和时间安排

（老镇圣地亚哥"鬼魂漫游"浏览项目说明。在美国，人们在旅游景点介绍的时候似乎都喜欢加上有关幽灵的内容，而且该内容还会得到政府部门的首肯或认同。在该镇上有两个地方专门提供鬼魂漫游。如"维里鬼屋"，内有很多出现鬼怪精灵的神乎其神的传说，这座房子还被美国商务部门确定为真正的鬼屋。这所房子是在过去的绞刑架上建立起来的，很多人曾经在这里丧命，有好几个故事中出现了无法解释的怪现象。比如有人看到房间内的一根铁链子自己摆动起来；还有人听见过楼上有沉重的脚步声等。）

32

BASED ON THE MOST RECENT INSPECTION BY THE DEPARTMENT OF ENVIRONMENTAL HEALTH THIS EASTABLISHMENT HAS COMPLIED WITH REQUIREMENTS FOR GRADE

A

A COPY OF THE MOST RECENT ENVIRONMENTAL HEALTH INSPECTION REPORT IS AVAILABLE AT THIS FACILITY FOR YOUR REVIEW UPON REQUEST COUNTY OF SAN DIEGO DEPARTMENT OF ENVIRONMENTAL HEALTH PENALTY FOR REMOVAL

根据最近环境卫生部的检测报告，本大楼符合A级要求

本处有最新环境卫生检测报告复印件，如需查看可以向本处索取。检测部门为圣地亚哥县环境卫生部。

撕毁本告示将受处罚

（美国环境卫生部门的评级公告）

二十、旅游景点

33

FREE WALKING TOURS At 11 AM
Please Meet on the FRONT Porch, NO Sign Up
TOUR is 55 Min LONG

免费徒步导游：集合时间上午11点；地点为前门廊，无需签约；游览时间55分钟。
（免费徒步导游讲解的告示牌）

34

PLEASE…
NO STROLLERS NO FOOD OR DRINKS
CAPACITY 30 VISITORS
WE OPEN AT 10:30 AM
SEVEN DAYS A WEEK

请勿使用童车，不吃零食，不喝饮料；
本室只可容纳30人参观，上午10点30分开放，每周七天开放。
（旅游点告示文字）

35

First Schoolhouse
BUILT IN 1865, THIS WAS THE FIRST PUBLIC SCHOOLHOUSE IN SAN DIEGO
HISTORIC SITE #538

第一校舍
建于1865年，是圣地亚哥历史上第一所公立校舍。
历史遗迹编号为538号
（加州圣地亚哥小镇一所具有150年历史的学校说明牌）

36

ATTENTION…
CHILDREN MUST BE SUPERVISED AT ALL TIMES YOU ARE RESPONSIBLE FOR THEIR ACTIONS
THANK YOU MASON ST. SCHOOL

注意……
家长要随时监管儿童，对他们的行为负责
谢谢
（旅游点警示牌）

37

Teachers who have taught The History of San Diego
Free Classes meet here: Wednesdays 7:00pm – 9:00pm

教授圣地亚哥历史的老师每周三晚7点至9点在此免费讲课
（免费历史课通知）

38

DIAMOND HEAD CRATER
OPEN TO THE PUBLIC 6:00 AM
TO 6:00 PM, DAILY. RESTRICTED
ACCESS FOR OFFICIAL
BUSINESS ONLY AT ALL OTHER
TIMES. VIOLATORS SUBJECT TO
PROSECUTION.

金刚钻头火山口
每天上午6点至下午6点向公众开放。其他时间因公务限制进入；违反者将受到起诉。
（夏威夷钻头火山口开放说明。该火山远看发亮被误认为有金刚钻，故有此名。）

39

Ernest Hemingway Home
Open 9 a.m. ~ 5 p.m. daily
Admission Adult $11 Child $6

海明威故居
开放时间上午9点至下午5点
入场费：成人11美元，儿童6美元。
（海明威故居门前说明。海明威故居位于佛罗里达州的基韦斯特小城。）

40

LOUIS M. MARTINI WINERY
TASTINGS TOURS PICNIC
AREA
OPEN DAILY 10 – 6

路易斯·M.马丁尼酿酒厂
品酒、游览和野餐
每天开放时间为10点至6点
（一家葡萄酒酿酒厂入口的标志牌。路易斯·M.马丁尼酿酒厂是位于加州的一家葡萄酒酿酒厂，建厂时间为1933年。在这家酒厂内游客可以品酒、参观酿酒生产过程或野餐。）

41

WELCOME TO VAN HELSING FORETRESS DRACULA
CODE OF CONDUCT
NO TOUCHING LIVE PERFORMERS
NO EATING, DRINKING, OR SMOKING
NO CARRYING CHILDREN
NO FLASH PHOTOGRAPHY OR VIDEO CAMERA LIGHTING
THIS ATTRACTION IS PG13. NOT RECOMMENDED FOR SMALL CHILDREN

二十、旅游景点

欢迎参观凡赫辛城堡
注意事项

禁止触碰城堡中表演者
禁止进食、喝水或吸烟
禁止带孩子
禁止使用闪光相机或摄像机照明设备
本娱乐项目属PG13等级（需要在父母陪伴下参观的项目），**不适宜幼小儿童**

（环球影城中一个恐怖游乐项目—凡赫辛城堡门口的告示。这一恐怖游乐项目是根据1931年环球影业经典恐怖片《吸血鬼凡赫辛》的场景设计。影片首次集结环球影史上最伟大的经典恐怖片怪物：吸血鬼、科学怪人和狼人。影片叙述19世纪末怪物猎人凡赫辛受托前往罗马尼亚西部的一个神秘之都德兰斯斐尼亚，那里是传说中吸血鬼德古拉公爵的故乡，希望能藉凡赫辛的力量消灭一股邪恶势力。凡赫辛是作家布拉姆·史托克笔下的传奇人物，从1931年之后陆续出现在小说《吸血鬼凡赫辛》一书为题材的电影中。2004年好莱坞重新拍摄了《吸血鬼凡赫辛》。）

42

PARENTAL DISCRETION
DUE TO THE INTENSE NATURE
OF THIS ATTRACTION
PARENTAL DISCRETION IS
ADVISED.
IF YOU WISH TO PARTICIPATE IN
OUR CHILD SWITCH PROGRAM
PLEASE SEE AN ATTENDANT
FOR ASSISTANCE.

父母审慎
由于本娱乐项目具有紧张性，提请父母谨慎；如果希望参与儿童引导课程，请找服务员帮助。
（游乐场所中提示父母的标识牌。为了避免孩子受刺激，在娱乐前可以对孩子进行一下心理引导。）

43

VOLUNTEER OPPORTUNITIES
Old Town San Diego State Historic Park is looking for individuals in the community, who seek to donate time, in order to enhance park's activities. Volunteers at Old Town share their passion for history and creative skills with the general public on a daily basis. Many volunteers bring the park alive by wearing period attire and demonstrating period activities.

新世纪美国公示语1000例

EXAMPLES OF VOLUNTEER ACTIVITIES

Blacksmiths	Gardeners	Printers
Office Staff	Seamstress	Singers
Dancers	Book Store Clerks	Computer Help
Historians	Writers	Museum Aides
Tour Guides	Livestock Help	Photographers

VOLUNTEER TRAINING

State Park staff anticipate training classes to begin the middle of October 2005. Please fill out a volunteer application, located at front desk in the Robinson Rose Building and someone will contact you at a later date.

CONTACT

Gregg Giacopuzzi, Volunteer Coordinator, (619)220-5373

加州圣地亚哥小镇志愿者招聘启事。古镇圣地亚哥州历史公园为加强公园活动正在招聘本区志愿者。志愿者每天和大家一起在古镇分享历史的热情和创造技能。许多志愿者通过身着昔日服装展示昔日活动给公园带来昔日气氛。志愿者参与的内容包括铁匠、花匠、印刷工、办公室职员、女裁缝、歌手、舞者、书店职员、计算机助手、历史学家、作家、博物馆助理、导游、畜牧助理、摄影师。志愿者培训预期2005年10月中旬开始，请填写大楼前台上的志愿者表格，届时有人会与你联系。

44

GENERAL PARK TOURS

Meeting Place: The Robinson Rose House
Time: 11:00am – 2:00pm
Conducted By: State Park Staff
Tour Length: One Hour
Content: A synopsis on the development of San Diego (Old Town) between the years of 1821–1872
Cost: Free

圣地亚哥公园内为普通游客提供的游览说明。公园普通游览集合地点、时间（上午11点至下午2点）、带领者（公园工作人员）、游览时间（1个小时）、内容（1821年至1872年圣地亚哥小镇的发展梗概），费用免收。

二十、旅游景点

45

LIVING HISTORY

Volunteers and Park Staff, dress in period attire, and bring the Old Town alive as they demonstrate and
provide stimulating historic activities. The activities
take place every Wednesday between 10:00a.m. and 1:00 p.m. and is free for the general public.

历史再现

志愿者和公园工作人员身着当时服饰,展示和表演激动人心的历史事件来复活古镇。活动每周三上午10点至下午1点进行,免费观看。

(圣地亚哥小镇旅游活动说明)

46

The World's Symbol for Liberty

世界自由的象征

(美国费城存放自由钟的室内说明。自由钟铸造于1752年,又称为独立钟,1753年重新铸造。上面刻有铭文:向全世界的人们宣布自由(参见下一条)。这口钟于1776年7月8日宣读《独立宣言》的时候敲响。英国占领费城期间,该钟被藏于爱伦镇,1778年又重新放回到独立大厅内。1835年7月8日,在为大法官约翰·马歇尔鸣丧钟时裂开。1976年,为了便于参观,自由钟被移到了独立宫边上的玻璃房内。)

47

Proclaim liberty throughout all the land unto all the inhabitants thereof.

向全世界的人们宣布自由。

(费城自由钟上铭文。这段文字来自于《圣经》利未记(Lev. 25:10)。)

48

NOTICE
ALL GOV'T BUILDINGS INSIDE THE CAPITOL COMPLEX ARE SMOKE-FREE

PENALTY FOR VIOLATION
1ST OFFENSE   200 Fine
2ND OFFENSE   500 Fine
3RD OFFENSE   500 Fine and
2 days IMPRISONMENT

注意

国会区域所有政府大楼禁止吸烟;
违者罚款:
第一次违犯罚款200美元;
第二次违犯罚款500美元;
第三次违犯罚款500美元以及2天监禁。

(进入美国国会大厦前告示牌)

49

Your Pictures are located at the end of this hallway on your way out. Thank you!!

你的相片位于出口大厅尽头。谢谢！
（纽约帝国大厦在排队入口处关于领取所拍摄相片的说明。美国许多旅游点会在游客排队的时候拍纪念照，然后将相片展示出来，如果游客需要可以交钱领取。）

50

CAMERAS OFF!
FOR THE CONVENIENCE OF EVERYONE, GUESTS ARE HEREBY ADVISED TO TURN OFF THEIR CAMERAS
WHILE INSIDE THIS AREA.
SOUVENIR PHOTOS ARE COPYRIGHTED AND CANNOT OR, SHOULD NOT BE PHOTOGRAPHED.

请勿拍照！
为了大家方便，请游客在本区域内关闭相机。
纪念照版权所有，不能也不应拍摄。
（纽约帝国大厦入口拍照处的说明。大厦内将游客的相片拍下来让需要的游客购买，但是也没有忘记保护被拍摄者的肖像权。）

51

THIS GALLERY HAS INSTALLED THE CHECKPOINT ELECTRONIC ANTISHOPLIFTING SYSTEM.
PLEASE PROCEED TO THE CASHIER IF YOU ARE PURCHASING YOUR PHOTOS

本展厅安装电子反偷窃检查系统。
购买你的相片，请前往收银台。
（纽约帝国大厦内纪念照拍摄处说明）

52

EMERGENCY EXIT ONLY
EXITING THIS DOOR WILL REMOVE YOU FROM THE THEME PARK WITH NO RE-ENTRY

紧急出口
从此门出，不得再入主题公园。
（主题公园出口说明）

53

NOTICE
HANAUMA BAY IS CLOSED TO THE PUBLIC EVERY TUESDAY

告示
每周二恐龙湾不对公众开放
（夏威夷一海湾开放时间告示）

二十、旅游景点

54

| Cirque Stadium Will Open 30 Minutes Prior To The Next Show Time | 马戏剧场将在下一场开始前30分钟开放 （观众可以根据提示确定观看表演的时间） |

55

Soak Zone

溅水区

（洛杉矶海洋公园内海豚等表演场所板凳或座位上的文字。美国一些娱乐场所，比如迪斯尼、海洋公园等场所内前几排座位上都有这样的文字说明，告知前排的观众在观看表演时会有水喷洒过来。通过饲养员的培训，动物故意将水洒到前几排的座位上，而不少观众为了刺激，尤其是青少年以及儿童比较喜欢选择在这样的座位上观看，有些人甚至还披上雨衣观看，免得浑身湿透。）

56

We took 40 pelicans under our wing so they could fly again.

When a summer storm blew 40 endangered brown pelicans off their migration path, we took them in.

Malnourished and too weak to fly, the birds needed a helping hand. So we cared for them at Sea World. When they were strong enough, we released them to continue on their way.

It's our hope that the entire brown pelican population takes off as smoothly as those 40 birds did.

A pledge and promise from the Anheuser-Bush Companies.

我们收养了40只鹈鹕，为了它们能再飞起来。

当一阵夏季风暴将40只濒危的棕色鹈鹕吹离迁徙路线，我们收养了它们。

这些鸟缺乏营养，无力飞行，需要帮助，所以我们在海洋世界里照料这些鸟儿。当它们养好身体，就会被放飞上路。

希望所有的棕色鹈鹕都会像这40只鸟一样顺利起飞。

安豪泽-布施公司的承诺和保证。

（加州海洋公园内收养了40只鹈鹕的说明。安豪泽-布施公司是美国一家荣登美国福布斯的企业，简称A-B公司。总部位于美国密苏里州圣路易斯市，旗下有世界最大的啤酒酿造公司，美国第二大铝制啤酒罐制造厂等。公司占领着本国啤酒市场的48%的份额，它的产品响誉世界，如Budweiser（百威），Busch（布士），Michelob（米狮龙）等。）

新世纪美国公示语1000例

57

This Facility is available for private company picnics, corporate dinner meetings, and award banquets. For more information on all of SeaWorld's special event opportunities.
Call our sales office.
(619)226-3845
POLAR BEAR PLAZA

本设施可以为私人公司提供餐饮、公司聚会或颁奖仪式。请与海洋世界销售公司咨询更多特殊庆典的信息。
北极熊区
（举办活动聚会或颁奖仪式的场地也可以在游乐场所内租赁）

58

ARCTIC ADVENTURE!!
PLEASE, NO EATING, DRINKING OR SMOKING BEYONG THIS POINT.
SHIRTS AND SHOES REQUIRED.
RIDE RESTRICTIONS:
DIRECT ROUTE TO EXHIBIT
NO RESTRICTIONS
MOTION EXPERIENCE RESTRICTIONS:
This helicopter ride is not recommended for elderly guests, expectant mothers, or those with heart, back or neck problems.
Travelers who experience claustrophobia or motion sickness should not ride.
Minimum height requirement for the helicopter ride is 42" (106cm.).
ENJOY YOUR JOURNEY!

北极探险
请勿在此区域内吃零食、喝饮料或吸烟；衣冠整齐。
乘坐须知：直达展示区；无任何限制。
动感体验要求：老人、孕妇或心脏、后背、颈部有问题的人不宜乘坐直升机。乘客如有灾难恐惧症或有晕动症者请勿乘坐。乘坐直升机的最低身高需42英寸（106厘米）。
祝旅途愉快！
（加州海洋公园内北极探险区的说明。对可能发生的危险，游乐场所都有文字警示。）

二十、旅游景点

59

TRAIL NOTES:
To protect the fragile environment and make your hike enjoyable:
Stay on marked trail.
Do not smoke or cause fires.
Wear loose clothing and appropriate hiking footwear.
Avoid dehydration by drinking fluids before and after hiking.
Keep your hands free to grasp handrails.
Proceed cautiously in dark passages.
Take your time, pace yourself.
Allow 1.5 hours from start to finish.
Trail and crater closed to public at 6:00 pm daily.

小径提示
为保护脆弱的环境
并提高徒步旅行的兴致：
沿有标记路径走
不要吸烟或点火
宽松服装舒适鞋
徒步前后多饮水
腾出手来抓栏杆
昏暗道上小心行
放松稳步莫心急
从头至尾九十分
每天下午6点徒步小道和
洞穴对外关闭
（公园徒步旅行提示）

60

NEW YORK CITY PARKS

Welcome to your park. This is a shared public space provided for your enjoyment and recreation. We want you to have a fun and safe time. Be courteous and respectful to others, and please keep the park clean.

Park Rules Prohibit:

- Adults in Play Equipment Area Except in the Company of Children
- Littering or Dumping of Debris
- Barbecuing Except in Designated Areas
- Unleashed Dogs Except in Designated Areas
- Using Illegal Drugs or Alcohol
- Amplifying Sounds, Except by Permit
- Feeding Birds or Squirrels
- Panhandling or Solicitation
- Entering the Park After It Is Closed
- Performing or Rallying, Except by Permit
- Engaging in Comercial Activity, Except by Permit
- Obstructing Entrances to the Park
- Rummaging Through Trash Receptacles
- Vehicles Without Specific Authorization From Parks & Recreation

This Parks Closes at Dusk

纽约城市公园

欢迎您来到自己的公园。这里是娱乐休闲的公共场地。希望您度过一个愉快而安全的时光。文明礼貌尊重他人,保持公园整洁。

纽约城市公园禁止:

成人在游乐设施区内(陪伴儿童除外);乱丢乱扔杂物;非指定区内烧烤;非指定区内放狗;使用非法毒品或酒精饮料;未经允许使用扩音设备;喂食鸟类或松鼠;乞讨或拉客;公园关闭后入内;无证表演或集会;无证进行商业活动;堵塞公园入口;在垃圾箱内翻找;未经公园特殊批准的车辆。

公园黄昏时关闭

(纽约城市公园管理规定)

61

WARNING

YOU ARE ENTERING A RARE OR ENDANGERED SPECIES HABITAT. WILLFUL DESTRUCTION OF A RARE OR ENDANGERED SPECIES HABITAT IS A VIOLATION OF FEDERAL LAW AND MAY BE PUNISHABLE BY FINE OF UP TO 10,000 AND/ OR IMPRISONMENT FOR SIX MONTHS OR BOTH. (U.S.C. 1540)
STAY ON DESIGNATED ROADWAYS.

注意!
你现在进入稀有
或濒危物种区域内

故意毁坏稀有或濒危物种区的行为是违反联邦法律的,可能会受到高达10,000美元的罚款或6个月监禁的处罚,或合并处罚。
请在指定路线内游览。

(野生动物保护区警示)

62

Prohibited Within the Washington Monument:	华盛顿纪念碑内禁止以下行为:
No Smoking	禁止吸烟
No Eating or Drinking, (except bottled water)	禁止饮食(瓶装水除外)
No Guns or ammunition	禁止枪支或弹药
No Knives	禁止刀具
No Mace or aerosol cans	禁止伤害性压缩液或气溶胶罐
	禁止大于18"×16"×8"的皮箱、

二十、旅游景点

| No Suitcases, duffel bags or backpacks larger than 18"× 16"×8"
No Strollers
No Animals (except guide dogs)
No Other objects that threaten security
For public safety all visitors and their belongings are subject to search | 行李袋或背包
禁止婴儿车
禁止携带动物（导盲犬除外）
禁止其他威胁安全的物品
为了公共安全，所有参观者及其物品均须检查。
（华盛顿纪念碑安全告示牌。1888年10月9日，华盛顿纪念碑正式免费向游人开放。碑内共有897级台阶盘旋直上顶端，而高速电梯只需70秒钟运行便可达到。在顶层，通过8个观览窗口，首都华盛顿一览无余。碑的内部有188块世界各国赠送的牌子。） |

63

| Coat Check Closes at 4:15 PM | 衣物寄存下午4:15 关闭
（国会大厦游客中心告示） |

64

The United States Capitol Visitor Center is not liable for loss or damage to property stored as a result of fire, theft, negligence or otherwise, to the extent allowed by law. All property must be retrieved within posted operating hours. Property cannot be retrieved after the coat check is closed.
The United States Capitol Visitor Center will not be liable for items left after 20 days.

美国国会大厦游客中心对存放物品因失火、盗窃、疏忽等原因遗失或损坏不负法律允许范围以内责任。所有存物必须在公布的工作时间以内取回。衣物寄存关闭后，存物不能取回。物品存放20天后，美国国会大厦游客中心概不负责。
（美国国会大厦游客中心说明。大厦位于华盛顿25米高的国会山上，是一幢全长233米的3层建筑，白色大理石为主料，中央顶楼上建大圆顶，顶上立有一尊6米高自由女神青铜雕像。大圆顶两侧的南北翼楼，分别为众议院和参议院办公地。众议院的会议厅是美国总统宣读年度国情咨文的地方。它仿照巴黎万神庙，极力表现雄伟，强调纪念性，是古典复兴风格建筑的代表作。）

FISHING IN CENTRAL PARK

Welcome to Central Park. Please help keep our lakes, streams and ponds clean and health by obeying official rules. Remember that the long-term health of Central Parks' water bodies depends on your cooperation and support.

- All fishing is catch-and-release. This means that every fish caught must be put back in the water immediately. Returning fish to their habitat is essential to maintain the ecological balance of the water body.
- Use hooks without barbs. Barbed hooks are difficult to remove fish and can injure them.
- Lead weights are not permitted. Lead is poisonous and can kill wildlife. Use stainless steel or other non-toxic materials.
- To prevent birds from getting tangled or hurt, take all fishing line fragments and hooks when you leave. Do not leave any tackle behind.
- All violators will be subject to a summons.

If you see any violators of these rules or have any questions about fishing, please call 311.

For more information about Parks, please call 311. You can also visit us on the web at www.nyc.gov/parks.

City of New York Parks & Recreation
Michael R. Bloomberg, Mayor
Adrian Benepe, Commissioner
Douglas Blonsky, Central Park Administrator

中央公园钓鱼须知

欢迎来到中央公园。请遵守政府规定，保持湖面、小溪和池塘清洁卫生。中央公园水体的长期卫生得益于您的合作和支持。

- 所有垂钓均为捕与放，即每一条捕得的鱼必须立即放回水中。让鱼回归栖息地是保持水体生态平衡的基本要求。
- 使用不带倒刺的鱼钩。带倒刺的鱼钩很难取下，也会伤害鱼。
- 不准使用铅块。铅有毒，对野生动植物有害，使用不锈钢或其他无毒材料。
- 离开时请带走所有鱼线和鱼钩，不要遗留任何用具以防鸟类被缠或受伤。
- 违者将被传唤。

如见有违反上述规定者或有任何钓鱼问题，请拨打311，或者访问以下网址：www.nyc.gov/parks。

（纽约中央公园钓鱼说明）

二十一、纪念文字

1

HUNDREDS OF THOUSANDS OF SAILORS
WENT TO SEA AND FOUGHT IN WORLD WAR II, PERHAPS
THE MOST SINGULAR UNIFYING EVENT IN THE HISTORY OF THE
UNITED STATES.
THESE YOUNG AMERICANS SET ASIDE THEIR INDIVIDUAL
HOPES AND ASPIRATIONS, LEFT FAMILIES, HOMES AND JOBS IN
A COLLECTIVE SACRIFICE TO DEFEND THEIR COUNTRY
AND THEIR COMMON IDEALS. THE MEN OF THE
USS SAN DIEGO (CL-53) REMEMBERED HERE
ARE EMBLEMATIC OF ALL WHO FOUGHT FOR VICTORY
IN THIS EPIC STRUGGLE.

成千上万的水兵应征来到大海上参加了第二次世界大战,也许这是美国历史上最统一的联合行动事件。这些美国青年为保卫国家和共同理想将个人希望和抱负抛在一边,离开亲人,离开故乡,放弃工作,集体牺牲。这里纪念的USS SAN DIEGO(CL-53)舰艇上的战士们代表所有为这次大战胜利而战斗的人们。

(美国"中途岛"号航空母舰纪念碑上文字。美国海军有4艘潜艇是以USS SAN DIEGO命名的。)

2

FREEDOM IS NOT FREE

自由是要付出代价的
或自由不是免费的
(美国首都华盛顿韩战纪念碑上的文字)

3

LET EVERY NATION KNOW
WHETHER IT WISHES US WELL OR ILL
THAT WE SHALL PAY ANY PRICE, BEAR ANY BURDEN,
MEET ANY HARDSHIP, SUPPORT ANY FRIENDS,
OPPOSE ANY FOE TO ASSURE THE SURVIVORS
AND THE SUCCESS OF LIBERTY

告天下善意或恶意的国家，
为保障自由的幸存者和胜利成果，
我们将不惜任何代价，担当任何负重，
应付任何艰难，支援任何朋友，反对任何敌人。
（美国阿灵顿国家公墓中一块石碑上的纪念文字。美国阿灵顿国家公墓在弗吉尼亚州阿灵顿县，临波多马克河（Potomac River），位于华盛顿市的正对面。占地500亩，呈半圆形。正中央是1802年仿照雅典忒修斯神庙（Theseum）建筑的殿堂。安葬在这里的有美国军事将领和杰出人物，以及历次战争中牺牲的官兵，无名烈士纪念碑就在这里。据统计，在墓地安葬的死者已超过163,000人。）

4

THE ENERGY, THE FAITH, THE DEVOTION WHICH WE BRING TO THIS ENDEAVOR WILL LIGHT OUR COUNTRY AND ALL WHO SERVE IT AND THE GLOW FROM THAT FIRE CAN TRULY LIGHT THE WORLD

我们为此付出的精力、信念和奉献照亮我们的国家和所有为之服务的人，而其光辉能够真正照亮世界。
（美国阿灵顿国家公墓中另外一块石碑上的纪念文字）

5

Tomb of the Unknown
HERE RESTS IN HONORED
GLORY AN AMERICAN
SOLDIER
KNOWN BUT TO GOD

无名烈士墓
这里长眠着一位光荣的美国军人，他的名字无人知晓。
（美国阿灵顿国家公墓中无名烈士纪念碑文）

二十一、纪念文字

6

THIS TABLET MARKS
THE BROOKLAND FERRY LANDING
FROM WHICH POINT THE AMERICAN
ARMY
EMBARKED DURING THE NIGHT
OF AUGUST 29TH 1776
UNDER THE DIRECTION OF
GENERAL GEORGE WASHINGTON
ABLY ASSISTED BY
COLONEL JOHN GLOVER
OF MARBLEHEAD, MASSACHUSETTS

本碑为纪念布鲁克兰渡口而建。1776年8月29日夜间,在来自萨诸塞州马勒赫特镇的约翰·格劳夫上校的巧妙帮助下,华盛顿将军指挥美国军队在此登船。

(纽约市布鲁克林大桥旁一码头上的纪念碑文字。马勒赫特是美国马萨诸塞州一旅游小镇,位于波士顿东北约25公里处,濒马萨诸塞湾。)

7

When the Constitutional Convention met in Independence Hall in 1787, Philadelphians of diverse backgrounds, incomes, and occupations lived side-by-side. Engraved on these stones are the names of the people who lived on this block.

1787年大陆会议在独立宫举行的时候,不同背景、不同收入和不同职业的费城人生活在一起。这些石头上镌刻着曾经在这一地区居住过的人们的名字。

(费城独立宫附近石头路上所刻的文字)

8

DEAD	MISSING
U. S. A. 54,246 U. N. 628,833	U. S. A. 8,177 U. N. 470,267

美国首都华盛顿的朝鲜战争纪念碑文字说明。纪念碑上显示美方死亡54,246人,联合国军队628,833人;美国军队失踪8,177人,联合国军队470,267人。在中国,朝鲜战争被称为"抗美援朝战争";在美国,被称为"韩战"。纪念碑1995年7月27日建成,由十九个真人大小的美国士兵不锈钢塑像,一人来高的黑色大理石纪念墙,以及喷泉水池等建筑集中在一起组成三角形花园。

9

IN THIS TEMPLE
AS IN THE HEARTS OF THE PEOPLE
FOR WHOM HE SAVED THE UNION
THE MEMORY OF ABRAHAM LINCOLN
IS ENSHRINED FOREVER

这座殿堂内敬奉着亚伯拉罕·林肯。他为人民拯救了联邦,他永远铭记在人民心中。

(林肯纪念堂内林肯座像上方的文字。纪念堂于1922年5月30日建成,是一座仿古希腊神庙式的建筑。纪念堂正中设有一尊由大理石雕刻而成的林肯坐像,大厅墙壁上刻有林肯在葛底斯堡的著名演说词。)

10

ON THIS SPOT STOOD
GORE HALL
ARCHITECT RICHARD BOND SUPERVISOR DANIEL TREADWELL
BUILT IN THE YEAR 1838 NAMED IN HONOR OF
CHRISTOPHER GORE
CLASS OF 1776
FELLOW OF THE COLLEGE OVERSEAS BENEFACTOR
GOVERNOR OF THE COMMONWEALTH SENATOR OF THE
UNITED STATES
THE FIRST USE OF MODERN BOOK-STACKS WAS IN THIS
LIBRARY
IN 1877 WHEN THE EASTERLY WING WAS ADDED
GORE HALL CONTAINED THE HARVARD LIBRARY UNTIL 1913
AND BEING THEN LONG OUTGROWN
WAS TORN DOWN TO MAKE PLACE FOR
THE HARRY ELKINS WIDENER MEMORIAL LIBRARY
THIS TABLET HAS BEEN PLACED HERE BY THE
UNIVERSITY LIBRARY COMMITTEE
1916

1838年建造的戈尔大厦原址,建筑师为里查·邦德,监理是丹尼尔·特雷德韦尔,为了纪念1776届学生克里斯托弗·戈尔而命名,他是哈佛海外捐赠成员之一,也是美国联邦参议院的首脑。这座图书馆首先使用了现代意义上的书架,1877年扩建东翼,戈尔大厦作为哈佛图书馆一直使用到1913年。由于馆藏容量有限,大厦被拆除而建造哈里·艾尔金·魏德纳纪念图书馆。
本说明牌哈佛大学图书馆协会1916年立。
（哈佛大学一图书馆的说明牌。该图书馆简称魏德纳图书馆，是为纪念哈里·艾尔金·魏德纳而建。他是哈佛1907届的毕业生，喜好藏书。1912年4月1日，在结束伦敦购书之行后，哈里和父母登上了"泰坦尼克"号，携带着从伦敦书店购买的大量书籍，其中包括一本1598年版的培根《随笔集》。中途"泰坦尼克"号失事，他的母亲和女仆登上了救生艇，得以幸存。为纪念儿子，母亲捐赠了350万美元筹建该图书馆。馆内有90公里长的书架和300万册图书。）

11

University Hall (1813-1815) was designed by Charles Bulfinch (Harvard Class of 1781) and is a National Historic Landmark. The statue is by Daniel Chester, French. It represents John Harvard, of whom no known likeness exists. The model was Sherman Hoar, Class of 1882.

John Harvard (1607—1638) was a graduate of Emmanuel College, Cambridge who emigrated to America in 1637. On his death he left his library and half his estate to the "college at Newtowne," which had been established by the Massachusetts Legislature in 1636.

In appreciation of John Harvard's generosity, the "college" was renamed Harvard College in 1638, when the first students enrolled.

大学馆为哈佛1781届学生查尔斯伯芬设计，是美国一座历史性建筑。雕像为法国人丹尼尔·切斯特设计，模特是哈佛大学1882届学生，不是哈佛本人。

约翰·哈佛（1607—1638）毕业于剑桥爱玛努艾学院，1637年移民美国，1638年去世的时候将自己的图书和一半财产捐给了纽镇（剑桥的旧称）学院，该院为马萨诸塞州立法机构1636年建立。为几年他的慷慨捐赠，1638年第一届新生入学时学院更名为哈佛大学。

（哈佛大学校园中一栋名为University Hall大楼前的说明。）

12

THESE BUILDINGS DEDICATED IN
THE YEAR NINETEEN
HUNDRED SIXTEEN STAND AS AN
ENDURING MONUMENT
RICHARD COCKBURN
MACLAURIN
WHOSE ENERGY VISION AND
LEADERSHIP AS PRESIDENT FROM
NINETEEN HUNDRED NINE TO
NINETEEN HUNDRED
TWENTY ESTABLISHED THE
MASSACHUSETTS INSTITUTE
OF TECHNOLOGY IN THIS MORE
AMPLE HOME AND GUIDED
IT INTO A NEW ERA OF STRENGTH
AND STABILITY

这些大楼建于1916年，永久纪念**理查德·考科苯·麦克劳林**1909年至1920年期间，他作为校长所表现出来的精力、远见和领导才能让麻省理工学院在这个知识更加富足的家园内更为稳固，并引导着学校走向强大和稳定的新时代。

（麻省理工学院内大楼的说明。理查德·考科苯·麦克劳林是一位教育家和数学物理学家，曾任麻省理工学院第六任校长。文字中的这幢大楼是麻省理工学院内一座有高大的古希腊爱奥尼亚式立柱和巨大圆屋顶的建筑，校内被称为10号楼。）

13

DEDICATED TO
JULIUS ADAMS STRATTON
CLASS OF 1923
ELEVENTH PRESIDENT
OF THE
MASSCHUSETTS INSTITUTE OF TECHNOLOGY
IN GRATEFUL APPRECIATION FOR HIS ABIDING CONCERN FOR THE
STUDENTS OF M.I.T.
THIS BUILDING STANDS AS AN ENDURING EXPRESSION OF THEIR
AFFECTION AND ESTEEM
HIS DEVOTED EFFORTS ON THEIR BEHALF
OCTOBER 9, 1965

献给朱立亚·亚当斯·斯特顿（1923届），麻省理工学院第十一任校长。感谢他对学生的不懈关怀，建造本楼以表达对他的爱戴和尊敬。
1965年10月9日
（麻省理工学院内西20号楼的纪念文字）

二十一、纪念文字

14

BETHANY COLLEGE
BETHANY, WEST VIRGINIA
HONORS ITS DISTINGUISHED GRADUATE
EDGAR ODELL LOVETT 1871—1957
IN THIS 75TH YEAR OF HIS BACCALAUREATE
AND THE 125TH YEAR OF THE COLLEGE
WITH A SALUTE TO RICE UNIVERSITY
WHOSE PIONEER PRESIDENT WAS A
CITIZEN OF THE WORLD AT HOME WITH
THE STARS
HE HELD BEFORE THE YOUNG
AN ABIDING VISION OF GREATNESS
WHICH IS EVER GRATEFULLY
REMEMBERED 1965

西弗吉尼亚州的贝斯尼学院
纪念优秀毕业生爱德加·欧戴尔·拉维(1871—1957)在其获得学士学位75周年以及学院成立125周年之际，向莱斯大学致敬。其首任校长立足宇内，仰望星空。高瞻远瞩，永远为青年人所感激怀念。1965年
（莱斯大学校园内一栋大楼（贝斯尼学院）的说明）

15

THE RICE INSTITUTE OF LIBERAL AND
TECHNICAL LEARNING FOUNDED BY
WILLIAM MARSH RICE
AND DEDICATED BY HIM TO THE
ADVANCEMENT
OF LETTERS SCIENCE AND ART

莱斯文科和技术学院由威廉·马士·莱斯创立并致力于促进文学、科学和艺术的进步。
（莱斯大学校园内一栋大楼的说明文字）

16

LOVETT HALL
IN GRATEFUL HOMAGE TO THE CLEAR VISION
UNFALTERING ZEAL AND BENEFICENT LABORS OF
EDGAR ODELL LOVETT
FIRST PRESIDENT OF THE RICE INSTITUTE
EXEGIT MONUMENTUM AERE PERENNIUS

向莱斯学院的第一任校长爱德加·欧戴尔·拉维特致敬，感谢他的远见卓识、不变的热情和慈善之举。我们立起了一座比青铜更永久的纪念碑
（休斯敦莱斯大学校园内的一座名叫拉维特主楼的碑文。碑文最后一句EXEGIT MONUMENTUM AERE PERENNIUS为拉丁文，是古罗马诗人贺拉斯《纪念碑》一诗中的第一句，意思是：我们立起了一座比青铜更永久的纪念碑（I have erected a monument more lasting than bronze）。）

17

CULLEN FAMILY PLAZA
THIS PLAZA, COMBINING NATURAL BEAUTY, ART AND UTILITY AS A KEY FACILITY WITHIN THE NEW MASTER PLAN OF THE UNIVERSITY OF HOUSTON, IS DEDICATED TO THE CULLEN FAMILY. ITS CENTRAL LOCATION AND SIGNFICANCE RECALL THE IMPORTANCE OF THE GENEROUS SUPPORT AND LASTING FRIENDSHIP OF THIS GREAT PHILANTHROPIC FAMILY. A TRADITION BEGUN BY HUGH ROY AND LILIE GRANZ CULLEN AND CONTINUED BY THEIR CHILDREN AND GRANDCHILDREN. 1972

卡伦家族广场
本广场兼自然美、艺术和实用为休斯敦大学新规划图中的一个主要场所,现敬献给卡伦家族。其中心位置和意义显示这一伟大慈善家族慷慨捐赠和永恒友谊的价值。这一传统始于卡伦夫妇,并由其子女和孙子孙女继承。
1972年
(休斯敦大学校园内卡伦家族广场说明文字)

18

ROY GUSTAV CULLEN
MEMORIAL BUILDING
GIVEN BY
MR. AND MRS. H. R. CULLEN
IN MEMORY OF THEIR SON

罗怡·葛斯塔夫·卡伦纪念大楼
卡伦夫妇捐赠以纪念其子
(休斯敦大学校园内一教学楼捐赠碑文)

19

Conrad N. Hilton
College of Hotel and Restaurant
Management
This complex is designed for the education of future hospitality managers. Many of the staff you come in contact with and who serve you, in all areas of the hotel and conference center, are students learning the many components of the hospitality industry. We look forward to your visit, and welcome you as our guests.

康拉德·N. 希尔顿酒店管理学院
学院是为培养未来的餐饮业经理。在酒店和会议中心各区域的管理人员和服务人员都是在学习餐饮业的各方面知识的学生。期待您来参观,欢迎您来做客。
(休斯敦大学中酒店饭店管理学院的一座酒店说明)

二十一、纪念文字

20

IN TRIBUTE TO MONROE D.
ANDERSON 1873—1939
WHOSE VISION FOR PROSPERITY
MADE POSSIBLE THIS USEFUL
BUILDING. A GENTLE MAN OF NOBLE
HEART, HE DEVOTED HIS LIFE TO
HARD WORK AND HIGH PURPOSE.
HE DEDICATED HIS FORTUNE TO
IMPROVING THE PHYSICAL, THE
INTELLECTUAL, AND THE SPIRITUAL
WELFARE OF HUMANKIND.

向蒙罗·D·安德逊致敬
(1873—1939)
他成功的远见使这栋大楼的建造成为可能。他心灵高尚，待人谦和，毕生辛勤工作，追求高尚理想。他将自己的财富奉献给提高人类的健康、知识和精神福祉。
（校园内一栋大楼捐赠说明）

21

Anne and Charles Duncan Hall
Named in their honor by the
Board of Governors
in recognition of their inspired
leadership and dedication to Rice
1996

董事会命名此楼为安娜和查尔斯·邓肯大楼，以纪念他们富有灵感的领导和对莱斯大学的贡献，1996年。
（莱斯大学校园内一栋大楼捐赠说明）

22

THE FOLLOWING DONORS HAVE
GENEROUSLY GIVEN TO THIS
FACILITY
(omitted)

以下人员为本楼的建设给予慷慨捐赠（略）
（莱斯大学校园内邓肯大楼内的捐赠说明）

23

CEILING MADE POSSIBLE THROUGH
THE GENEROSITY OF STEVE & SUE SHAPER

天花板由斯蒂威·夏波和苏·夏波慷慨捐赠
（莱斯大学校园内邓肯大楼天花板捐赠说明文字。邓肯楼有无数自己的特点，设计师为约翰·奥特兰。这座大楼是为工程学院中的计算工程各专业而建，其中包括当今最兴旺的计算与应用数学、计算机科学、统计学等，楼内大约有200名教职工和学生。邓肯楼与大学校园的主题思想相呼应，其中最突出的是河谷文化的主题。邓肯楼的入口处圆柱上就有象征河谷文化的图案。）

24

Dedicated to Minerva M. McCauley
Chemical Engineering Department
Employed: 1966 – Retired 1989
Live Oak
Family: Fagaceae
Range: Southeastern United States

敬献给化学工程系米纳维·M.麦考雷
(在职时间：1966年—1989年)
槲树，豆科
生长范围：美国东南部
（美国德州莱斯大学校园内树下水泥块中镶嵌的铜牌。该大学的教师退休以后可以要求将自己的工作时间镌刻在校园内某一棵树下作为纪念。Fagaceae为拉丁文。）

25

RICE UNIVERSITY
ATHLETIC ENDOWMENT FUND
Recognizing the generosity of our friends who have established scholarships to benefit The Rice University Athletic Program.
（omitted）

莱斯大学
体育项目捐赠基金会
感谢各位友人慷慨设立的奖学金，使莱斯大学体育项目受益（略）
（莱斯大学体育馆墙壁上捐赠人员和机构名单文字）

26

SHELL OIL COMPANY
FOUNDATION
AUDITORIUM

壳牌石油公司基金会捐赠装修
会议室
（会议室门上方说明）

27

JONES EXECUTIVE OFFICES
made possible through
a generous gift from
HOUSTON
ENDOWMENT INC.,
a philanthropy endowed by
Mr. and Mrs. Jesse H. Jones

琼斯行政办公室
杰斯·H.琼斯先生和夫人资助的慈善事业休斯敦捐赠基金公司慷慨捐赠
（莱斯大学图书馆大楼捐赠说明）

二十一、纪念文字

28

WEST HALL named in honor of
JOSEPHINE ABERCROMBIE
TRUSTEE EMERITA

西大厅
以荣誉受托人约瑟芬·阿贝科隆比命名
（大楼捐赠说明）

29

RAYZOR HALL DEDICATED TO
HUMANISTIC STUDIES AND
MADE POSSIBLE BY THE
DEVOTION OF
NEWTON RAYZOR AND EUGENIA
PORTER RAYZOR
TO WILLIAM MARSH RICE
UNIVERSITY 1961
STAUB RATHER AND HOWZE
ARCHITECTS

瑞瑟尔大楼敬献给人文研究
牛顿·瑞瑟尔和尤吉尼尔·伯特·瑞瑟尔
1961年捐赠给莱斯大学
建筑师为斯特伯·拉瑟和斯特伯·郝泽
（瑞瑟尔大楼捐赠和建设说明）

30

115
CONFERENCE ROOM
GIVEN BY Phoebe and Bobby Tudor
In Honor of the Late
John Parish, Professor of English

115会议室
佛比·图德和博比·图德捐赠
纪念已故英语教授约翰·帕里悉
（会议室捐助说明）

31

GIVEN BY Walter and
Karen Loewenstern

沃尔特·罗文斯特恩和凯伦·罗文斯特恩捐赠
（教学大楼捐赠文字说明。这可能是最简单的捐赠文字说明。）

32

HERMAN BROWN HALL
FOR MATHEMATICAL SCIENCES HONORING HERMAN BROWN
A PROGRESSIVE LEADER OF MEN 1892 – 1962
WHOSE DEDICATION, INTEGRITY AND CREATIVE CONCEPTS
INSPIRED BOTH THE WEAK AND THE STRONG AS HE ENGINEERED

新世纪美国公示语 1000 例

> GREAT PROJECTS AT HOME AND ABROAD
> ad astra per aspera
> ERECTED WITH GENEROUS SUPPORT FROM
> THE BROWN FOUNDATION AND
> THE NATIONAL SCIENCE FOUNDATION DEDICATED 26 AUGUST 1971
>
> 赫曼·布朗大楼
> 用于数学科学,纪念进步领袖赫曼·布朗(1892—1962)。
> 他的奉献、正直和创造思想通过他设计的国内外伟大工程激励了弱者和强者
>
> 排万难而达星斗
> 大楼建设由布朗基金会和国家科学基金会慷慨资助,1971年8月26日敬献。
> (大楼题献和捐赠说明。其中的ad astra per aspera(排万难而达星斗)为拉丁文格言。)

33

| This plaque was donated to Rice by the class of 1950 honoring the 1950 championship football team. | 本牌匾由1950届学生献给莱斯大学,纪念1950年橄榄球队获得冠军。(大学内纪念匾文字。在美国,footballl是橄榄球。) |

34

| THE ALLEN CENTER FOR BUSINESS ACTIVITIES HERBERT AND HELEN ALLEN 1967 | 埃伦商务活动中心 捐赠人赫伯特·埃伦和海伦·埃伦 1967年 (商务大楼捐赠说明) |

35

| City of Houston
Friends of Hermann Park
Miller Theatre Advisory Board
Gratefully acknowledge the generosity of
The Wortham Foundation, Inc.
Karen and Arthur Rogers
Turner Charitable Foundation | 休斯敦市
赫蒙公园的朋友
米勒露天剧场咨询委员会
感激沃尔汉姆基金会、卡伦·罗杰斯和亚瑟·罗杰斯以及特纳慈善基金会
(休斯敦市米勒露天剧场捐赠说明) |

二十一、纪念文字

As a crusader for human rights and liberty, thinker, writer, and social reformer, Mahatma Gandhi successfully united millions of people of all faiths across India in a mass movement of civil disobedience against British colonial rule.

Mahatma Gandhi said: "An eye for eye will only make the whole world blind." "I have nothing new to teach the world. Truth and Non-violence are as old as the hills."

A Gift from the People of India and the Indo-American Community. Facilitated by India Culture Center, Houston and Indian Council of Cultural Relations October 2, 2004

Albert Einstein on Gandhi: "Generations to come, it may be, will scarce believe that such one as this ever in flesh and blood walked upon this earth."

Dr. Martin Luther King, Jr. on Gandhi: "… If humanity is to progress, Gandhi is inescapable. He lived, thought and acted, inspired by the vision of humanity evolving onward a world of peace and harmony…"

MAHATMA GANDHI
October 2, 1896 – January 30, 1948
An apostle of truth, peace and non-violence who led India to Freedom from British rule in 1947, and is hailed as the Father of the Nation.

莫罕默德·甘地，人权和自由的战斗者、思想家、作家和社会改革家，在非暴力反抗英国殖民统治的群众运动中，成功地将全印度各种信仰的人团结起来。

莫罕默德·甘地说：以眼还眼只会让整个世界变瞎；我没有新的东西教给世人，真理和非暴力像山岭一样古老。

印度人民和印美协会捐赠

休斯敦和印度文化关系协会印度文化中心于2004年10月2日设立。

爱因斯坦对甘地的评语：后世人也许不相信，地球上行走过这样一位血肉之躯者。

小马丁·路德·金对甘地的评语：如果人类要进步，甘地是必然会有的。他生活过，思想过，行动过，是人类向着和平与和谐的世界进化的远见激励了他。

莫哈默德·甘地生于1896年10月2日，卒于1948年1月30日。一位真理、和平和非暴力的圣徒，1947年引导着印度摆脱英国的统治，被奉为国父。

（休斯敦一名人雕塑园内莫罕默德·甘地雕塑四周的说明文字）

37

Here in the Presence of Washington and Lincoln,
One the Eighteenth Century Father and the Other
the Nineteenth Century Preserver of our Nation,
We Honor Those Twentieth Century Americans
Who Took Up the Struggle During the Second World
War and Made the Sacrifices to Perpetuate
the Gift Our Forefathers Entrusted to Us:
A Nation Conceived in Liberty and Justice.

在此面对华盛顿和林肯，一位是18世纪的国父，另一位是19世纪民族的护卫者，我们向那些20世纪的美国人致敬。他们在第二次世界大战中奋斗牺牲，为了永葆先辈对我们的嘱托：一个自由和正义孕育的国家。
（首都华盛顿第二次世界大战纪念碑入口碑文。2004年4月29日，美国第二次世界大战纪念碑在首都华盛顿落成后正式向公众开放。纪念碑坐落在林肯纪念堂和华盛顿纪念碑之间，为纪念在二战期间服役的美国军人而建。）

38

THIS GATEWAY PRESENTED BY
THOMAS W. SMITH
OF THE CLASS OF 1871
IN APPRECIATION OF HIS
INSTRUCTORS
A.M. SHIPP DAVID DUNCAN
WHITEFOORD SMITH JAMES H.
CARLISLE WARREN DUPRE
A.M. LESTER

这座大门由1871届学生**托马斯·W.施密特**捐助，感谢以下恩师（略）。
（哈佛大学学生捐赠学校大门的纪念文字。这里the class of 1871表示1871年毕业的学生。）

39

BENEFACTORS
⊙DEBORAH & CARL RHEUBAN
⊙THE NEWHALL LAND AND FARMING COMPANY
⊙MRS. ALAN HAY MEANS SHELL COMPANIES FOUNDATION INC. THE JONES FOUNDATION HARRY ROTH & LOUIS ROTH – IN MEMORIAM LEONARD & JANICE WEIL
⊙DEAN M. & REBECCA WILLARD
⊙DISTINGUISHED PATRON OF THE ARTS

剧场捐赠人的名牌。有个人、组织和企业等。最后一个注释说明其中带星号的为著名的文艺美术赞助人。

二十二、购票说明

1

PURCHASE INTERPID MUSEUM TICKETS HERE

"勇猛号"航空母舰博物馆参观券在此购买

2

PLEASE PURCHASE TICKETS FROM TOURMOBILE DRIVERS THIS BOOTH IS TEMPORARILY CLOSED THANK YOU

请从游览车司机处购票,本售票亭暂时关闭。
谢谢
(旅游购票指示牌)

3

Admission Prices

		combo tickets
daily single show		
admission (13-59)	$8.50	$7.00 per ticket
youth (2-12)	$7.00	$6.00 per ticket
senior (60+)	$7.50	$6.00 per ticket

入场券价格表。每天单场表演的入场券价格分别为13-59岁成人8.50美元;2-12岁儿童7美元;60岁以上的7.50美元。购买套票每张分别为7美元、6美元和6美元。

4

TICKETS AND INFORMATION ARE THREE DOORS DOWN ON YOUR LEFT

购票和问讯处位于左边第四个门
(临时张贴的游船购票说明)

5

PAID FARE ZONE. Valid fare item required while on the platform and before boarding the train.

购票区:轻轨站台上需购买有效票上车。
(轻轨站台上的购票说明文字。轻轨站台上有机器自动售票,购票人按触摸屏上的指令操作,使用现金、信用卡等方式支付。)

6

Please select your transaction		轻轨站台上自动售票系统的说明文字。选择交易方式：单程成人票（有效时间3小时）；代用币和其他单程票（有效时间3小时）；往返票/当日票（有效时间24小时）；多选票（单程/往返/当日）；所有票即刻使用。另外，自动售货机上还有购买新票、充值、查验余额等功能。
Purchase a ticket	METRORide Card	
One Way Adult Ticket (Valid 3 hours)	METRORide Card Touch & Ride	
Token & Other One Way Tickets (Valid 3 hours)	Add to METRORide Card	
Round Trip/ One Day Pass (Valid 24 hours)	Check METRORide Card Status	
Multiple Tickets (One Way/Round Trip/Day Pass)		
All Tickets For Immediate Use		

7

In the event of problems with this TVM, please contact METRO at 713-658-0180 and provide the device number.

自动售票机发生问题，请通过所示电话联系，并提供机器号码。（TVM（=Ticket Vending Machine）是轻轨车站上自动售票系统。）

8

TICKET PRICES

	Exhibit Halls All Day	Butterfly Center All Day	Planetarium Per Show	IMAX Per Show	VALUE PASS All 4 Venues
Member	Free	3.00	3.00	4.00	10.00
Adult	9.00	8.00	6.00	8.00	25.00
Child [3-11] Senior [62+] College Students [w/valid I.D.]	6.00	5.00	4.00	5.00	15.00

二十二、购票说明

博物馆票价说明。该馆共有四个收费项目：展览大厅、蝴蝶中心、天文馆和IMAX电影。会员可免费参观展厅，而其他各场所都有优惠；成人价格最高；3-11岁儿童、62岁以上老人和持有效证件大学生参观都有一定的优惠。另外还可以将博物馆内的四个场所放在一起购买一张超值4+1的票。这里IMAX是Image Maximum的缩写，意为"最大影像"，汉语音译为"艾麦克斯"，是一种能够放映比传统胶片更大和更高解像度的电影放映系统，宽幅可达20米以上。

9

RIVER OAKS THEATER	
2009 West Gray	
General:	$8.25
Seniors 62+:	$6.00
Children 12 & under:	$6:00
Bargain (see below):	$6:00
Student (with valid ID):	$6:00

All shows before 6:00pm, Mon-Fri, (except holidays) & the first show of the day Sat. & Sun discounted

休斯敦一老剧场张贴票价告示。普通票8.25美元；62岁以上老人6美元；12岁及以下儿童6美元；优惠票（见注）6美元；学生票（出示有效证件）6美元。

注：周一至周五下午6点前所有场次（节日除外）以及每天第一场，周六和周日场次均为优惠价。

10

MULTI-PARK PASSES

SAN DIEGO 3-FOR-1 PASS Five consecutive days admission to SeaWorld, San Diego Zoo and San Diego Wild Animal Park
Ages 10+ $99.95 Ages 3-9 $76.95

SOUTHERN CALIFORNIA VALUE PASS Unlimited admission for up to 14 consecutive days to SeaWorld and Universal Studios Hollywood
Ages 10+ $99 Ages 3-9 $79

SOUTHERN CALIFORNIA ATTRACTIONS CITYPASS Includes one-day admission to SeaWorld, San Diego Zoo or Wild Animal Park, Universal Studios Hollywood and a 3-Day Disneyland Resort Park Hopper to Disneyland and Disney's California Adventure Park.
Must be used within 14 consecutive days from first use.
Ages 10+ $199 Ages 3-9 $159

新世纪美国公示语1000例

美国加州圣地亚哥海洋世界公园门口张贴的通票信息。一种票是圣地亚哥三合一通票，该票可连续5天进入海洋世界、动物园和野生动物园，10岁以上99.95美元，3到9岁的孩子76.95美元。第二种是南加州超值通票，该票可以无限制连续14天游玩海洋世界和好莱坞环球影城，10岁以上99美元，3到9岁的孩子79美元。第三种是南加州城市景点通票，包含1天进入海洋世界、圣地亚哥动物园或者野生动物园，好莱坞环球影城以及3天的迪斯尼休闲公园、迪斯尼公园和迪斯尼加州冒险乐园。但是该票从第一次使用开始后连续14天内有效，10岁以上199美元，3到9岁的孩子159美元。为了更好利用游乐资源，美国许多临近甚至有一定距离的游乐场所会联合起来出售通票，以这样的方式吸引更多游客。

11

GENERAL ADMISSION	Ages 10+	Ages 3-9
FUN CARD *black-out dates, May 28 and Sept. 3 *unlimited admission through Dec. 31 2006	$59.00	$49.00
SINGLE DAY TICKET	$54.00	$44.00
DELUXE ADMISSION Includes park admission, Behind-the-Scenes Tour, and second day return visit within seven days of purchase.	$63.00	$53.00

美国加州圣地亚哥海洋世界公园门口2006年7月31日的普通门票信息。第一个普通门票有关娱乐卡信息，10岁以上59美元，3至9岁49美元，但是5月28日和9月3日不包含在内，其他时间一直到2006年12月31日无限进园游乐；第二个信息有关一天游乐的价格，年龄10岁以上54美元，3至9岁44美元；第三个信息有关豪华门票的信息，年龄10岁以上63美元，3至9岁53美元，包括进入公园大门、幕后游览以及自购票之日起7天内可二次入园游览。美国很多游乐场所为游人提供各种价格优惠的门票，以吸引更多的游人，尤其是一张票可在规定时间内二次以上进入游览区很常见。

二十二、购票说明

12

PASSPORT MEMBERSHIP		
	Ages 10+	Ages 3-9
SILVER		Ages 50+
One-year unlimited admission	$89.00	$74.00 $79.00
PLATINUM		
One-year unlimited admission plus elite benefits	$147.00	$127.00 $132.00

美国加州圣地亚哥海洋世界公园门口护照会员门票信息。这里提供了两种票的信息,第一种是银卡,10岁以上89美元,3至9岁74美元,50岁以上79美元,一年之内进入无限制;第二种为铂金卡,10岁以上147美元,3至9岁127美元,50岁以上132美元,一年之内进入无限制,并且还有会员优惠(elite benefits)。由于在美国持护照的人比较多,因此在公园等场所优惠政策也考虑到了这些人。

13

PLEASE HAVE YOUR FASTPASS TICKET AVAILABLE

请将快速通行卡准备好

(迪斯尼乐园内要求在快速通道内排队的游客将快速通行票准备好的说明文字。美国迪斯尼公园内因为有些项目排队时间比较长,因此游客可以在某些项目开始前去快速通行机器上插入自己的票根,然后取得一张快速通行票,这样按照票上规定的时间前往该游乐点通过快速通道进入该区域游玩。)

14

NOTICE
THIS PARK CLOSES
AT 6:00 PM DAILY
ALL ENTRANCES WILL BE
SECURED AT THAT TIME

告示
本公园每天下午6点关闭
此时所有入口紧闭
(公园开放时间通告)

15

Star Line Tours
MOVIE STARS' HOMES TOUR
SEE OVER 40 STARS' HOMES
VEVERLY HILLS, RODEO
DRIVE AND MORE!
2-HOUR NARRATED TOUR
Adult: $37 Child: $27

明星路线游
游览电影明星宅邸,参观维弗利山庄40多位明星居所、罗德大道以及更多景点;
2小时讲解游览;成人37美元,儿童27美元。
(这是一幅参观明星居所的游览广告)

16

THE SYMPHONIANS OF THE MUSIC CENTER
COMPLIMENTARY GUIDED TOURS
August 1–August 5, 2006

No Tours Scheduled on Sundays or Mondays

Tuesday, August 1	Thursday, August 3
10:00 public	10:00 public
10:30 public	10:30 public
11:30 public	11:30 public
12:00 public	12:00 public
1:00 public	1:00 schedule
1:30 public	1:30 public
Wednesday, August 2	**Friday, August 4**
10:00 public	10:00 public
10:30 public	10:30 no tour
11:30 public	11:30 public
12:00 public	12:00 no tours
1:00 public	1:00 public
1:30 public	1:30 no tours
	Saturday, August 5
	10:00 public
	10:30 schedule
	11:30 public
	12:00 public

Tour availability and start times are subject to change. Tours last approximately 60–75 minutes. For a daily schedule, or to make a school group reservation call 213-972-7483.

洛杉矶音乐中心阿曼森剧院游览项目说明文字。说明开始告知2006年的8月1日至5日由音乐中心的交响乐团的团员讲解游览；周日或周一不安排；其他为游览的具体时间，具体时间后为散客游览和预定游览以及无游览；告示最后还说明是否安排参观以及开始时间都可能会发生变化；参观时间大约为60分钟至75分钟；每天的游览安排或者学校集体参观可通过电话联系预定。

17

WILL CALL
Ahmanson Theatre
Please examine day and Date of tickets. No mistakes Rectified after leaving window. No exchanges or refunds.

预定票务
阿曼森剧院请观众检查票上日期和星期离开售票窗口后不得更改、换票或退票（洛杉矶音乐中心阿曼森剧院有关WILL CALL购票方式的文字告示。Will Call是美国剧场常用的一种售票服务方式，观众通过电话或网络预订，然后前往取票进入剧场观看。）

二十二、购票说明

18

| Void If Detached | 撕下作废（票根上的说明文字） |

19

| BULK ADMISSION TICKET TICKET VALID FOR ONE YEAR FROM DATE OF ISSUE, NO REFUNDS SEE IMPORTANT TERMS AND CONDITIONS | 团体票
从发出之日起有效期一年；不得退款；请看主要条款。
（游船船票上的说明文字。除了这些内容，还有游船出发码头、船票发出时间及性质等信息。） |

20

1-DAY $59.00 AGES 10+VALID AT ONE RESORT THEME PARK ONLY NOT VALID AFTER 03/31/2007

Not for resale. Nonrefundable. Nontransferable; must be used by the same person on any and all days. Hand stamp and ticket are required for same day readmission to same park and, if applicable, crossover to the other Park. Guest assumes the inherent risks associated with the operation of all rides and attractions. Read any obey all safety signage; instructions and rules. Parks or attractions may change operating hours, close temporarily, or may otherwise change or be discontinued with notice and without liability to the owners of the Parks. Entry into any Park constitutes consent for Disney to use any film, video or reproduction of image and / or voice of bearer for any purpose whatsoever without any payment to the bearer. Not responsible for lost or stolen tickets or property. Other restrictions may apply.

当日票售价59美元，年龄在10岁以上，且只适用于一个主题公园，有效期至2007年3月31日。不得转售；不得退款；不得转让；只可同一人在任何一天使用。同一天进入同一个公园，需手章和票据；如适用，可转到其他游园；游客承担所有乘坐和娱乐固有的风险性；请阅读并遵守所有安全提示、指令和规定。景点可能会更改开放时间、临时关闭或其他改变或者通知中断运行，公园一方不承担责任。进入公园就意味着同意迪斯尼乐园使用被拍摄人的胶片、摄像或其音像复制品，可无偿用于任何目的，门票或财物丢失或被盗公园不负责；其他限制可以适用。
（这是迪斯尼乐园提供一日游门票上的信息，使用日期为2006年7月31日。门票背面的文字几乎涵盖所有能够想到的责任。）

21

| SKYTOWER RIDE
SINGLE RIDE 3.00
BOTH RIDES 5.00 | BOTH NOW AND
SAVE | 乘坐通天塔：单次3美元，两次5美元。购买两次乘座票，可以省钱。
（加州海洋世界内通天塔票的信息。通天塔会以每小时65英里（104公里）的速度上升到15层楼高的地方。） |

22

The Metropolitan Museum of Art
FAMILY PASS
Explore 5000 years of art
- European paintings
- a Chinese garden
- Central and South
- American gold
- African sculpture
- an Egyptian temple
- knights in armor
and much more!

纽约大都会艺术博物馆家庭门票
探索5,000年的艺术，包括欧洲绘画、中国园林、美国中南部、美国黄金、非洲雕塑、埃及神庙、铠甲武士，还有更多内容。
（纽约大都会艺术博物馆家庭门票）

23

PLEASE PRESENT YOUR PERMIT ON REQUEST.

许可证承索 请出示
（票面上的要求）

24

SEE ATTENDANT
PAY STATION AHEAD
                         SINGLE ENTRY   ANNUAL PASS
1) INDIVIDUAL (WALK-IN) $1:00 $10:00
2) PRIVATE VEHICLE $5:00 $30:00
3) COMMERCIAL VEHICLE
   SEDAN/VAN (15-CAP) $10:00
   MINI-BUS (16-25 CAP) $20:00
   BUS   (26+ CAP) $40:00

二十二、购票说明

前往收费点有服务员
个人单次步行1美元,年票10美元;
私车单次进入5美元,年票30美元;
商务车单次进入
中小型(15人以下)10美元、小型公共车(16-25人)20美元、公共汽车(26人以上)40美元。

(旅游点门票说明)

25

HANAUMA BAY NATURE PRESERVE
ADMISSION FEE: $5.00 PER PERSON 13 YEARS AND OLDER
FREE FOR PERSON 12 YEARS AND YOUNGER
NO PERSONAL CHECKS, AND BILLS OVER $50.00 ACCEPTED
PLEASE KEEP YOUR RECEIPT WHILE IN PRESERVE
HOURS OPEN: 6:00AM TO 6:00PM DAILY
CLOSED TUESDAYS
ALCOHOL BEVERAGE NOT ALLOWED
SMOKING NOT PERMITTED IN LOWER PARK AREA

海湾自然保护区
门票费用:13岁以上每人5美元,12岁和以下免费;不得使用个人支票,接受50美元以上票据;在保护区内请留好自己的收据。开放时间为每天上午6点至下午6点;周二关闭;不得喝酒精饮料。公园地势低的区域不得吸烟。

(自然保护区门票费用和开放说明)

26

The Ticket Booth is CLOSED for Non-Peak Season
(August through February)
TICKETS ARE NOT REQUIRED AT THIS TIME OF YEAR.
Please go to the Visitor Entrance at 14th and C. Street
Tour Information Line (202) 874-2330

非高峰季节(8月至次年2月),本售票亭关闭
每年该时段免票
请前往14大街和C大街的游客入口
旅游信息电话(202)874-2330

(公园购票说明)

27

VISITING THE WASHINGTON MONUMENT
Open Daily 9 a.m. – 5 p.m.   Monument is Fully Accessible
Last Tour at 4:30 p.m.   Free Timed Tickets are Required for All Visitors

TICKETING INFORMATION

Same Day Free Tickets	Advance Reservation Tickets
Available Daily Beginning at 8:30 a.m. from the Ticket Kiosk on a First Come Basis Up to Six Tickets Per Adult	Available by Calling (800)967-2283 or Visiting http://reservations.nps.gov Convenience Fees Will Apply

The Washington Monument May Close in Case of Severe Weather or Emergency. Refunds are Available by Calling (800)967-2283.

华盛顿纪念碑参观须知
每日开放时间：9 a.m. — 5 p.m.   纪念碑完全开放
最后进入时间：4:30 p.m.   所有参观人员需要出示定时免票

票务信息：	提前预定票
当天免票 上午8:30开始在售票处领票 先来先得，每个成人最多6张。	电话订票(800)967-2283 或访问http://reservations.nps.gov 收取便利费

华盛顿纪念碑在恶劣天气或紧急情况下关闭。电话退款(800)967-2283。

28

Empire State Building Observatory	Adult	
	Subject to early closure due to customer volume. Good For 1 Admission Tickets are Non-Refundable.	Ticket Expires 2 Years From Dated Printed.

纽约帝国大厦观景台成人票
可能会因游客量过多而提前关门；1人进入有效；本票不退款。本票印刷之日起2年之内有效。
（纽约帝国大厦票面上的说明）

二十三、博物馆

博物馆

1

Please do not enter during the performance
Door opens automatically, prior to next show

表演中请勿入内
下一场表演前,大门自动开启
(美国康宁玻璃博物馆剧场门上说明。剧场每天大约表演10场吹玻璃。)

2

Ring around the Rosy
Stand hand-to-hand with a friend to make a circle with your reflections.

美国小镇康宁玻璃博物馆内一个展览项目说明。只要你和朋友手拉手地站着就可以看到镜子里的影子形成一个圆圈。馆内有一些与观众互动的项目。

3

The nature of glass theater
Experience the film Glass into Dreams a dramatic introduction to this amazing material that has intrigued mankind for more than 3500 years.
1999 New York Festival—
Best of Show World Gold Award

玻璃溯源大剧场
体验一下已经让人类痴迷3500年玻璃的科教片《玻璃之梦》,该片曾经于1999年获得纽约节上的全球表演金奖。(美国小镇康宁玻璃博物馆内剧场演出节目介绍。美国"纽约节"也叫"纽约广告节",是当今世界三大广告节之一。)

4

Micromosaics
Micromosaics are glass pictures made from tiny sections of colored glass rods. As many as 1,400 glass sections fit into a square inch, creating the illusion of a painting. By the 1880s, mosaic artists had found ways to make these labor-intensive panels faster. They used multicolored, fused rods to repeat border

新世纪美国公示语 1000 例

designs.
In Rome, mosaicists copied paintings and prints, and they also created new designs. These ranged from jewelry to large furniture inlays.

微型马赛克画

微型马赛克画是由细小的彩色玻璃柱构成的。在每平方英寸的面积范围内，嵌入了1400块玻璃片，宛如画作。19世纪80年代之前，马赛克艺术家就已经想出方法来让这种耗力的画制作更快一些。他们使用各种颜色的融化金属条进行边角设计。

罗马的马赛克画艺术家复制绘画和印刷品，他们也设计新作品，这些作品包括从珠宝到大型家具的内嵌装饰等。

（美国纽约州康宁玻璃博物馆微型马赛克画的介绍）

5

Touch Roman bottle
This was made by Roman glassblowers in the second century.

请触摸罗马瓶
这个瓶子是公元2世纪罗马吹玻璃工吹制而成的。
（博物馆有一些项目邀请观众参与互动。）

6

MUSEUM POLICIES
Thank you for not smoking or chewing gum while on the aircraft carrier Intrepid, submarine Growler, Concorde or Pier.
Only food and beverages purchased on the premises are permitted unless authorized by museum management.
Strollers are NOT permitted in the Growler or Concorde.
Children under age 6 are NOT permitted aboard the submarine Growler.
Flight Simulator requirements: 4D-X Must be 42" & over; G-Force Must be 48" & over. Must be 6 years or older.
Due to original design construction the submarine Growler and Concorde are NOT wheelchair accessible.

二十三、博物馆

博物馆守则

感谢你在航母、潜水艇、协和号飞机以及码头上不吸烟不嚼口香糖；未经博物馆允许，只可食用博物馆范围内购买的食品和饮料；潜水艇和协和号飞机上不得使用童车；6岁以下儿童不允许上潜水艇；进行飞行模拟的孩子要6岁以上，观看4D-X电影必须是高于42英寸的儿童，体验G-Force飞行模拟器要48英寸以上。鉴于原始设计规格，"黑鲈号"潜水艇和"协和号"飞机上不能使用轮椅。

（纽约"无畏号"航空母舰博物馆参观要求。该馆还包含其周围的"黑鲈号"潜水艇、"协和号"飞机以及码头。纽约"无畏号"航空母舰上机库中有大展览厅，从舰首至舰尾分别是戏院(Cartier Operations Theatre，放映舰艇作业的影片)、美国海军厅(U. S. Navy Hall，展出美国海军制服、装备和多架军用飞机)，无畏号厅(Intrepid Hall，展出二次大战中太平洋战争的海战史物)、先锋厅(Pioneer Hall，展出海军航空界的先驱)、科技厅(Technologies Hall，展出登月太空计划等航天科技)及餐厅等；其他小展区则散布其间，而在下层甲板则是较小的D-Day展示厅，与前苏联在二次大战的展示厅。）

7

GENERAL INFORMATION

The Intrepid Museum is a private, non-for-profit educational institution chartered by the New York State Board of Regents.

Hours of Operation

SPRING/SUMMER HOURS
April 1–September 30
Mon-Fri 10–5 Last Admission @ 4 pm
Sat-Sun 10–6 Last Admission @ 5 pm
Holidays 10–6 Last Admission @ 5 pm

FALL/WINTER HOURS
October 1–March 31
Tues-Sun 10–5 Last Admission @ 4 pm
Holidays 10–5 Last Admission @ 4 pm
Open all Holidays except Thanksgiving Day and Christmas Day

简 介

"无畏号"航空母舰博物馆是一家私人、非盈利性教育机构,由纽约州董事会承包。

春夏营业时段4月1日至9月30日,

周一至周五上午10点至下午5点,最后入馆时间下午4点;

周六至周日上午10点至下午6点,最后入馆时间下午5点;

节假日为上午10点至下午6点,最后入馆时间下午5点。

秋冬营业时段每年10月1日至次年3月31日,

周二至周日上午10点至下午5点,最后入馆时间下午4点;

节假日上午10点至下午5点,最后入馆时间下午4点。

除感恩节和圣诞节,其他假日全部开放。

("无畏号"航空母舰博物馆的总体开放时间介绍)

8

Museums are open daily 10AM–5:30PM

All Smithsonian museums and the National Zoo are free. All are closed December 25. Information subject to change. Check at any museum information desk.

博物馆每天上午10点至下午5点30开放

所有史密森尼博物馆和国家动物园均为免费参观,所有博物馆12月25日闭馆。

信息可变,请查询博物馆信息台。

(华盛顿地区博物馆开放说明)

9

Dates follow Daylight Saving Time

approx. April–October

Grounds: 6AM–8 PM

Buildings: 10AM–6PM

approx. October–April

Grounds: 6AM–6 PM

Buildings: 10AM–4:30PM

夏令时开放安排

大约4月至10月

室外参观上午6点至下午8点

室内参观上午10点至下午6点

每年10月至4月

室外上午6点至下午6点

室内上午10点至下午4点30分。

(博物馆开放时间说明)

二十三、博物馆

10

SECURITY CHECK
Bag Check in Progress

安全检查
正在验包
（博物馆入口处的安检指示牌。遭受911恐怖袭击以后，美国很多场馆都开始实行进门验包规定。）

11

Look… listen… explore…
But please don't touch.

看……听……探索……，但请勿触摸
（博物馆内告示牌）

12

BENEFITS OF SMITHSONIAN MEMBERSHIP
- Smithsonian Magazine (12 issues)
- Reduced tickets to IMAX and Planetarium Shows
- 10% off meal purchases
- 10% Shopping discounts, in person and online!
- Special invitations to programs throughout the US
   *Ask a Theater Host for Details and Start Saving TODAY!

史密森尼博物馆会员优惠
协会12期杂志
IMAX和水族馆表演门票减价
餐饮九折优惠
店内或网上购物享受九折优惠
特邀参加全美的一些项目
详情请咨询剧院工作人员，省钱从今天开始！
（华盛顿地区博物馆会员说明。在美国，很多参观或者娱乐的地方都可以通过成为会员而得到一定的优惠。）

13

Please Ask About Our Smithsonian Brochures in Alternative Formats:
- Audio Cassette
- Braille

请索取各种形式的史密森尼博物馆宣传材料：
- 卡式录音带
- 盲文

- Compact Disc (CD)
- Computer Diskette
- Large Print

- 光盘
- 磁盘
- 大字印刷品
（博物馆入口处咨询台上有关博物馆的介绍说明。边上有一个残疾人的标志，显示资料提供的对象。）

14

Audrey Jones Beck Building
Admission
Admission on Thursday is free thanks to a generous grant from Shell Oil Company Foundation. Museum members admitted free every day. No admission charge required for Café Express, MFA Stores or Library.

因壳牌石油基金会慷慨赞助，休斯敦艺术博物馆每周四免费开放；本馆会员每天免费参观；咖啡店、商店和图书馆不收入场费。
（休斯敦艺术博物馆入馆说明）

15

Contemporary Arts Museum
5216 Montrose
Hours:
Tuesday – Saturday: 10:00 a.m. – 5:00 p.m.
Sunday: 12:00 p.m. – 5:00 p.m.
Closed Monday
Admission is Free
due to the generosity of Less Marks and Marks Automotive Group.

当代艺术博物馆
蒙特罗斯大街5216号
开放时间：
周二至周六：上午10点至下午5点
周一闭馆
免费入馆（马科斯汽车集团慷慨资助）
（休斯敦当代艺术博物馆入馆说明）

16

Lillie and Hugh Roy Cullen
Sculpture Garden
A partnership between The Museum of Fine Arts, Houston and the City of Houston. Made possible by generous contributions from:

二十三、博物馆

The Cullen Foundation The Brown Foundation, Inc. Antonette and Isaac Arnold, Jr.
Mr. And Mrs. Meredith J. Long William James Hill The River Oaks Garden Club Mr. and Mrs. M. S. Stude The Garden Club of Houston Mr. and Mrs. Theodore N. Law Douglas B. Marshall, Jr. Sculptor: Isamu Noguchi
Dedicated: April 15, 1986

休斯敦美术博物馆附属的一座雕塑园的文字说明。该园由休斯敦美术博物馆、休斯敦市合作建立，由以下机构和个人慷慨捐赠。其中卡伦基金会排列第一，因此以卡伦命名该雕塑园，后面还有系列个人和机构。落成日为1986年4月15日。

17
Please,
do not touch the exhibits

请勿触摸展品
（博物馆内告示牌）

18
**TEACHERS'
REPORTING POINT**
STUDENTS FORM
SINGLE LINE

教师报到点
学生排成单行
（博物馆内专门设置了带队老师集合学生参观的报到点）

19
Due to the popularity of Member programs, please present a form of ID with your Membership Card when purchasing ticket.

由于会员项目非常受欢迎，请在购票时出示会员卡和身份证。
（使用会员卡购票说明）

20
Guided Tours Begin Here
Guided Tours are free with museum admission, and topics change daily!

导游讲解从这里开始
持博物馆门票导游讲解免费，话题每日更换！

Ask for a complete tour schedule at the Information Desk.	全程导游安排请向咨询台询问。 （博物馆内提供导游讲解的说明文字）

21

PLEASE ENTER MUSEUM THROUGH MIDSUMMER BOOKS FREE ADMISSION	请通过仲夏书店进入本博物馆免费参观 （一座小型博物馆说明，外间为书店，里间为博物馆。）

22

Please Do Not Touch Works of Art	请勿触摸艺术作品

23

FREE General Admission* all day on Thursdays Thanks to a generous grant from Shell Oil Company Foundation Does not apply to specially ticketed exhibitions: Reduced rate is available on Thursdays only	由于壳牌石油公司基金会慷慨捐赠 普通参观周四全天免费 不适用于特殊购票展览： 仅周四门票减价 （博物馆免费参观说明文字）

24

Please do not place MFAH stickers on silk, leather or suede fabric.	请勿将MFAH（休斯敦艺术博物馆）粘贴贴在丝织物、皮革或麂皮织物上。 （博物馆有关参观标志的粘贴说明文字。博物馆在免费参观的日子会给每个参观者一个粘贴，这里的提示是为了避免粘贴损坏参观者的衣服。）

25

SEELEY STABLE MUSEUM
THIS BUILDING IS A RECONSTRUCITON OF THE ORIGINAL
STABLE BUILT AND USED BY ALBERT SEELEY IN 1967.

SEELEY USED THE STABLE FOR HORSE AND CARRIAGE STORAGE.

TODAY, THE BUILDING IS AN OLD TOWN SAN DIEGO STATE HISTORIC PARK MUSEUM DISPLAYING HORSE DRAWN VEHICLES AND WESTERN MEMORARBILIA

DONATIONS ARE ACCEPTED
PLEASE… NO FOOD DRINKS OR SMOKING

西迪马厩博物馆

本建筑是原马厩的复制件,由埃尔伯特·西迪于1967年重建使用。主人曾经用来存放马车。今天这栋建筑已经成为圣地亚哥古镇历史公园内的一座博物馆,里面展出的是马拉车以及和西部有关的纪念物品;欢迎捐款;请勿在馆内吃零食、喝饮料或吸烟。(马厩博物馆说明牌)

26

COME INSIDE
SEE THE RECREATED
COMMERCIAL RESTAURANT.
ESTABLISHED IN 1854 WITHIN THE CASA DE MACHADO DE SILVAS. A HOME BUILT C. 1843.

MUSEUM OPEN 10AM TO 5PM
FOOD OR DRINKS
NOT ALLOWED IN
THIS RESTAURANT.

请入室参观重新创建的商业饭店,始建于1854年。该建筑为1843年建的一户人家。上午10点开放,下午5点关闭;不得携带食品或饮料进入本饭店。
(圣地亚哥镇上一家小型博物馆告示)

27

Welcome to the **WELLS FARGO HISTORY MUSEUM**
OPEN DAILY 10-5 ADMISSION IS FREE
PLEASE, NO SMOKING, NO FOOD, NO DRINK
NOR STROLLERS.

欢迎参观"富国"
历史博物馆
开放时间上午10点至下午5点,免费参观。
参观时请勿吸烟、吃零食、喝饮料,不得使用童车。
(历史博物馆的公告牌)

28

DEWETT GODFREY
American, born 1960
Untitled 1989 Welded steel
Museum purchase with funds provided by Duke Energy

休斯敦美术博物馆附属的一座雕塑园内的一组雕塑文字介绍。从中可以看出作者、作者的国籍、出生年份、作品的创作时间和名称、雕塑的材质以及博物馆使用哪个组织提供的资金购买的。博物馆将一些有价值的雕塑作品收集在一个花园内展出。

29

Henri Matisse
French, 1869—1954
Woman in a Purple Coat
1937
Oil on canvas
Gift of Audrey Jones Beck

This painting is a masterpiece of Henri Martisse's mature decorative style. Matisse depicts his model and companion of many years, Lydia Delectorskaya, reclining in an exotic Moroccan costume, surrounded by exuberant patterns. The pulsating color and ingenious variety of lines energize the painting. Matisse used both ends of the brush – he dipped bristles thickly in black for bold outlines, and he scraped away wet paint with the blunt end of the handle to create white lines of exposed canvas beneath.

亨利·马蒂斯（1869—1954）
法国人
穿紫袍的女人（1937）
画布油画
奥德瑞·琼斯·贝克赠品

这幅画作是亨利·马提斯成熟装饰风格的代表作。作品描绘了他多年的模特和伴侣利迪亚·德雷托斯卡亚，身着具有异国情调的摩洛哥服饰斜躺着，周围装饰华丽。画中脉动的色彩和灵巧的线条变化使得整幅画作充满生机。马蒂斯使用画笔的两端——他将画笔沾上厚厚的黑色用于勾画粗框线条，而他则用钝的那头刮去未干的颜料通过下面的画布来表现白色线条。

（博物馆内一幅马蒂斯作品的说明文字）

30

The Houston Museum of natural science
Hours of Operation Monday–Sunday
9 a.m. – 9 p.m.

休斯敦自然科学博物馆的开放时间。

二十三、博物馆

31

**CHRISTOPHER COLUMBUS
EXPLORER/MAP MAKER**

Donated to the City of Houston by the Federation of Italian American Organization of Greater Houston, Inc. October 11, 1992

Sculptor Joe L. Incrapera

克里斯托弗·哥伦布
探险家/地图绘制者
1992年10月11日大休斯敦意美组织协会敬献休斯敦市
（公园雕塑说明，后面为雕塑家的名字。）

32

**PEACE ON EARTH
BY JACQUES LIPCHITZ
GIVEN AS A SYMBOL OF PEACE
TO THE PEOPLE OF THE WORLD BY
LLOYD E. RIGLER LAWRENCE E.
DEUTSCH 1969**

洛杉矶音乐厅广场上的一雕塑说明。雕塑的名称叫"地球上的和平"，另外还有作者和捐赠人的信息，捐赠时间以及捐赠目的。

33

COPIES OF THIS DOCUMENT ARE AVAILABLE FOR DOWNLOAD ON OUR WEB SITE AT WWW.BAKERINSTITUTE.ORG OR WITH THE RECEPTIONIST IN SUITE 120.

本文件的复印件可从网站WWW. BAKERINSTITUTE. ORG下载或咨询120室的接待员。
（一展览馆内有关索取资料的说明）

34

Closed Today

The Museum is closed on Mondays-except for certain Holiday Mondays-and also closed on Thanksgiving Day, Christmas Day, and New Year's Day. Please visit again.

今日闭馆
博物馆每逢周一闭关，节假日周一除外。其他闭关时间还包括感恩节、圣诞节和新年，欢迎再次光临。
（博物馆闭馆说明）

35

The 21st-Century Met... building from within

Please pardon the inconvenience.
Renovation of the Main Steps
The Museum's main steps are undergoing repair and restoration. The project will include removing the granite steps, cleaning and resetting the existing stone, and installing a snow-melt system that is energy-saving and will minimize the use of salt-a green solution for the Museum.
The project is expected to be completed in May 2009.

Plaza Entrance
←Public Entrance
←Wheelchair Access Entrance
←School Group Entrance

21世纪Met……内部整理

请恕不便
主台阶装修
博物馆的主台阶在整修，本项目包括移除花岗石台阶，清洗和调整现有石块，安装节能的融雪系统，该项目将降低盐的使用，是博物馆的一项绿色方案。
项目预计2009年5月完成。

广场入口

←公共入口
←轮椅入口
←学生团体入口
（纽约大都会艺术博物馆名为21st Century Met内部装修项目告示）

36

Place all items containing metal in bins

请将含有金属的物件放在箱子内
（博物馆安检提示）

37

NOTICE: Airport-style security ahead
To keep the line moving, place all items containing metal into purses, jackets, and backpacks for quick scanning.
　All persons and property are subject to search.

注意：前方机场模式安检
为了提高安检速度，请将所有含金属的物品放入手提包、夹克和背包中以便快速扫描。
所有人员和物品都要接受检查。
（博物馆安检说明）

二十四、超市商店

1
| THESE ITEMS ARE PRICED PER POUND | 商品以磅为单位计价（超市价格标签说明。美国的重量单位基本以磅和盎司为单位计量。1磅等于453.59克；1盎司等于28.3452克。） |

2
| Pork with Vegetables | 猪肉素菜（超市产品标签说明。超市提供很多成品菜，这是成品菜上的标签。） |

3
| NO REFUND OR EXCHANGE | 不退款 不退换（商场退货说明） |

4
| SELF-SERVE WOKERY $6.49LB. | 自助餐 每磅6.49美元（自助菜说明标签。WOKERY是美国一家自助餐馆的名字，提供的饭菜以中国餐为主。wokery一词来自于wok（锅）。） |

5
| WOKERY WILL CLOSE AT 4PM ON TUESDAY JULY 4TH | WOKERY将在7月4日（周二）下午4点关闭。（超市自助餐厅临时停业时间。7月4日为美国国庆日。） |

6
| Mix & Match Your Favorites $ 6.49lb. | 混合搭配自己喜爱的饭菜 6.49美元1磅（超市自助餐厅说明。各种菜品可自由搭配，按重量计价。） |

新世纪美国公示语 1000 例

7

Summer Vegetable Orzo Soup
Roasted corn & tomatoes with tender orzo pasta; vegan.
Each serving (1 cup) contains 90calories,
17g carbohydrates, 2g fiber, and 1.5g fat
LC LOW CALORIE LF LOW FAT A ALLERGENS: Contains Wheat

夏令素菜意大利粒状面食汤
烤玉米和西红柿加意大利粒状嫩面食；全部素食。
每份（1杯）含90卡路里，17克碳水化合物，2克纤维和1.5克脂肪。
低热量；低脂肪；过敏物质：含小麦。
（超市烹制成品菜说明文字。美国很多现场制作的食品说明会提供相应的营养成份。）

8

Steamed White Rice

蒸白米饭（超市食物提示牌）

9

MINORS MAY OPERATE BUT NOT CLEAN, WIPE, OIL, OR DRAIN

未成年人可以操作，但是请勿清洗、擦拭、用油或烧干锅。
（超市内米饭锅上的说明文字。为了避免不必要的麻烦，美国各类场所时时在提醒安全问题。）

10

Steamed Rice containers must be full to be charged $ 1.99 or you will be charged by the pound.

盛蒸米饭的容器一定要装满了才会按照1.99美元收费，否则将以磅计费。
（超市自助餐厅取餐提示）

11

-bake at home-
Gourmet Pizzas
Now in the cold case!
Take one home today!

家里烤制
美食家比萨
现在储存在凉盒中！
今天就带一个回家吧！
（超市自助餐厅取餐提示。美国的超市中常常提供比萨的半成品，只要买回家放在烤箱里面烘烤一下即可食用。）

12

consistent low prices	永远低价
Large Traditional Pizza w/1 Topping 10 Wings & a 2 liter Wpop YOU PAY $ 14.99 WITHOUT SHOPPERS CLUB CARD $16.49	大型传统比萨，配品多，10个鸡翅加2升含气的水，只需支付14.99美元；无购物会员卡16.49美元。（超市内的比萨说明。比萨的配品是放在饼的上方，因此用topping表示。比萨饼的配品可以是素菜、坚果、肉类、海鲜、奶酪等。）

13

Pizza Menu & Toppings

	Medium 12"	Large 17"	Sheet 18"×26"	Choose from...	
Plain w/cheese	$ 7.75	$ 10.75	$ 17.00	Extra Cheese	Ham
				Extra Cheese	Broccoli
				Pepperoni	Spinach
1-Topping	$ 8.75	$ 12.75	$ 19.00	Italian Sausage	Pineapple
				Mushrooms	Ricotta
2-Toppings	$ 9.75	$ 13.75	$ 17.00	Sweet Peppers	Chicken
				Black Olives	Garlic
3-Toppings	$ 10.75	$ 15.75	$ 23.00	Anchovies	
				Ground Beef	
4-Toppings	$ 11.75	$ 16.75	$ 25.00	When available…	
				Seasoned Tomatoes	Zucchini
Beverages	Medium $1.09	Large $1.29		Feta Cheese	Artichokes
				Asiago Parmesan	

快餐店比萨菜单。比萨饼和配品；该店所提供的比萨有三大类：中号（12英寸）、大号（17英寸）和方形（18英寸X26英寸）；每个型号中还有普通芝士的、1层配品、2层配品、3层和4层配品，此外各种备选的配料包括芝士、花椰菜、火腿、乳酪和番茄酱、菠菜、意大利香肠、菠萝、蘑菇、意大利乳清干酪、甜椒、鸡肉、黑橄榄、大蒜、鱼酱油、牛肉泥，可能的话还有调味番茄、美洲南瓜、希腊菲达奶酪、洋蓟意大利脱脂干酪等。美国文化的多样化从其提供的食品种类上也可见一斑。

14

Have Food Allergies?
You should know that despite taking every precaution, cross-contact with **peanuts, tree nuts, soy, milk, eggs, wheat, fish, or crustacean shellfish** can occur in our food production areas.

有食物过敏症吗？
尽管采取各种预防措施，但是坚果、树果、大豆、牛奶、鸡蛋、麦子、鱼类或甲壳贝壳类都有可能在我们的食品生产区域内发生交叉接触。
（餐厅内提醒顾客可能会引起过敏的食物）

15

New England Clam Chowder
All fresh clams, peeled potatoes, bacon & real cream with fresh vegetables.
ALLERGENS: Contains Milk, Shellfish (clams), Soy, & Wheat

新英格兰牡蛎浓汤
全部使用新鲜牡蛎、去皮土豆、培根和纯奶酪加新鲜素菜。
过敏提示：本菜品含牛奶、贝类（牡蛎）、黄豆和小麦。
（超市烹制好的菜品介绍）

16

Cream of Broccoli Soup
A creamy vegetarian soup flavored
with cheddar cheese
ALLERGENS: Contain Milk, Soy & Wheat

花椰菜奶油汤
奶油素菜汤加切达奶酪调味
过敏提示：内含牛奶、大豆和小麦。
（超市烹制好的菜品介绍。切达奶酪又叫车打奶酪，来源于16世纪的英国原产地切达郡，是英国索莫塞特郡车达地方产的一种硬质全脂牛乳奶酪，历史悠久。色白或金黄，组织细腻，口味柔和，含乳脂45%。）

17

Italian Wedding Soup
Fresh spinach, tiny pasta, and tender meatballs made
With pork & beef in a rich chicken broth.
Each serving (1 cup) contains 100 calories,
8g carbohydrates, 2g fiber, and 6g fat
LOW CALORIE
ALLERGENS: Contains Egg, Milk, Soy and Wheat

意大利婚宴汤
新鲜菠菜、小通心粉、嫩肉团加猪肉牛肉于浓汁鸡汤中煮成。每份（即每杯）含100卡路里，8克碳水化合物，2克纤维和6克脂肪，低热量
过敏提示：本菜品含牛奶、贝类（牡蛎）、黄豆和小麦。
（超市餐厅内关于汤的介绍）

二十四、超市商店

18

Shrimp Bisque
Creamy shrimp pureed with tomatoes, wine & fine seasonings.
ALLERGIES: Contains Milk, Shellfish (shrimp, clam & lobster), and wheat

浓汁虾
番茄泥奶油虾，加葡萄酒和精选佐料。
过敏提示：含牛奶、介壳类海产（虾、蛤和龙虾）和小麦。
（超市浓虾汤说明）

19

ATTENTION
All Newspapers and Magazines must be accompanied by a Valid receipt as proof of purchase. Thank you!

注意
所有报刊需购物证明的有效收据
谢谢！
（超市内赠送报刊的提示。在超市购物达到一定数额可以领取一份报刊。）

20

CAUTION
HOT WATER CAN REACH TEMPS. OF 150°F OR 70°C
(Studies show this may cause 3rd degree Burns within ½ a second of contact.)
Please use caution, especially with children.

小心！
热水可以达到华氏150度或摄氏70度（研究表明这样的温度接触0.5秒可能造成3度烫伤）。
请小心使用，尤其是儿童。
（餐厅内的热水提示。美国表示温度常用"华氏"，但同时提供"摄氏"温度作为参照。）

21

"Please Do not bring unpaid merchandise into the Restrooms"
Thank You

请勿将未付款的商品带入卫生间。
谢谢。
（超市卫生间门口的提示）

22

A Reminder to Part-Time Employees
Make sure you work an average of
20 HOURS PER WEEK
During your anniversary year

非全日工作人员请注意
务必工作平均
每周20小时
满一年才有资格享受2006

159

新世纪美国公示语 1000 例

To stay eligible for
VACATION & HOLIDAY PAY
After October 31, 2006
If your next anniversary date is after October 31,
Then you should be working 20 hours per week
NOW!
Any questions?
Please see your Department Manager or your
Employee Representative.

年10月31日后带薪休假。如果下一个周年日在10月31日以后，现在就需每周工作20小时。
如有问题，请咨询部门经理或招聘主管。
（超市内对非全日制工作人员的劳动休假提示）

23

Congratulations to Kandy
and George Baier on the
birth of their son,
Dylan George
Born Tuesday, 6/27/06 at
10:34pm
Weighing 9lbs., 12oz.
21 inches long.

祝贺卡迪·贝尔和乔治·贝尔喜得贵子
达兰·乔治
于2006年6月27日晚10点34分出生
重量9磅12盎司
长21英寸
（超市为自己的员工喜得贵子表示祝贺。9磅12盎司等于4.42公斤，21英寸等于53.34厘米。）

24

SHELF TAGS
For Complete Price Information
The shelf tag tells you:
1. The selling price—the price you will pay for the product.
2. The unit price—the price you would pay if you were buying by the pound, the quart, the square 100 feet, or other common unit of measure.
Use this pricing information to compare among sizes and brands.

货架标签
完整价格信息货架标签提供
1. 售价——商品的价格。
2. 单价——以磅、夸脱、100平方英尺或其他常用单位计量购物的价格。
请用这些价格信息比较商品的大小和品牌。
（货架标签上说明。在美制液量中，1夸脱=2品脱= 946.35毫升，在美制干量中，1夸脱=2品脱=1101毫升，但是在英制中1夸脱=2品脱=1136毫升，另外100平方英尺= 9.29平方米。）

25

THIS IS PRIVATE PROPERTY
THE SIDEWALKS AND BUILDINGS ARE PROVIDED FOR THE CONVENIENCE OF WEGMANS CUSTOMERS, EMPLOYEES, AND VENDORS ONLY.
For your protection and convenience, the following activities are not permitted on the sidewalks and in the building: solicitation, distribution of literature, picketing, wearing or carrying of placards, loitering, any interference with or annoyance of customers, employees, or vendors.

私人领地
人行道和大楼仅为本超市顾客、雇员和供应商提供方便。
为了您的安全和方便,人行道和建筑内禁止以下行为:乞讨、散发印刷品、扒窃、佩戴或携带广告牌、逗留、打扰或纠缠顾客、职员或供应商。
(超市门口告示。Wegmans是美国一家具有40年历史的食品连锁超市。)

26

We Reserve The Right to Inspect all Packages. Please no eating, drinking or smoking in the Store

商店保留检查包裹的权利,请勿在本店内吃东西、喝饮料或吸烟。
(商店门口告示)

27

Sorry we're
CLOSED
BUSINESS HOURS

	A.M	P.M
MONDAY	7:00	9:00
TUESDAY	7:00	9:00
WEDNESDAY	7:00	9:00
THURSDAY	7:00	9:00
FRIDAY	7:00	9:00
SATURDAY	8:00	9:00
SUNDAY	8:00	6:00

商店打烊标识牌。这里商店并没有简单地使用一个CLOSED而是向顾客道歉后再提供一个完整的营业时间表以尊重商店关门后前来的顾客,也是方便顾客再次光临。

28

EXPRESS **Check Out** 10 Items or Fewer

10件或以下的东西从快速通道结算
(超市说明)

29

Red Potatoes
Smooth texture, very moist potato.
YOU PAY 99¢ PER POUND

红土豆
质地光滑，水分充足 每磅99美分
（红土豆销售牌）

30

White Potatoes
Best for boiling, soups,
stews, and salads
YOU PAY 99¢ PER POUND

白土豆
适宜煮菜、堡汤、煨炖和沙拉
每磅99美分
（白土豆销售牌）

31

Red Creamer Potatoes
Great for boiling or oven roasting.
YOU PAY 99¢ PER POUND

红色小土豆
适宜煮菜或微波炉内烤
每磅99美分
（红色小土豆销售说明。red creamer potato 指在成熟前收割的直径1厘米的土豆，还有一种是 yellow creamer potato，指在成熟前收割的黄色土豆。）

32

Red Creamer Potatoes
Lower starch makes
them great for boiling.
YOU PAY $1.69 PER POUND

红色小土豆
淀粉含量低
适宜炖煮
每磅1.69美元
（红色小土豆销售说明）

33

Micro-Sweet Potatoes
Convenient and easy,
Great for lunches
YOU PAY $ 2 PER POUND

小红薯
方便简单
适宜午餐
每磅2美元
（小红薯的销售说明。sweet potato 表示"红薯"，也叫"白薯"、"山芋"、"地瓜"等。）

二十四、超市商店

34

Yams
Very sweet vivid orange flesh
YOU PAY $.99 PER POUND

甘薯
非常甜,色泽鲜艳,肉质橘色,每磅99美分。
（一种甘薯销售说明）

35

Greenhouse Grown Tomatoes on the Vine **$1.99lb.**

温室内生长带根茎西红柿,每磅1.99美元。（西红柿销售说明）

36

Mini Pork Egg Roll

迷你猪肉蛋卷（超市食品说明）

37

FOR CUSTOMER ASSISTANCE USE BLUE LIGHT TELEPHONE

如果顾客需要帮助,请使用蓝灯电话拨打。
（商场内顾客服务电话告示）

38

Women's Shoe Sizes

English	2	2.5	3	3.5	4	4.5	5	5.5	6	6.5	7	7.5	8
European	34	35	35.5	36	37	37.5	38	39	39.5	40	40.5	41	42
American	4.5	5	5.5	6	6.5	7	7.5	8	8.5	9	9.5	10	10.5
Japanese	21.5	22	22.5	23	23	23.5	24	24	24.5	25	25.5	26	26.5

商场内提供的四种女士鞋号换算表。其中包括英制鞋号、欧制鞋号、美制鞋号和日制鞋号。美国鞋码与中国鞋码对应为美国5（35）、美国5.5（36）、美国6（37）、美国6.5（38）、美国7（39）、美国7.5（39）、美国8（40）、美国8.5（40）、美国9（41）、美国9.5（41）等。

39

Men's Shoe Sizes

English	5	5.5	6	6.5	7	7.5	8	8.5	9	9.5	10	10.5	11	11.5	12
European	38	38.7	39.3	40	40.5	41	42	42.5	43	44	44.5	45	46	46.5	47
American	5	5.5	6	6.5	7	7.5	8	8.5	9	9.5	10	10.5	11	11.5	12
Japanese	23.5	24	24.5	25	25.5	26	26.5	27	27.5	28	28.5	29	29.5	30	30.5

商场内提供的四种男士鞋号换算表。其中包括英制鞋号、欧制鞋号、美制鞋号和日制鞋号。美国男鞋与中国男鞋对应码为美国7（39）、美国7.5（40）、美国8（41）、美国8.5（42）、美国9（43）、美国9.5（44）、美国10（45）、美国10.5（46）等。

40

NEW ARRIVALS   新品上市（商场告示牌）

41

Outdoor World
COMMITTED TO HELPING YOU HAVE FUN OUTDOORS
OUR GOALS
PRICE
WE WILL NEVER KNOWINGLY BE UNDERSOLD!
SERVICE
100% SATISFACTION GUARANTEED ON EVERY PURCHASE!
QUALITY
WE STAND BEHIND EVERY ITEM WE SELL!
SELECTION
FIRST WITH THE PRODUCTS YOU WANT!

户外世界：
我们承诺会帮助你在户外玩得高兴!
我们的目标
价格
决不故意廉价出售!
服务
保证购买100%满意!
质量
出售商品绝对负责!
选择
首先提供中意产品!
（野外设备专供商店门口告示）

42

Engraving On
Glass wine/perfume bottle, flutes, frames
Silver necklaces, bracelets, dog tags

刻字店的说明。该店可以在玻璃酒瓶/香水瓶、香槟酒杯、玻璃框架、银项链、银手镯、犬

Stainless Steel flash, keychain
Plastic name tags, gift box
Wedding Bands inside-outside engraving
Name Rings Necklaces Bracelets While You are Shopping

牌、不锈钢长颈瓶、钥匙链、塑料名牌、塑料礼盒、结婚手镯(婚箍)(内外刻字)、姓名戒指、项链和手镯上雕刻，不耽误您购物。

43

TV on DVD SALE

光盘销售说明。这里销售的是重新制作在DVD光盘上的电视节目。

44

Mature Viewing

成人光盘
（光盘销售说明）

45

YES!
All the produce here is
LOCAL!
Naturally Grown
No Synthetic Fertilizers
No Pesticides

没错!
这里全部为本地农产品!
天然种植，无化肥农药。
（超市绿色蔬菜招牌）

46

Care Instructions

We recommend you protect your investment from normal soiling by using a cotton protective cover. To maintain plumpness and even distribution of the Natural Fill, refluff or shake as needed. Spot clean as necessary with a mild detergent and warm water. If necessary your product may be professionally dry cleaned.

衣服标签上有关衣服保养的说明。厂家建议使用棉质材料覆盖以免弄脏；为了保证本产品保持蓬松以及填料自然匀整，必要时抖动衣服。污点清洗需用适度的洗涤剂和温水。必要时请专业人员干洗。

47

ALTERATION PICK-UP
ALL ALTERATIONS ARE PROMISED FOR 5 PM ON THE DUE DAY WE ARE NOT RESPONSIBLE FOR ALTERED MERCHANDISE LEFT OVER 30 DAYS

修改衣服领取点
修改的衣服到期日5点前领取，30天以后未领取，商店概不负责。（购买的衣服如不合适，可在商店内修改，一般第二天可领取，这是领取修改衣服窗口的标识。）

48

WARNING: Oil will catch fire if overheated. Damage or serious burns may result.
DO heat oil carefully, uncovered, on medium heat.
DO reduce heat if smoking occurs.
DO NOT leave unattended while heating.
DO NOT refill bottle with hot oil.
IF OIL CATCHES FIRE:
DO turn off heat.
DO cover pot until cooled to room temperature to avoid reignition.
DO NOT carry pot until cool.
DO NOT put water on hot or flaming oil.

警示：食用油过热会着火，可能造成损害或严重烧伤。用中等热度小心加热食用油，不加盖；如果冒烟，务必降低热度；加热时不要离开；热油不要重新倒入瓶中。如食用油着火：关闭热源；盖上锅盖直至冷却到室温以避免复燃；冷却后才拿锅具；切莫在热油或燃烧的油上浇水。
（食用油瓶上的安全警示文字）

49

SEE NUTRITION INFORMATION FOR FACT CONTENT.
VEGETABLE OIL IS A CHOLESTERALFREE FOOD WITH 14g OF TOTAL FAT PER SERVING.

实际含量请看营养信息。植物油不含胆固醇，每份中含有14克全脂肪。
（食用油上说明文字）

50

FRESH GROUND BEEF ROUND
SELL BY: 07/17/06
NET WT   UNIT PRICE   TOTAL PRICE
0.92lb $3.09/lb $2.84
SAFE HANDLING INSTRUCITONS
THIS PRODUCT WAS PREPARED FROM INSPECTED AND PASSED MEAT AND/

新绞牛腿肉
06年7月17日前售出
净重0.92磅
单位价格每磅3.09美元
共计2.84美元
安全操作指示
本产品用通过检验的肉

OR POULTRY. SOME FOOD PRODUCTS MAY CONTAIN BACTERIA THAT COULD CAUSE ILLNESS IF THE PRODUCT IS MISHANDLED OR COOKED IMPROPERLY. FOR YOUR PROTECTION, FOLLOW THESE SAFE HANDLING INSTRUCTION.
KEEP RAW MEAT AND POULTRY SEPARATE FROM OTHER FOODS. WASH WORKING SURFACES (INCLUDING CUTTING BOARDS), UTENSILS, AND HANDS AFTER TOUCHING RAW MEAT OR POULTRY.
COOK THOROUGHLY
KEEP HOT FOODS HOT. REFRIGERATE LEFTOVERS IMMEDIATELY OR DISCARD.

类和/或家禽制作。有些食品如处理或烹饪不当可能含有病菌。请按照以下安全指示操作。
将生肉及家禽与其他食品分开；在触摸生肉或家禽后，将操作台（包括切菜板）、餐具和手洗净；烹饪彻底；将熟食保温，剩菜立即置入冰箱或扔弃。
（超市鲜肉包装袋上说明）

51

ALL NATURAL FORTUNE COOKIES
NO TRANS FAT
NO PRESERVATIVES
NO ARTIFICIAL COLORS
NO ARTIFICIAL FLAVORS
LOW SODIUM
Many Healthy Messages
It is impossible to please everybody. Please yourself first.
0g Trans Fat No Hydrogenated Oils

全天然幸运饼
不含反式脂肪；不含防腐剂；不含人造色素；不含人造香料；低钠。
健康信息很多。
不可能使人人满意，让自己先满意。
0克反式脂肪酸，不含氢化植物油。
（幸运饼说明文字。trans fat 为反式脂肪酸，又叫转基因脂肪酸；hydrogenated oil又称为hydrogenated palm oil（氢化棕榈油）。在美国食品的包装上会有营养要素，其中有饱和脂肪（saturated fat）、反式脂肪（trans fat）、胆固醇（cholesterol）等。1993年，FDA（美国食品和药物管理局）要求把饱和脂肪和胆固醇含量标示在食品上。2006年，FDA要求标示反式脂肪酸含量。）

52

SAFE HANDLING INSTRUCTIONS: TO PREVENT ILLNESS FROM BACTERIA: KEEP EGGS REFRIGERATED, COOK EGGS UNTIL YOLKS ARE FIRM, AND COOK FOODS CONTAINING EGGS THOROUGHLY.

Some food products may contain bacteria that could cause illness if the product has been cross-contaminated, mishandled or cooked improperly. For your protection, follow these safe handling instructions.

Keep eggs refrigerated after purchase. Discard broken or cracked eggs. Use or cook eggs immediately after cracking.

Wash working furfaces, utensils and hands before and after handling eggs. Do not touch yolks or whites with your hands.

Cook thoroughly until whites are firmly set and yolks thicken. Avoid eating raw eggs and foods containing raw eggs.

Keep hot foods hot (above 140ºF) and cold foods cold (below 40ºF).

安全操作指示：为了避免病菌，要将鸡蛋保持冷藏，烹饪鸡蛋至蛋黄变硬，将带有鸡蛋的食物彻底做熟。

有些食物如果交叉感染，操作不当或烹饪不彻底，可能会含有致病病菌。为了你的安全，请遵守以下操作规程。

鸡蛋购买后保持冷藏。扔弃已破或有裂纹的鸡蛋。鸡蛋有裂纹后马上烹饪。

在做鸡蛋以前，请清洗台面、刀具和手，不要用手触摸蛋黄或蛋清。

鸡蛋要彻底烹制，直至蛋白凝固，蛋黄成块，不要食用生鸡蛋和含有生鸡蛋的食物。

使热鸡蛋保持在高温（140ºF），冷却鸡蛋保持在低温（40ºF）

（超市鸡蛋包装上的说明）

53

We are not liable for vehicle damage caused by shopping carts.

Please also remember to leave your cart on the premises for others to use.

本超市对购物车给您车辆造成的损坏概不负责。请将购物车留在超市内以便他人使用。

（超市门口提示牌）

54

50 CENTS PER PLAY
2 PLAYS PER $1.00
10 PLAYS PER $5.00
  PLAY AT YOUR OWN RISK
  NO CHANGE GIVEN
  NO REFUNDS

游戏一次50分
游戏两次1元
游戏10次5元
  风险自负
  不找零
  不退款

（商店机械手抓毛绒玩具装置说明）

二十四、超市商店

55 Reg. 16.00 11.99 — 原价16美元,现价11.99美元。(商场降价牌)

56 5.99 SALE! $9.98 Value — 5.99美元廉价出售!原价9.98美元。(商场降价牌)

57 14.97 Our 19.97Ea — 现价每件14.97美元,原价19.97美元。(商场降价牌)

58 Was $14.50-now $12.50! — 原价14.50美元——现售12.50美元(商场降价牌)

59 List￥495…￥395 — 原价495美元,现卖395美元。(商场降价牌)

60 Regular price $11.50 —SPECIAL PRICE $7.50 — 原价11.50美元,特价7.50美元(商场降价牌)

61 Reg. $99 $20 down — 原价99美元 降20美元(商场降价牌)

62 All Redline Items originally priced up to $10, now 15 for $5 — 所有带红线的商品 原价10美元 现5美元买15(商品降价广告)

63
Valuable Coupons Here!

这里提供超值兑换券!
（兑换券告示）

64
UP TO 50% OFF FACTORY STORE PRICES

厂价基础上减半
（商场降价信息）

65
Take An Additional 40% OFF

再买一件，打六折。
（商店促销告示）

66
THE COLOR OF SAVINGS

Spot a colored logo stamp on one of our price tags—it means you'll enjoy extra savings off the lowest marked price. How much more you save depends on the color.

LAST CALL(RED) = 20% OFF
LAST CALL (PURPLE) = 35% OFF
LAST CALL (BLUE) = 50% OFF
LAST CALL (GREEN) = 75% OFF
The Lowest Marked Price

减价之色
发现商品价格标签上有彩色标志粘贴——即在最低标注价格上享受再次打折，折扣多少按颜色不同。
最后打折（红色）20%
最后打折（紫色）35%；
最后打折（蓝色）50%；
最后打折（绿色）75%。
最低标价
（商场内的减价花样之一）

67
Cynthia Steffe
Now: $52
Compared To: $150

现价52美元，原价150美元。
（职业妇女名品"史黛菲"服饰降价广告）

68
THE SUMMER SALE

夏季优惠销售
（商场打折告示）

We happily accept our competitors'
TRIPLE COUPONS!
Simply present any of our competitor's valid triple coupons at the registers for discount.*

*Some restrictions may apply based on Wegmans coupon policy.
Please see Service Desk for details.

超市通过特殊优惠券来进行促销的文字。美国超市经常通过手头广告或者报纸广告的方式来发放优惠券，有的时候还有发放double coupon或者triple coupon。如果使用了这样的优惠券，顾客就可以享受到两倍或三倍的折扣。这家超市的招数更加奇特，竟然允许顾客使用其他商家的优惠券来自己的超市享受购物优惠。

新世纪美国公示语1000例

临时告示

1

Earn $$$ for Participating in a Psychology Experiment
You will receive $25 for participating in an experiment

参与心理实验可以赚取美元
每次实验可以获得25美元报酬
（校园内招聘参与实验人员的广告）

2

NOTICE
IN THE EVENT OF LOSS OF POWER, THIS BUILDING MAY NOT BE SUPPORTED WITH AIR CONDITIONING, ELECTRICAL OR WATER SERVICES.

通 知
如遇停电，本楼可能不提供空调、水电服务。
（大楼门口有关停电的提示）

3

NOTICE
A REQUEST TO ABANDON THIS STREET
HAS BEEN RECEIVED BY THE CITY
CALL THE CITY OF HOUSTON AT
(713)837-0597
TO REGISTER YOUR COMMENT

通 知
休斯敦市已经接到废弃这条道路的意见，请拨打市政府电话，登记意见。
（政府征求一条道路是否废弃的意见通知。在城市的发展过程中，可能有些道路已经没有多大的用途，于是人们可以提出自己的建议，而市政府在接到这类信息多了以后就可以征求广大市民的意见来决定是否废弃这条道路。）

二十五、临时告示

4

Happiness: A Guide to Life's Most Important Skill
Thursday, May 11 4–5 p.m.
M. D. Anderson, SBC Auditorium
1515 Holcombe Blvd.
Free Admission, Registration Not Required Co-sponsored by:
Institute of Religion and Health.

幸福：生活中最重要的技能指南
5月11日（周四）下午4点至5点
赫尔寇姆大道1515号SBC礼堂
演讲人M. D. 安德森
讲座免费 无需登记
合作主办方：宗教健康学院
（校园讲座宣传内容）

5

Welcome to the Rice University Student Center!
A Building Manager is not currently available to assist you. They have gone on errand.
WE WILL BE BACK SHORTLY.
In case of an emergency, please contact the Campus Police at x6000.

欢迎来到莱斯大学学生活动中心！
大楼经理目前不在，无法帮助你，他们因公外出。
我们很快就回来。
紧急情况，请拨电话x6000联系校园警察。
（大学学生活动中心的临时说明文字）

6

UTILITY OUTAGE EXTENSION NOTIFICATION
TYPE OF OUTAGE–DOMESTIC WATER
LOCATION OF OUTAGE–LOVETT COLLEGE
REASON FOR OUTAGE–TO REPLACE SHOWER FIXTURES
COMMENTS:
OUTAGE SCHEDULED–Monday June 26, 2006 @ 8:00 AM through Wednesday July 12, 2006@8:00 AM
HOUSING AND DINING

停水延长通告
停水类型：家庭用水；
停水位置：拉维学院；
停水原因：更换喷头。
备注：停水安排时间段：2006年6月26日（周一）上午8点至2006年7月12日上午8点（周三）。
房屋餐饮管理部发布
（临时停水通知）

新世纪美国公示语 1000 例

7

NOTIFICATION

Facilities Technicians will be changing Air Condition Filters in Will Rice College the week of Wednesday July 5th, 2006.
Housing and Dining

通　告

设备处技术人员将于2006年7月5日（周三开始的一周）在威尔·莱斯学院更换空调过滤网。
房屋餐饮管理部发布
（维修空调的临时通知）

8

Announcement

On July 06, 2006 at 9:00 am the Rice University IT Department will be conducting an x-ray of the floors in Old Will Rice College. During this time, for safety reasons, EVERYONE needs to be outside and away from the building. The testing should be finished roughly by 10:00am.
Thank you for your cooperation and understanding in this situation.

通　告

2006年7月6日上午9点，莱斯大学信息技术部门将对老威尔·莱斯学院的地板进行X光扫描。在此期间，为了安全，每一个人都需要离开这栋大楼。测试大约会在上午10点之前结束。
感谢您的合作和理解。
（学校临时通知）

9

SUBLET

AVAILABLE FOR RENT
Furn., 2+1, hrdwdFlrs, frplc, W/D, A.C., C.H., GRT VU, Roof Access
1660 Mason St. (415)5650174

转租

有现房，带家具，2室1卫，硬木地板，壁炉，洗衣机/烘干机，空调，长沙发，视野好，可达房顶，梅森大街1660号，电话(415)5650174。
（学校内临时张贴的房屋租赁广告）

在美国租赁房屋的广告上往往会为了节省篇幅而创造出一些常用的缩略词，这里是一些美国租房信息中常用的缩略词：

4/2 or 2/1 (eg) = number of bedrooms/ number of bathrooms

lndry = laundry
lr or lvrm = living room

174

二十五、临时告示

a/c = air conditioning
aek = all electric kitchen
apls = appliances
apt(s) = apartment(s)
avl = available
ba or bth or bthrm = bathroom
balc = balcony
bd or bdrm = bedroom
bicc = built-in china closet
bldg = building
bsmt = basement
c/a or cac = central air conditioning
c/vac or cvac = central vacuum
cbl = cable
cln = clean
condo = condominium
cpt = carpet
d/d = dishwasher/disposal
d/w or dw = dishwasher
det = detached
dr = dining room
eik = eat-in kitchen 厨房兼餐厅
elev = elevator
exp = exposure 朝向
fpl or frpl = fireplace
fr or fmrm or fam rm
　 = family room 家庭娱乐室
fridg = refrigerator
furn = furnished
ga or ga r = garage
gdo = garage door opener
　 车库门遥控器
grt = great
h/w or hdwd flr = hardwood floors
ht/hw = heat/hot water
incl = included
kit = kitchen

lrg or lg = large
lux = luxury or luxurious
mbr = master bedroom
mo = month
mod = modern
mw = microwave
negot = negotiable
ns = non smoker
ono = or near offer 依买方接近
　　　　　　　　 的价格出价
osp = off street parking
pd = paid
ph = penthouse
pl = swimming pool
prkg = parking
pvt = private
rm = room
sec = security or secure
sec dep = security deposit 押金
sep entr = separate entrance
sm = small
spac = spacious
sq ft or sf = square feet
stu = studio 有卧室、卫生间和
　　　　　　 厨房的小套间
trans = transportation
twnhse = town house
unfurn = unfurnished
util = utilities
vict = Victorian
vu = view
w/ = with
w/d or wd = washer/dryer
w/w or w/w cpt = wall-to-wall
　　　　　　　　　carpeting
wd hkup = washer/dryer hookup
wic = walk-in closet 大型衣柜
yd or yrd = yard

United States Department of the Interior
June 26, 2006
NOTICE TO THE PUBLIC

Sherman Park and Hamilton Place, the First Division Monument and State Place, E Street and its adjacent north and south sidewalks from 15th Street to 17th Street, N. W., and the northern half of the Ellipse will be closed to the public from 6 a.m. to approximately 11:00 a.m., Thursday, June 29.

The park area will be closed to the public to provide security and ensure pubic safety during the official visit of the Prime Minister of Japan.

Persons demonstrating or otherwise using this park are should remove themselves and any personal property from the closed park areas by 6 a.m., June 29.

The National Park Service appreciates the public's cooperation in this matter.

美国内政部
2006年6月26日
公告

6月29日（周四）上午6点至11点左右，谢尔曼公园、汉密尔顿剧院、第一师纪念碑和白宫、E大街及其临近15大街至西北17大街的南北人行道，以及爱里斯公园的北半部予以关闭。

为了日本首相正式访问期间的保安和确保公众安全，公园区不对公众开放。

示威人员或其他使用本公园的人以及个人物品必须在6月29日上午6点以前撤离关闭的公园区。

国家公园服务中心感谢大家合作。

（日本首相正式访问美国首都华盛顿时发布的一个公告；第一师纪念碑是纪念第一次世界大战阵亡将士；the Ellipse指白宫南面的椭圆形草坪，又叫爱里斯公园。）

二十六、办公场所

1

| PLEASE **SIGN-IN** AND HAVE A SEAT
SOMEONE WILL HELP YOU | 请在登记簿上签名，坐等服务。
（办公室的门口放着一个对来办事人员的提示牌） |

2

| Office of Admissions
Graduate
Undergraduate
Post-Baccalaureate | 学校招生办公室办公内容说明。办理有关硕士生、本科生和学士后生的事务。学士后是指获得了学士学位后再读一个学位，但还未取得硕士的学生。post-baccalaureate 还可以简写为postbacs。 |

3

| PLEASE WAIT HERE FOR THE NEXT AVAILABLE ASSISTANT TO CALL YOU & BE PREPARED TO SHOW ID
THANK YOU | 请在这里等待下一个助手叫你，随时出示证件。
（校园办公室门前指示牌） |

4

| UNIVERSITY OF HOUSTON
PRESIDENTIAL
ENDOWED SCHOLARSHIPS (omitted) | 休斯敦大学总统奖学金名单的公示牌
（人员名单略） |

5

| UNIVERSITY OF HOUSTON
LANGUAGE & CULTURE CENTER
JOYCE MERRILL VALDES
SCHOLARSHIP
RECIPIENTS (omitted) | 休斯敦大学语言文化中心一种奖学金获得者的铜牌。该大学将所有曾经获得过某一奖学金的学生名单铭刻在铜牌上，并悬挂在办公室的墙上，每天来办公室的人都会看见历届奖学金的获得者（人员名单略）。 |

新世纪美国公示语1000例

6

| FELLOWSHIP OPPORTUNITIES IN THE HUMANITIES | HUMANITIES NEWS | HUMANITIES SPONSORED EVENTS | CAMPUS NEWS |

学校人文学院告示栏的上方要求告示栏内张贴海报的时候要按照四个区域来张贴，即人文学院奖学金目录、人文学院新闻、人文学院主办的活动和校园新闻四个栏目。

7

Athletic Business and Ticket Office

体育事务和售票处
（体育馆内一间小办公室门上的文字）

8

113 STUDY OF WOMEN & GENDER

113 妇女及性别研究室
（教学大楼内一办公室上的说明）

二十七、邮政服务

邮政服务

1

STOP!
Important Customer Information Because of heightened security, the following types of mail may not be placed in this receptacle:
 All domestic mail, weighing 16 ounces or over, that bears stamps.
 International mail and military APO/FPO mail weighing 16 ounces or over.
Please take this mail, in person, to a retail clerk in a post office.

注意！重要信息
为了加强安全，以下邮件不得投入本邮箱：
所有已经贴上邮票，重16盎司或以上的国内邮件；
重16盎司或以上的国际邮件以及军人邮件。
请将上述邮件亲自带往邮局零售助理处投寄。
（信箱上有关邮寄信件的要求说明。APO/FPO分别表示Army Post Office/Fleet Post Office，指美国专门用于军人寄往海外或者军人寄往国内的邮件系统。）

2

Rice University Mail Service

莱斯大学邮政所
（休斯敦莱斯大学邮政所的标识）

3

CAMPUS POST OFFICE
Hours:
Monday-Friday 8:00 am-4:00 pm
Closed on Weekends and Federal and University Holidays

校园邮局
营业时间：
周一至周五每天上午8点至下午4点；
周末、联邦休息日以及学校放假日邮局不营业。
（邮局门上的营业时间说明）

4

BUY STAMPS HERE
This establishment and the United States Postal Service have made it easy for you to buy stamps at no extra charge.

请在这里购买邮票
本营业所和美国邮政服务处会让您方便购买邮票，不收额外费用。
（邮局购买邮票说明）

5

| AEI MUSIC EXPRESSLY PROGRAMMED MUSIC FOR THIS ESTABLISHMENT | 1996 LICENSE ALL CLEARANCES AND PERFORMANCE RIGHTS FEES PAID IN FULL |

AEI专为本场所编程的音乐；
许可证1996年颁发；
许可费和播放费已全额支付。
（邮局门上有关室内播放音乐版权的说明文字）

6

CASH OR CHECKS ONLY
THE RICE UNIVERSITY POST OFFICE CANNOT ACCEPT DEBIT OR CREDIT CARDS FOR PAYMENT!

只收取现金或支票
莱斯大学邮局不接受借记卡或信用卡付款！
（邮局内付款说明）

7

Extra Services   All charges in addition to postage
Delivery Confirmation   45¢ – Priority Mail
                           55¢ – Parcel Post
Signature Confirmation $1.80
Return Receipt $1.75
Insurance $1.30 and up
Certified Mail $2.30

附加费用说明：以下所有费用都不包含邮资。
投递确认
　　优先投递　45美分
　　包裹投递　55美分
签字确认　　1.8美元
回执单　　　1.75美元
保险　　　　1.3美元及以上
保证投递邮件 2.3美元
（邮局附加服务说明）

二十七、邮政服务

8

U. S. Shipping
Priority Mail　from $3.85
Delivery averages 2–3 days.
Express Mail　from $13.65
Guaranteed next day delivery to many locations.
Some restrictions apply. Ask retail professional for guarantee details

美国邮局有关邮件寄送的说明。如果使用优先邮件寄送起步价为3.85美元，寄送时间平均2至3天；如果使用快递邮件寄送，起步价为13.65美元，保证第二天到达，可以投送很多地方。但是有一些限制，详细保证细节请咨询零售专业人员。

9

FLAT RATE ENVELOPE
FLAT RATE POSTAGE REGARDLESS OF WEIGHT
DOMESTIC USE ONLY

平信信封
统一邮资，不记重量
仅限国内
（信封上提示文字）

10

UNITED STATES POSTAL SERVICE
POSTAL SERVICES AVAILABLE
AT THIS LOCATION
DOMESTIC SERVICE:
• EXPRESS MAIL-OVERNIGHT
• PRIORITY MAIL-2-3 DAYS
• FIRST CLASS-3 DAYS OR LESS
• PARCEL POST-9 DAYS OR LESS
INTERNATIONAL SERVICE:
• EXPRESS MAIL
• GLOBAL PRIORITY MAIL
• PARCEL POST
LEGAL PROOF AND SECURITY:
• CERTIFIED MAIL
• REGISTERED MAIL
• INSURED MAIL
• RETURN RECEIPT

美国邮政
此处提供邮政服务
国内服务：快递（隔天达到）；优先邮件（2–3天）；一等信件（3天或者少于3天）；包裹投递（9天或者少于9天）。
国际邮政服务：快递；全球优先邮件；包裹邮寄。
法律证明和安全服务：保证投递信件；挂号信件；保险信件；回执。
（美国邮政服务局张贴的邮政服务种类说明）

11

Notice
If the Mail room is closed……
Please deliver mail packages to Room 259.
Thank you.

注　意
如果邮件收发室关闭……
请将邮件包裹送往259室，谢谢。
（邮件收发室有关说明）

12

On-Campus
Mail Only

只投校园邮件
（邮箱上的投递说明）

13

There are two convenient ways to purchase stamps:
• **The Information Center,** located in the Ley portion of the Student Center. This outlet sells single stamps (up to 5 stamps per transaction) whenever the center is open;
• **The Rice University Post Office,** A full-service post office is located in the Annex Building (facing the Stadium) at Entrance 8. Service hours are 8 a.m. through 4 p.m. Monday through Friday.

购买邮票的两种简便方式：
信息中心：位于学生中心的Ley部位。中心开放时候，本代理处出售单枚邮票（每次交易至多5张邮票）。
莱斯大学邮局：位于校园8号门的安耐科斯大楼（体育场对面）内，营业时间为周一至周五每天上午8点至下午4点。
（购买邮票说明）

14

NOTICE
CHECK TO SEE IF YOUR LETTER HAS 39¢ POSTAGE!!!
The cost to mail is a one-ounce letter has changed from
37¢ to 39¢ effective 1/8/06.
Your Rice University Post Office has the new First-Class Stamp and 2¢
Makeup Stamp for Sale now!!!

注　意
请检查一下你邮件的邮资是否39美分！！！
投递一盎司重的信件从2006年8月1日起已经从37美分改成39美分。莱斯大学邮局出售新的一级邮票和2美分的补足邮票！！！
（新邮资增加后提醒检查邮资的告示）

15

1092 MAIL/COPY ROOM   1092室为邮件/复印室（校园用房说明）

16

LETTERS ONLY   只可投放信件（邮筒上说明）

17

For collection information…
PULL MAIL DEPOSIT DOOR HANDLE
MAIL COLLECTION SERVICES
The Postal Service provides many different services to insure that your mail is sent on to its destination quickly. The Postal Service collects mail with postage affixed:
FROM YOUR HOME MAILBOX—when your carrier has a delivery for your residence.
FROM YOUR CURBLINE MAILBOX—when the mailbox flag is raised.
FROM A COLLECTION BOX—no later than "last collection" time displayed.
FROM YOUR LOCAL POST OFFICE—until the "last collection" time displayed.
FROM YOUR BUSINESS—when your carrier has a delivery for your business.
Your mail will receive the same high quality, consistent service regardless of the collection method used. Please use the most convenient method for you. For additional information, contact your local postmaster.
A fine of $ 1,000 or three years imprisonment for tampering with this box, lock or contents.

邮件收集
拉开邮箱门

邮件收集服务
邮政服务部门提供各种服务以保证信件尽快送达目的地。邮政服务部门收取贴上邮资的邮件：
从家庭邮箱收取——当邮递员有你处的投递
从路边邮箱收取——当邮箱旗竖起
从收集箱收取——不晚于所表明的末次取件时间
从当地邮局收取——直至所表明的末次取件时间
从商行取件——当邮递员有贵行的投递
无论以何种方式收取，邮件都将得到同样高质量稳定的服务，更多信息请咨询当地邮政局长。
损坏本邮箱、邮箱锁或邮件，罚款1000美元或3年拘役。

新世纪美国公示语 1000 例

二十八

图书馆

1

BOOK RETURN　　　　　图书归还

（图书馆露天还书处。为了方便读者还书，美国很多图书馆会在馆外设立一个箱子方便读者。）

2

REFERENCE COMPUTER　　　　查询计算机

Reference workstations are open to the public. Access does not require login/password

查询平台向公众开放，不需要登陆/密码

Public reference computer are reserved for:

公共查询计算机专用于：

- Searching WEBCAT, the online catalog
- Accessing research-related web sites
- Reading full-text journal articles
- Searching for citations in online databases

(examples: WorldCat, EBSCO, MLA, Psychinfo)

- 查询WEBCAT网络图书目录
- 查询与研究相关的网址
- 阅读杂志全文
- 搜寻网上数据库中的引文

公共查询计算机不能用于：

Public reference computers may not be used for:

- Reading and sending email via Yahoo, Hotmail, AOL, and other major email sites: Use of these sites is blocked from these computers. Trying to access one of them may cause these computers to free up
- Word processing-Microsoft Word, Notepad, and Wordpad are not installed on public workstations
- Participating in chat-room dialogues
- More than 30 minutes if others are waiting

- 通过Yahoo，Hotmail，AOL等其他主要电邮站收发电邮（使用这些网址会受到阻挡，试图进入，计算机可能出问题。
- 公共计算机平台上没有安装Word，Notepad和Wordpad软件
- 聊天室对话
- 有人等用，使用不能超过30分钟。

PRINTING

Printing files from this computer requires a copy card. Copy cards may be purchased in the machine next to the print station. Cards cost 50 cents each and copies are ten cents per page.

LAST UPDATED APRIL 19, 2006

打印说明

从计算机打印文档需要复印卡，复印卡可以从打印站边上的机器上购买，每张卡50美分，复印每页10美分。

本说明更新于2006年4月19日

（图书馆内资料查询计算机说明。其中WEBCAT为莱斯大学校园计算机系统。）

二十八、图书馆

3

The On/Off button is located on the back of the monitor—on the lower, left side. If Mac is frozen, hold down button until monitor powers off. Press again to power on.
While restoring connections, a "no internet connection" message will appear. Wait a few minutes before clicking on it.

开/关钮位于显示器后左下方，如果计算机死机，按住按钮直至关机，然后再按钮启动电源。恢复连接时，会显示"无互连网连接"，等几分钟再点击。
（图书馆内计算机上的标签说明）

4

This machine DOES NOT give change back, make change, or dispense Rice COPY/PRINT cards! Cards can be purchased near Vending machine in the hallway by the reference desk.
ADD VALUE to your Rice U. COPY/PRINT card here!
Insert ONLY dollar amount needed for use with copiers or to PRINT from Computers.

本机不找、不换零钱，也不售复印卡！复印卡可以在咨询台附近过道上的售卖机上购买。
复印卡在此充值！
插入美元，数额为使用复印机或从计算机打印所需。
（图书馆内自动出售复印卡的机器上的说明）

5

ADD VALUE STATION
This machine does not give change!
How to add value to Card:
- Insert card (above)
- Insert $1, $5, $10, or $20 bill(s) (below)
- WAIT 3 SECONDS, push button to eject card
  INSERT BILL FACE UP

充值点
本机不找零
充值方法：
- 首先插入卡（上槽口）；
- 插入1美元、5美元、10美元或者20美元纸币（下槽口）；
- 等待3秒钟，按钮，卡弹出。

纸币面向上插入
（图书馆内自动出售复印卡的机器说明）

6

Purchase Copier/Access Cards here

复印/上网卡在此购买
（购卡指示牌）

7

TO BUY A NEW PRINT/COPY CARD
1. Push the Black Button FIRST!
2. Insert $1, $5, $10, or $20 bill(s)
(There is a 50¢ charge deducted for the cost of the new card)
3. Push Black Button below to eject card. This card can be revalued and used again hundreds of times!

NO CHANGE IS GIVEN BACK BY THIS UNIT

New Cards cost 50¢ each!

购买新的打印/复印卡
1. 先按下黑色键!
2. 插入1、5、10或20美元纸币（新卡将扣除成本费50美分）；
3. 按下面的黑色键将卡退出。本卡可多次充值使用!
本机不找零；新卡成本每张50美分。
（图书馆内购卡说明文字）

8

To Add Value to a Student ID Card or Print/Copy Card:
1. Insert Copy/Print Card (face up) first!
2. Insert $1, $5, $10, or $20 bill(s).
3. Push Black Button (below) to eject card.

学生卡或打印/复印卡充值：
1. 首先（面朝上）插入复印/打印卡；
2. 插入1美元、5美元、10美元或20美元纸币；
3. 按（下面的）黑色键将卡弹出。
（复印/打印卡充值说明文字）

9

Please Do Not Reshelve Books
Thank you

请勿将图书重新上架
（图书馆书架上的告示文字。图书馆中往往会提示读者不要自己向书架上放书，以免放错位置。）

10

Books are being moved to facilitate the renovation.
Please ask at circulation or reference desk for current locations.

为便于装修，图书搬移。当前位置，请咨询流通处或咨询台。
（图书馆临时通知。）

11

CIRCULATION DESK HAS MOVED TO NEW LOCATION BESIDE WEST ENTRANCE

图书流通处已经迁往西门
（图书馆的临时通知）

二十八、图书馆

12

The
**Elizabeth Neathery Smith
Reading Room**
Given By
Elizabeth Neathery Smith,
In memory of her parents
Sam and Willie Bounds Neathery

这是校友捐赠建立的阅览室铜牌上的文字。
为纪念其父母,伊丽莎白·尼瑟丽·史密斯捐赠修建该阅览室,因此该阅览室以她的名字命名。美国几乎所有私立大学内的建筑都由校友捐赠建立,如果捐赠达到一定的数额就可以将其姓名铭刻在墙壁或者铜牌上。

13

ARE YOU HERE TO GET A LIBRARY CARD?
Please fill out an application in blue or black in ink and you MUST show proof of your current address
As proof of address you may show:
Tx Drivers License, Tx ID, mail, or your checkbook.
Thank you

你来这里是办理图书馆借书证的吗?请使用蓝色或者黑色墨水笔来填写申请表,必须出示现在地址的证明。
作为现在地址证明,你可出示:
得克萨斯州驾驶证、得克萨斯州身份证、邮件或支票簿。谢谢。
(休斯敦图书馆办理图书证说明文字。在美国,通常人们证明自己的身份是驾驶证,有些州也颁发身份证,但没有全国性的身份证。)

14

Persons with disabilities needing assistance should contact an employee at the information counter.

需要帮助的残疾人士请联系问询台工作人员。
(图书馆的文字提示)

15

Babytime!
Is your baby between 6 and 18 months old? Join our baby storytime!
We offer singing, stories, and fingerplays for babies and their caregivers, as well as playtime afterwards.
MONDAYS at 10:30 a.m.
Montrose Meeting Room
**Older siblings welcome, but MUST BE CLOSELY SUPERVISED.

宝贝时光!
你的孩子是6—18个月大吗?参与我们的宝贝故事时光吧!我们为孩子和保姆提供唱歌、故事和手指游戏,以及之后的娱乐时光。周一10点30分,蒙图斯分馆会客厅。
**欢迎年龄稍大的孩子参加,但必须有人严格监管。
(图书馆招生广告)

16

REDEDICATED
MARCH 5, 1995
ELEANOR K. FREED
MONTROSE BRANCH
HOUSTON PUBLIC LIBRARY

1995年3月5日再次捐赠
捐赠埃莉诺·K.弗里德蒙图斯分馆
休斯敦公共图书馆立
（休斯敦图书馆分馆的捐赠说明）

17

SMOKING IS PROHIBITED WITHIN
25 FEET OF DOORWAYS
AND WHEELCHAIR RAMPS
AT PUBLIC ENTRANCES PER
CITY ORDINANCE NO. 2002-800
ARTICLE IX, SECTION 21-236 –
21-246 PUBLIC PLACE – NO. 11

入口25英尺以内禁止吸烟
轮椅缓坡位于公共入口处，本规定依据为城市法令。
（图书馆禁烟告示。最后列出公共场所相关法规条文出处。）

18

PLEASE
NO FOOD OR DRINK
IN THE LIBRARY
(EXCEPT BOTTLED WATER)

请勿将食品或饮料带入馆内（瓶装水除外）
（图书馆内告示）

19

Welcome To
Freed-Montrose
Branch Library
4100 Montrose 77006
PLEASE NOTE OUR NEW HOURS
Effective January 1, 2006

Monday	Thursday
10–8	12–8
Tuesday	Friday
10–6	12–6
Wednesday	Saturday
10–6	10–6

欢迎光临
蒙图斯大街4100号
休斯敦图书馆蒙图斯分馆
请注意我馆新的开放时间
2006年1月1日生效
周一（上午10点—晚8点）
周二（上午10点—晚6点）
周三（上午10点—晚6点）
周四（中午12点—晚8点）
周五（中午12点—晚6点）
周六（上午10点—晚6点）
（休斯敦市图书馆开放时间）

二十八、图书馆

20

THIS IS YOUR LIBRARY.
HELP KEEP IT SAFE AND CLEAN
BY OBSERVING THE FOLLOWING
NO SOLICITING
USE LITTER BARRELS AND ASH CANS
NO SKATING OF ANY KIND
NO LOITERING OR SLEEPING
VIOLATORS WILL BE ARRESTED FOR CRIMINAL TRESPASSING

这里是你的图书馆
请协助保持本馆的安全和卫生
注意遵守以下规定：
不得乞讨
使用垃圾桶和烟灰缸
不得使用任何滑行工具
不得逗留或睡觉
违者将因非法入侵遭逮捕。
（图书馆规定）

21

Widener Library Receiving Hours
Monday–Friday 8am–noon
And 1pm–4:30pm

哈佛大学图书馆开放时间说明

22

NOTICE TO ALL USERS OF HOUSTON PUBLIC LIBRARY

The Library is for reading, studying, writing, participating in scheduled programs or meetings, and using library materials. We ask your cooperation in maintaining an environment in which all library customers can use and enjoy library resources, services, and facilities. These rules are posted for the comfort and protection of all who use the Library. They will be firmly but courteously enforced by library staff/ security. Customers must comply with these rules and regulations.

The following behaviors and activities are prohibited on library property (inside or outside library buildings):

Acts that are subject to prosecution under criminal or civil codes of law.
Physical abuse, assault, public lewdness, indecent exposure or disorderly conduct.
Use of obscene, abusive, insulting or threatening language.
Possessing or being under the influence of alcohol or illegal drugs.
Damaging or destroying library property.
Unlawfully carrying a weapon.
Staring, stalking, harassment, or other behavior that reasonably can be expected to disturb others.
Tampering with security or safety devices.
Smoking within 25 feet of a public entrance.

Selling/ soliciting (approaching citizens with items for sale or pleas for donations).

Spreading out the contents or bags on library property. Unattended bags represent a safety and security and may not be left on library property.

The following behaviors and activities are prohibited in library buildings:

- Abuse or vandalism of library facilities, materials, or equipment.
- Producing or allowing any loud, unreasonable, or disturbing noises, including those from electronic and communication devices.
- Smoking or other tobacco use.
- Eating or drinking (except water in covered containers), except in designated areas.
- Bringing in packaged or unpackaged food, except into designated areas.
- Bringing in any animals, except animals assisting persons with abilities.
- Not wearing shoes or a shirt.
- Sleeping or putting your head on a table (except for infants), and putting your feet or legs on furniture.
- Taking library materials into rest rooms.
- Using library rest rooms for changing clothes, shaving, bathing or any purpose other than for which rest rooms are intended.
- Offensive bodily hygiene that constitutes a nuisance to others.
- Bringing in bedrolls, blankets, frame backpacks, suitcases, or bags measuring more than two feet in length or height. A maximum of two bags of any type will be allowed.
- Bringing in any items that could potentially be used as weapons, including but not limited to sporting equipment such as baseball bats, skateboards, etc.
- Distributing or posting printed materials/literature not in accordance with library regulations.
- Viewing material deemed to be obscene, child pornography, or harmful to minors, as those terms are defined in the Children's Internet Protection Act and the Texas Penal Code.

Parents/ guardians/ caregivers are responsible for monitoring the activities and for regulating the behavior of their children while in the library. Children under the age of seven may not be left unattended at any time. Children between the ages of seven and fourteen should not be left unattended for extended periods of time or at closing time.

All library materials must be properly checked out. If library staff/security has reasonable individualized suspicion that a library patron is attempting to exit the library with library materials that have not been checked out, the patron may be questioned and may be asked to open any item of sufficient size to contain library materials for inspection. Theft of library materials is a serious offense and will result in permanent exclusion from the library and arrest.

Anyone known to have violated any of the above rules may be asked to leave from the library as a matter of administrative policy or arrested, as permitted by law. Severe offenses may result in exclusion from the library.

If confronted with the violation of any of the above rules, please immediately inform library staff/security.

Violation of criminal trespass laws or of these rules and regulations may result in prosecution. These rules and regulations have been promulgated under the authority of Section 24-5 Article DC, Chapter 21 of the Code of Ordinances, City of Houston, Texas. See also Texas Penal Codes 30.05 (relating to criminal trespass) and 31.03 (regarding theft).

These rules were approved by City Council on April 27, 2006.

休斯敦公共图书馆读者须知

本馆供阅读、研究、写作、参与安排项目或会议以及使用藏书资料。敬请合作保持馆内环境使所有用户能使用并享受图书馆的资源、服务和设施。告示本规则是为了读者的舒适和安全，规则由本馆管理和保安人员严格但有礼貌地执行，读者必须遵守。

图书馆内外禁止以下行为和活动：
应受刑法和民法起诉的行为。
殴打、袭击，公开淫秽、露阴或行为不检。
使用淫秽、辱骂、侮辱或威胁性语言。
拥有或沾染酒精和非法毒品。
损毁或砸坏图书馆财物。
非法持有枪支。
盯视、潜随、骚扰或者其他有理由认为干扰他人的行为。
擅自摆弄安全或安检设施。
公共入口25英尺范围内吸烟。
销售/索求（接近他人销售物品或索求捐赠）。
将包裹或包裹内的东西摊铺在图书馆内外。无主包裹涉及安全，不得留在图书馆内。

图书馆内禁止以下行为和活动：
• 肆意毁坏图书馆设施、材料或设备。
• 产生或任其音量大、不合理或扰人的噪声，包括来自于电子和通讯设

新世纪美国公示语1000例

备的噪音。
- 吸烟或吸其他烟草。
- 吃东西或喝水（带盖容器饮料除外），指定区域除外。
- 带入包装或未包装食品，指定区域除外。
- 带入动物，但助残动物除外。
- 未穿鞋子或衬衣。
- 在桌子上睡觉或将头放在桌子上（婴儿除外）以及将脚或腿放在桌椅上。
- 将图书馆资料带入卫生间。
- 利用图书馆卫生间换衣服、剃须、洗浴或其他非卫生间允许进行的活动。
- 身体气味导致干扰他人。
- 带入被褥、毯子、带架背包、行李箱或长度高度大于两英尺的包裹，允许最多两件任何类型的包。
- 带入任何可能被用作武器的物品，包括但不限于运动器材，如棒球棍、滑板等。
- 未按图书馆的规定散发或张贴印刷材料。
- 翻阅被认为含有淫秽、儿童色情或对青少年有害的资料，如儿童互联网保护条例和得克萨斯州惩戒法规所规定的。
- 父母/监护人/保育员有责任监控孩子在图书馆期间的活动和行为。七岁以下儿童在任何时间不得无人照看。七岁至十四岁的儿童不得长时间或在闭馆时无人照看。
- 所有图书馆的材料必须经过出馆手续。图书馆的管理或保安人员如有理由怀疑图书馆用户试图将未经出馆手续的资料带出本馆，可进行查问和要求打开可能装有图书馆资料的物品进行检查。偷窃图书馆资料是一项严重的犯罪行为，将导致永久不准入馆和逮捕。
- 违反以上规则者将按行政令要求离开本馆或依法逮捕，严重违规者不准进入图书馆。
- 如遇以上违法行为，请立即通知图书馆管理或安保人员。

违反刑事侵犯法或上述规章者将受到起诉。本规章根据得克萨斯州休斯敦市法规第21章，24-5款颁布。同时参见得克萨斯州处罚条例30.05（有关违法行为）以及31.03（有关偷窃行为）。

本规则于2006年4月27日市议会通过

二十九、医院诊所

医院诊所

1

Morton L. Rich
Health and Wellness Center

休斯敦莱斯大学保健中心
（该中心治疗学生的生理和心理疾病；莫顿·L.里奇捐赠建立，故此命名。）

2

24 hr nurse triage line
1-800-556-1555
(Chickering Student Health Insurance Plan)

24小时护士分诊热线
（医院大门上有关学生健康保险计划的说明。分诊工作是急诊科工作的第一步，而急诊科分诊护士往往是患者及其家属来院就诊所接触的第一个医务人员。Chickering为人名。）

3

Health Services 2006 Summer Hours

BY APPOINTMENT ONLY
THE CLINIC STARTS MAY 15 AND WILL HAVE PART TIME HOURS WHICH ARE LISTED BELOW:
THE HOURS IN MAY:
MAY 15, 16,17   9AM–4 PM
MAY 30TH, 31ST   9AM–4 PM
SUMMER HOURS ARE:
MONDAY–TUESDAY   9AM–4 PM
WEDNESDAY   9AM–3 PM
THURSDAY   9AM–3PM
THERE WILL BE NO CLINIC HOWEVER THERE WILL BE A SECRETARY AVAILABLE TO ANSWER QUESTIONS. MAY, 22-29TH JULY 3-7TH AUGUST 7-9TH

健康服务2006年夏令时间
只提供预约就诊
本门诊5月15日开始 将按照以下部分时段开放。
5月时间安排：
5月15、16、17日每天上午9点至下午4点；
5月30日和31日每天上午9点至下午4点。
夏令时间安排：
周一至周二每天上午9点至下午4点；
周三上午9点至下午3点；
周四上午9点至下午3点。
其他时间停诊，但有秘书回答询问。
5月22日至29日，7月3日至7日，8月7日至9日。
（学校医院的夏季服务时间）

4

| NO DRUGS OR MONEY KEPT IN BOX
BLOOD AND URINE SPECIMENS ONLY | 盒内无药物或钱款，仅血样和尿样。
（校医院侧门附近墙上一个外挂盒子上的文字说明。这是学校医院为了让就诊的人提供血样和尿样而设立的一个专门的盒子，文字说明是为了不让人有非份之念。） |

5

| STOP
No One Beyond This Point Without Surgical Attire
Stop Here | 止步
未穿手术服者不得越过此点
（医院禁行说明） |

6

| Please Pick Up Phone on the Wall Behind You To Access SICU | 请拿起身后墙上电话联系外科监护室
（SICU的全称为surgical intensive care unit，为外科监护室。） |

7

| SICU Surgical Intensive Care Unit
No visitors
6:00 AM–8:00 AM
6:00 PM–8:00 PM
No Visitors After 9 PM
2 Visitors at a Time
30 Minutes Per Visit
No Children Under 14 Years of Age
No Outside Food or Drinks Allowed in SICU | 外科监护室
上午6点至8点 下午6点至8点 不准探望；晚9点后禁止探望；
一次2人探望，每次探望30分钟；14岁以下儿童不准探望；外带食品或饮料不得进入外科监护室
（外科监护室规定） |

8

| If You Are Here After 8:00 PM, Please Sign in at The 2nd Floor Security Desk North Tower | 如晚8点后在这里，请前往北楼2层保安处登记。
（探望病人说明） |

二十九、医院诊所

9

STOP
Please Wash Hands
Upon Entering The Unit

止步！进入本单元请洗手
（医院卫生说明）

10

Post Surgical Conference Rooms Behind These Doors Push Button to Enter →

术后会议室在门后，请按门钮进入。
（医院会议室标志牌）

11

NOTICE OF PRIVACY PRACTICES
THIS NOTICE DESCRIBES HOW MEDICAL INFORMATION ABOUT YOU MAY BE USED AND DISCLOSED AND HOW YOU CAN GET ACCESS TO THIS INFORMATION. PLEASE REVIEW IT CAREFULLY.

隐私惯例告示
本告示说明您的医疗信息如何可能被使用和透露，以及您如何可查阅此信息，请仔细阅读。
（医院有关病人隐私的告示）

12

These Valves
Service Hemodialysis
Rooms 1-8

这些阀门专为1号至8号房提供血液透析
（医院楼道内阀门说明）

13

1ST floor
< PHYSICAL THERAPY
< RESTROOMS
NURSES STATION >
ELEVATORS >
X-RAY ROOMS >

一楼
< 理疗室
< 洗手间
护士站 >
电梯 >
X光室 >
（医院内指示牌）

14

QUIET HOSPITAL ZONE

医院区域 保持安静
（医院外围的告示）

15

ROCK CREEK VETERINARY HOSPITAL
EVENING SERVICES
—OPEN 7 DAYS—
DOGS CATS BIRDS

洛克溪宠物医院　晚上服务
—7天营业—
治疗狗、猫、鸟。
（宠物医院营业告示）

16

C.A.T. Scan Control
LADIES: About to be X-rayed
If you are PREGNANT or feel you might be pregnant, please tell the technologist so appropriate protective measures can be taken.

CAT扫描管理
致女士（X光检查前）：
如果怀孕或感觉可能怀孕，请告知技术人员以便采取恰当保护措施。

17

Oxygen Shut Off Protocol
When to Shut Off
Fire/Smoke is More than One Patient Room
Who Can Shut Off
Charge/ Sr. Nurse in Collaboration with Respiratory Therapy

氧气关闭公约
何时关闭：火/烟超过一个病房
何人关闭：主管/高级护士联合呼吸治疗室
（医院氧气关闭提示）

18

CAUTION
Radiation Area

小心！辐射区域
（医院内警示牌）

19

PREGNANT
IF YOU ARE PREGNANT, OR THINK YOU MAY BE, TELL THE X-RAY TECHNOLOGIST BEFORE HAVING AN X-RAY TAKEN.

孕妇小心！
如果怀孕或认为可能怀孕，请在X光检查前告知X光技师。
（医院内给孕妇警示牌）

20

SMOKING PROHIBITED BY CITY ORDINANCE

城市法令禁止吸烟
（医院禁烟标示牌）

二十九、医院诊所

21

ATTENTION!
ALL WOMEN OF CHILD-BEARING YEARS (UP TO 50 YEARS OLD)
PLEASE Complete one of the "Pregnancy" Forms in the Box. Give the form to the Radiology Tech just before you go to the Exam Room.
Thank you!

注意!
育龄妇女(50岁以下),请填写盒中的孕妇表格一份,将表格交给X光技师后去检查室。谢谢!
(医院给孕妇的检查指示)

22

VALUABLES
PLEASE TAKE YOUR VALUABLES WITH YOU

贵重物品提示
请随身携带贵重物品
(医院检查室门口对患者的提示)

23

Please do not leave any articles in the dressing rooms such as money, credit cards or jewelry.
The Hospital is not responsible for lost articles.

请勿留现金、信用卡或珠宝等物品在更衣室。物品丢失医院概不负责。
(医院关于私人物品的提示)

24

PREGNANCY FORMS

孕妇检查表
(表格盒上的说明文字)

25

ALL EMPTY TANKS ARE TO BE TAKEN TO EMPTY TANK ROOM ON THE LOWER LEVEL

所有空箱将被运往底层空箱室存放
(医院有关存放脏衣服的箱子说明。医院的空箱内存放的是患者检查身体时穿过的衣服,但是如果有患者不小心将自己的东西随衣服一起丢弃,就可以知道该去什么地方寻找。)

26

If the volunteer is away Please Dial "0" for Patient Information

如志愿者不在,请拨0获取病人信息。
(医院内进入一道门之前看见的说明)

Target 100
OUR COMMITMENT TO YOU GIVING PERFECT 10 SERVICE

I. WE WILL ESCORT, NOT POINT, VISITORS AND PATIENTS TO THEIR DESTINATION.

II. WE WILL USE KEY WORDS AT KEY TIMES.

III. WE WILL OBSERVE THE SANCTITY OF PEACE AND QUIET BY KEEPING NOISE TO A MINIMUM.

IV. WE WILL INTRODUCE OURSELVES TO PATIENTS AND FAMILIES.

V. WE WILL RECOGNIZE EACH OTHER'S EFFORTS AND NEEDS, AND GIVE THANKS TO EACH OTHER.

VI. WE WILL HONOR OUR PATIENTS DIGNITY BY ENSURING THEIR PRIVACY, ENSURING THAT THEY ARE COVERED AT ALL TIMES DURING TRANSPORT, AND BY KNOCKING BEFORE ENTERING THEIR ROOMS.

VII. WE WILL PROVIDE EXCELLENT FOOD AND FOOD SERVICE.

VIII. WE WILL RECOGNIZE PAIN AS THE FIFTH VITAL SIGN AND ENSURE THE PATIENTS COMFORT.

IX. WE WILL PRACTICE WHAT WE PREACH BY ASKING OUR CUSTOMERS, "I HOPE WE HAVE GIVEN YOU PERFECT '10' SERVICE."

X. WE WILL ANSWER CALL LIGHTS PROMPTLY AND COURTEOUSLY.

目标100分
我们承诺提供完美的10项服务。
第一，陪同而不是指点访客和患者前往目的地；
第二，关键时刻使用关键词语表达；
第三，使噪声降到最小，保持宁静的神圣；
第四，向病人及其家属作自我介绍；
第五，尊重彼此的努力和需求并互相致谢；
第六，敬重病人尊严，确保病人隐私，病人在转运中身上一直有覆盖物，以及敲门后进入病房；
第七，提供优质食品和就餐服务；
第八，把疼痛看作第五生命指征，保证患者舒适；
第九，通过询问顾客"希望我给您提供了完美的10项服务"来履行我们的诺言；
第十，及时礼貌地应答呼叫灯。
（医院张贴的责任目标）

二十九、医院诊所

28
PATHOLOGY ACCESS IS AVAILABLE BY KEYLOCK ENTRY OR THROUGH THE CLINICAL LABORATORY ← (NEXT DOOR TO YOUR LEFT)

病理室可按键盘锁进入或通过临床实验室进入（位于左边下一道门）
（医院病理检查室指示说明）

29
Please Use This Phone For Assistance To Hospital

请使用本电话求助
（医院内部电话说明）

30
Since 1976 Park Plaza Hospital has had a tradition of issuing Holiday mugs. Enjoy looking at all the different ones!

自1976年以来，本院形成了发放假日杯的传统。请欣赏各种不同的杯子！
（医院展示假日杯的说明）

31
Holiday mugs and other items donated by Mathew Daniel, Director of Facilities And Park Plaza Employee since the hospital opened in 1975.

这里展示的假日杯和其他展品由设备处处长马修·丹尼尔和本院职工自1975年医院开业后捐赠
（医院展示的纪念杯捐赠说明）

32
IT'S THE LAW!
IF YOU HAVE A MEDICAL EMERGENCY OR ARE IN LABOR, YOU HAVE THE RIGHT TO RECEIVE, within the capabilities of this hospital's staff and facilities:
An appropriate medical SCREENING EXAMINATION
Necessary STABILIZING TREATMENT (including treatment for an unborn child) and, if necessary,
An appropriate TRANSFER to another facility

法律规定：
如有医疗急诊或分娩，即使你无法支付或无医疗保险，或无权享受医疗救助或医疗补助，你仍有权接受本医院人员和设施的能力范围内适当的医疗筛查、必要的稳定性治疗(包括对未出生儿的治疗)，如有必要，给予适当的转院。
本医院参与医疗补助项目。

Even if YOU CANNOT PAY or DO NOT HAVE
MEDICAL INSURANCE Or
YOU ARE NOT ENTITLED TO MEDICARE
OR MEDICAID
This hospital does participate in the Medicaid program.

（在美国，medical insurance 指人人可以参加的医疗保险；medicare主要针对65岁以上的老人或65岁以下身体永久残疾的人；medicaid主要针对低收入者的医疗补助项目。）

33

LOSE WEIGHT NOW!
Special $25.00
Includes:
Doctor's Visit
Consultation
Prescription
Weight Loss Injection
1-888-301-1004

现在就来减肥
特价25美元
项目包括医生出诊、咨询、开药方和减肥针注射。
（减肥注射针广告）

34

VIDEO AND AUDIO MONITORING AND RECORDING DEVICES IN USE ON THESE PREMISES

本场所内音像监控和录制设备在使用中
（医院门口监控提示）

三十、体育场馆

1

UP STAIRS FOR SECTIONS G-H-I-J-K-L
CONCESSIONS-RESTROOMS
NO SMOKING IN BUILDING

楼上为G至L各部分的看台
办理租地或商铺的办公室、卫生间
楼内禁止吸烟
（体育馆内说明）

2

MEN'S BASKETBALL
LOCKER ROOM

篮球男队员更衣房
（体育馆内衣柜说明）

3

CAUTION:
Consult a physician before using this equipment. Stop exercising if you feel pain, faint, dizzy or short of breath. Not suitable for therapeutic purposes.

注意：
使用本器械前，请咨询医生；如感觉疼痛、无力、眩晕或气短，请停止锻炼；本器械不适于治疗疾病。
（跑步器械上的说明文字）

4

PUBLIC SKATE TIMES
MON.-THURS.　11:00 a.m.—5:00 p.m.
　　　　　　　8:00 a.m.—10:00 p.m.
FRIDAY　　　 11:00 a.m.—10:00 p.m.
SATURDAY　　12:30 p.m.—10:00 p.m.
SUNDAY　　　1:00 p.m.—9:00 p.m.
　ADMISSION　　　　　　$7.50
　CHILDREN UNDER 12　　$6.50
　SENIORS AND
　ACTIVE MILITARY　　　$4.00
　SKATE RENTAL　　　　 $3.00
SKATE AT YOUR OWN RISK!

这里提供的是溜冰场的开放时间，还有各类人员入场的票价。其中包括普通大众、12岁以下儿童、老人、现役军人、租赁滑冰鞋。最后的安全提示相当于"责任自负"。

新世纪美国公示语 1000 例

5

POOL HOURS
Alarm will sound if pool gates are opened after facility is opened.

游泳池开放时间（略）
泳池大门关闭后再开，警铃会响。
（游泳池告示牌）

6

WARNING
NO LIFEGUARDS ON DUTY
NO GLASS CONTAINERS OR COOLERS
NO DIVING AND RUNNING
CHILDREN UNDER 14 MUST BE ACCOMPANIED BY AN ADULT.
POOL IS RESTRICTED TO GUESTS AND MEMBERS ONLY.

注意
泳池没有救生员值班；
禁用玻璃容器或者冷藏盒；
禁止潜水或者奔跑；
14岁以下儿童需成人陪伴，
本泳池只向房客和会员开放。
（旅馆泳池的告示牌）

7

Spa Fitness Center
SWIM DIAPER REQUIRED
FOR ALL CHILDREN UNDER THE AGE OF FOUR

Spa健身中心
4岁以下儿童需穿游泳尿布
（加州科罗纳酒店内的SPA中心告示对4岁以下儿童有严格的衣着要求）

8

TO ACCESS ANY HOTEL PUBLIC AREA:
COVER-UPS, PROPER LEISURE ATTIRE & FOOTWEAR ARE REQUIRED
Thank You

游泳者前往宾馆内其他公共场所：
需身披衣物，穿上休闲服和鞋子。
（游泳池提示。游泳池就在酒店20米开外的地方，但对游泳者衣着要求严格。）

9

CAUTION
RUNNERS ON THE ROAD

小心！
路上有径赛人员
（比赛场地告示）

三十、体育场馆

10. **RACE TODAY** / ROAD CLOSED — 今日比赛 道路封闭（比赛场地周围道路告示）

11. EVENT PARKING — 赛场停车处（比赛场地外告示）

12. **LANE CLOSED** / RACE TRAFFIC ONLY — 本车道关闭 只可行驶比赛车辆（用于比赛的车道说明）

13. **CAUTION** / RACE IN PROGRESS — 小心！比赛正在进行（比赛场地周围告示）

新世纪美国公示语1000例

影院剧院

1

NOTICE
UNAUTHORIZED COPYING OF MOVIES IS ILLEGAL
It is illegal to use any recording device, including any video camorder or audio recorder, to record any portion of the movies being shown in this theater.
Anyone who makes unauthorized copies of motion pictures in this theater or who assists others in those illegal activities, may be subject to individual civil or criminal liability.
It you witness anyone with a video recorder in this theater please notify the manager immediately.

公告
未经允许复制电影是非法的
利用任何录制设备，包括摄像机或录音机录制本院正在上映的电影的任何一部分都属于违法行为。
任何人在本院内未经允许复制电影或者协助他人进行以上违法活动，均负个人民事或刑事责任。
如发现本院内有人带摄像机，请马上通知管理人员。
（剧院版权告示）

2

A. M. Cinema
Start your day off right with a movie at AMC.
All shows before noon on Friday, Saturday and Sunday, just $4.00.

请在综合性多厅影院内观看电影，享受假期。周五、周六和周日午前放映的影片只需4美元。
（美国综合性多厅影院优惠广告。A. M. Cinema的英文全称为American Multiplex Cinema，即美国综合性多厅影院，指的是在同一屋顶下可以多厅放映多部电影，同时又往往与其他娱乐业、餐饮业、零售商业等综合经营。）

3

| ASSISTIVE LISTENING DEVICES ARE AVAILABLE | R-RATING MUST BE 17 WE CHECK ID 25 AND UNDER | SHOW YOUR CARD GET FREE STUFF | ALL AUDITORIUMS WHEELCHAIR ACCESSIBLE |

三十一、影院剧院

本院提供助听设备
R级电影必须达到17岁，25岁以下要检查身份证件
出示证卡获得赠品
所有影厅可通行轮椅
（多厅综合影院的说明）

4

Show us your picture.
We'll show you ours.
25 years & under must show I. D. for R-rated movies.
We check I. D. on R-rated movies.
Under 17 must be with parent or adult guardian 21 or older.
AMC THEATER

出示你的相片，我们给你看影片。
25岁以下需出示身份证件才可观看R级别电影。
我们会检查R级别电影观众的身份证。
17岁以下需有父母或21岁以上成年监护人陪伴。
AMC剧场
（电影院关于电影观看者年龄的告示。美国电影分为G级(general)，适合于所有观众；PG级(parental guidance)，10岁以下儿童在父母或其他成年人陪同下观看；PG-13级，13岁以下儿童由家长或成年人陪同观看；R级(restricted)，限制级别，17岁以下在成人陪同下观看；NC-17级(no children under 17)，17岁以下禁止观看。）

5

GLASS CONTAINERS PROHIBITED

禁止携带玻璃容器
（露天剧场地面文字说明）

6

NO GLASS CONTAINERS

禁止携带玻璃容器
（露天剧场地面文字说明。内容和前一个标示语功能一样，主要是为了避免玻璃容器碎裂后伤人。）

7

Blankets
To The Right
(Facing The Stage)

毯子铺在右边
（面向舞台）
（露天剧场座位说明。该露天剧场据说是全世界最大的露天剧场，一般观看的票都是通过免费发放的，因此很多没有领到票的人可以将毯子铺在露天剧场座位后面的草地上观看演出；要求将毯子铺在右边目的是为了统一管理。）

8

PLEASE SELECT ONE PAIR OF SAFETY VISORS

请选择一副安全护目镜
（剧院观看立体电影之前的提示）

9

The following is not permitted while in the theater:
No Wet Clothes
No Food or Drink
No Smoking
No Photography or Video Taping

在本影院中
请勿穿湿衣服；
请勿吃零食或喝饮料
请勿吸烟
请勿拍照或摄像
（进入剧院之前的标识牌）

10

WARNING

Terminator 2: 3D involves loud noises, strobe lights fog effects and sudden movements.
Due to the intense nature of this attraction, parental guidance is advised.
Persons with the following conditions should not experience this attraction:
Heart Conditions
Back, Neck or Similar Physical Condition
Expectant Mothers
Motion Sickness or Dizziness
Medical Sensitivity to Strobe Effects
Medical sensitivity to Fog Effects
Sensitivity to loud or sudden noises
Guests may remain in their standard motorized wheelchairs or Electric Convenience Vehicles.
Guest with service animals please see attendant for assistance.
Closed Caption please see attendant for assistance.
Reflective Captioning please see attendant for assistance.

告示

《终结者II》属于3D影片，有巨大声响、频闪灯光、雾效和强烈的动作，由于本项目动感极强，父母要照顾好孩子。有以下情况者不要参与该项目：心脏病、背痛、颈部和类似身体情况；孕妇；晕动症或眩晕；频闪效果过敏；雾效过敏；对高分贝和突发的噪声敏感。游客可以坐在标准的轮椅中或电动便利车中。带有服务犬的客人请向服务人员咨询。需要隐匿式字幕或者反射式字幕的观众请向服务人员咨询。
（好莱坞影视城内《终结者II》3D剧场外告示，告示中考虑到了各种可能发生的情况。）

三十一、影院剧院

11

Closed Captioning/ Assistive Listening Devices available upon request. Please see the nearest attendant for assistance.

本影院备有隐匿式字幕或者助听设备可索取
请就近让服务员帮助
（3D影院门票上的文字提示）

12

Discounted Admission Under 48"
CHECK HERE!

身高48英寸（121厘米）以下
打折票请在此验票！
（剧院门口验票提示文字）

13

Welcome to Universal City
For the comfort and security of all our guests, we strictly enforce our **Code of Conduct.**

欢迎来到环球影城
为了大家的舒适和安全，我们严格执行行为准则
（美国洛杉矶环球影城内行为准则提示语）

14

SAVE $20
WHEN YOU USE YOUR MASTERCARD
NOW!
GET A DELUXE ANNUAL PASS FOR ONLY $69
WHEN YOU USE YOUR MASTERCARD
HURRY LIMITED TIME OFFER!
No Black-Out Dates!

现在使用万事达卡可以节省20美元，一张豪华年票仅69美元。
使用万事达卡，从速，限期优惠！
无失效日！
（好莱坞影城门票优惠说明）

15

BUY A DAY GET 2006 FREE!

购买一张当天票可以免费获得一张2006年年票！
（好莱坞影城的门票优惠说明）

16

Take The Grauman's Chinese Theatre **VIP Tour!**
Discover
Sid Grauman's World-Famous Movie Palace!
Visit Backstage At The Chinese!
And See Authentic Grauman's Theatre Antiques!
Check Out The NEW VIP Lounge!
Grauman's Chinese Theatre
Inquire Inside The Retail Store

请参与中国大剧院的VIP游览项目！
世界著名的格劳曼电影宫殿的发现之旅！
参观大剧院的后台！
欣赏剧院内真正的古董！
全新VIP休息厅！
请在剧院内的零售店里咨询。
（洛杉矶明星大道上中国剧院参观告示）

学校

1

| CAMPUS DIRECTORY | 校园地图指示说明。进入校园之后往往都有一块地图,告知如何前往目的地。 |

2

| **1872 INSTRUCTIONS TO THE TEACHERS**
1) Teachers will fill lamps, clean chimneys and trim wicks each day.
2) Each teacher will bring a scuttle of coal and a bucket of water for the day's use.
3) Make your pens carefully. You may whittle nibs for the individual tastes of children.
4) Men teachers may take one evening each week for courting purposes or two evenings a week if they go to church regularly.
5) After ten hours in the school the teacher should spend the remaining time reading the Bible and other good books.
6) Women teachers who marry or engage in other unseemly conduct will be dismissed.
7) The teacher who performs his labors faithfully without fault for five years will be given an increase of 25 cents a week in his pay—providing the Board of Education approves. | **1872年教师守则**
1) 教师每天添加灯油、清扫烟囱、修剪树枝。
2)每天带一桶煤和一桶水作当日之用。
3)小心制作鹅毛管笔,根据儿童个人爱好削尖鹅毛管笔。
4)男教师每周可有一个晚上去求爱或每周两个晚上定期去教堂。
5)在校十个小时后,剩余的时间教师要阅读《圣经》或其他好书。
6)女教师结婚或有不体面行为将被解聘。
7)工作勤勤恳恳连续5年无差错的教师将获得每周增加25分钱的奖励,条件是教育署同意。
(圣地亚哥小镇上展示的1872年的教师守则。以上内容可以让我们看到140年前的美国教育和人权状况。) |

Punishments	Lashes
1. Boys and Girls Playing Together	4
2. Fighting at School	5
3. Quarreling at School	5
4. Gambling or betting at School	4
5. Playing at Cards at School	10
6. Climbing for Every Foot Over Three Feet up a Tree	1
7. Telling Lies	7
8. Telling Tales Out of School	8
9. Giving Each Other Ill Names	3
10. Swearing at School	8
11. For Misbehaving to Girls	10
12. For Drinking Spirituous Liquors at School	8
13. Making Swings and Swing on Them	7
14. For Wearing Long Finger Nails	2
15. Misbehaving to Persons on the Road	4
16. For Girls Going to Boys Play Places	3
17. Coming to School With Dirty Faces and Hands	2
18. For Calling Each Other Liars	3
19. For Wrestling at School	4
20. For Wetting Each Other Washing at Playtime	2
21. Scuffling at School	4
22. For Going and Playing about the Mill or Creek	6
23. For Going about the Barn or Doing any Mischief about the Place	7

这是美国140多年前圣地亚哥一所学校的处罚条例。男女生一起玩耍鞭打4下；在校打架或吵架鞭打5下；在校赌博或打赌鞭打4下；在校玩扑克鞭打10下；爬树3英尺以上每英尺鞭打1下；在校撒谎鞭打7下；在校外造谣鞭打8下；互相骂人鞭打3下；在校诅咒鞭打8下；对女生无理鞭打10下；在校饮酒鞭打8下；制作秋千并荡秋千鞭打7下；留长指甲鞭打2下；对路人无理鞭打4下；女生去男生玩耍的地方鞭打3下；脸和手不清洁上学鞭打2下；彼此互骂撒谎者鞭打3下；在校扭打鞭打4下；在游玩时间用水互相弄湿鞭打2下；在校拖脚走鞭打4下；去磨坊或小溪边玩耍鞭打6下；去谷仓周围或在那里胡闹鞭打7下。140多年前美国学校的体罚现在看来令人瞠目。但截至2009年4月，美国仍然有21个州可以在学校里体罚学生，一般由校长执行。

三十二、学校

4

DRUG FREE
GUN FREE
SCHOOL ZONE
VIOLATORS WILL FACE SEVERE
FEDERAL STATE AND LOCAL
CRIMINAL PENALTIES

学校区域，禁毒！禁枪！
违者将受到联邦、州和地方政府的刑事惩罚。

（学校安全告示牌）

5

QUIET PLEASE
Testing in Progress Thank You

请安静
考试正在进行。谢谢！

（教室门上的提示）

6

1042
CLASSROOM MAXIMUM
OCCUPANCY 46

1042号教室
本教室不得超过46人

（教室门口说明）

7

NO FOOD OR DRINKS IN
AUDITORIUM
FOR LATE ENTRY TO AUDITORIUM,
USE SECOND FLOOR ENTRY

礼堂内禁止零食或饮料
迟到者从二楼入口进入

（礼堂内提示晚来的人如何进入）

8

1055
AUDITORIUM MAXIMUM
OCCUPANCY 240

礼堂编号1055
最大容量不得超过240人

（礼堂容量说明文字）

9

PLEASE DO NOT MOVE CHAIRS FROM
ONE CLASSROOM TO ANOTHER
Please report chair shortages to the Registrar.
Thank you.
Humanities Dean's Office

不要在教室之间搬动座椅
座椅不够，请向管理人员报告。
人文学院院长办公室

（莱斯大学人文学院院长办公室的告示）

新世纪美国公示语1000例

10

PLEASE DO NOT STORE FILES ON THIS COMPUTER. THIS IS A PUBLIC MACHINE THAT MAY BE WIPED AT ANY TIME.

请勿在本机内储存文件。公用机器，随时删除。
（公用计算机键盘上说明文字）

11

LAPTOP CONNECTION

教室桌子上手提电脑连接指示说明。台式电脑为desktop computer，而laptop指坐着时可放在腿上使用的电脑，即"笔记本电脑"。

12

Humanities Conference Room
115 Humanities Building
Humanities Building Rooms 103-114 are located in the next wing

人文学院会议室位于人文大楼115室
人文学院大楼的103至114房间位于翼楼内
（教学楼内教室指示文字）

13

Attention
Practice Room Users
Please finish all sessions by 1 a.m. Our apartment is directly over this room, and while we normally appreciate music, we do not do so when it wakes us up at 3 o'clock in the morning. Cory and Kevin

音乐练习室使用者请注意
请在凌晨1点前完成所有学习任务。我们的公寓就在本室的上方，尽管我们通常喜欢音乐，但不喜欢凌晨3点被叫醒。科利和凯文
（两个学生在音乐练习室门上的临时告示。带着幽默提意见更容易为人所接受。）

14

LECTURE HALL
Assistive Listening System Available

演讲厅
本厅内有助听设施（演讲厅辅助说明）

15

102
SEMINAR ROOM
MAXIMUM OCCUPANCY 74
ASSISTED LISTENING DEVICES AVAILABLE

102研讨室
最多人数不得超过74人
内有助听设备
（研讨室说明文字）

16

No Drinks
No Food
No Cell Phone Use In Lab
No Kidding

实验室内请勿喝饮料、吃东西、打手机
我们是认真的
（大学实验室门口告示）

17

No food, drink or tobacco products are permitted past this point. This also includes all beverage containers. Either store them in your backpack or leave them in the Student Lounge. Thank you for your cooperation.

禁止食品、饮料或烟草制品越过此点，包括各种饮料容器。请将这类物品储存在背包里，或留在学生休息室。谢谢合作！
（大学实验室门口告示）

18

INTERNATIONAL STUDENT AND SCHOLAR SERVICES OFFICE
Office Hours: Monday and Tuesday, 8:00AM–6:00 PM
Wednesday, Thursday, and Friday, 8:00AM–5:00 PM

休斯敦大学国际交流学生和学者服务办公室的办公时间。

19

W20 DIRECTORY STRATTON STUDENT CENTER

0 LOWER LEVEL SERVICES
United States Post Office   003
Alpha Cleaners   005
Parking Office   022
Latino Cultural center   001
New Tech Barber & Styling Salon   023
Card Services   021
Technicuts   025
MIT Police Detail Office   020B
MIT Optical   027
FSILG Cooperative, Inc. (FCI)   020A
    1 First Floor   YOU ARE HERE
Anna's Taqueria   100
LaVerde's market   105

3 THIRD FLOOR
MEZZANINE Lounge   307
Stratton Balcony   300
Twenty Chimneys   306
Private Dining Room #1   301
Private Dining Room #2   302
Private Dining Room #3   303
Private Dining Room #4   304
Coffeehouse Lounge   308A
    4 FOURTH FLOOR
Student Organizations' Offices/Conference Room
Room   400
Room   407

Alpine Bagel Café' & Cambridge Grill 101	Room 491
Copy Tech Express 102	Student Art Association 429
MIT COOP 103	Room 414
Bank of America 104	Room 438
Gameroom 106	Room 440
2 SECOND FLOOR	**5 FIFTH FLOOR**
Wiesner Student Art Gallery 209	Campus Activities Complex Office 500
Stratton Lounge 200	Student Life Programs Office 549
West Lounge 201	Reading Room 526
Sala de Puerto Rico 202	540
Lobdell Dining Hall 208	Athena Cluster 575
	Student Information Processing Board Office 557
	Office of Campus Dining 500
	Community Development and Substance Abuse 507
	Student Mediation and Community Standards 507

麻省理工学院内西20号楼即学生中心的指南。从指南上可以看出，从地下一层到地上五层几乎涵盖了涉及学生学习和生活的所有办事处。地下一层有邮局、清洁公司、停车服务、拉丁文化中心、美发厅、校园卡服务处、理发厅、警察局、配镜处、服务公司；一楼有墨西哥风味餐厅、市场、咖啡烧烤厅、快速复印室、书籍杂货店、银行和游戏室；二楼有学生艺术馆、休息室、西休息室、小剧院、餐厅、咖啡厅以及私人就餐室；四楼则有学生组织办公室/会议室、学生艺术协会；五楼有校园活动办公室、学生生活项目办公室、电脑房、学生信息处理办公室、校园餐饮办公室、社区发展及禁毒中心以及学生媒体和社区标准处。FSILG Cooperative, Inc. 为学院内的一家服务公司，能够提供一条龙购物服务；Anna's Taqueria是一座提供墨西哥风味食品的餐厅；MIT COOP已经从1882年的一个小书店发展到现在可以向学生提供几乎校园内所有的用品，而成为其会员只需要1美元，与100多年前成立的时候一个价格；Athena Cluster为麻省理工学院内的电脑房，其中Athena为该学校电脑操作系统的名称。

三十三、施工工地

1

DANGER
CONSTRUCTION AREA
KEEP OUT

危险!
施工区域
请勿入内
（工地告示牌）

2

DANGER
HARD HAT AREA

工地告示牌，提示进入本区域一定要带安全帽。

3

WE ARE NOW CLOSED
DUE TO CONSTRUCTION

由于施工
本店现在停业
（场所关闭的临时通知）

4

RICE UNIVERSITY BOOKSTORE
WILL BE **CLOSED**
BEGINNING JUNE 30, 2006 **DUE TO CONSTRUCTION**
PLEASE CALL 713-348-4202 FOR SERVICE AND INQUIRIES

莱斯大学书店
因施工2006年6月30日开始停业，需要服务或咨询，请拨电话713-348-4202。
（书店暂停营业的临时通知）

5

Work Zone
Pedestrians Detour

施工区域 行人绕道
（工地告示牌）

6

Ends Work Zone

施工区域终止（公路上施工区域截止指示牌）

7

| Construction Zone Ahead | 前方施工（施工区域指示牌） |

8

| Fines Doubled for Speed in Work Zone | 施工地段超速行驶加倍罚款（施工区域指示牌） |

9

| Pardon the inconvenience while we make improvements to this attraction. Please join us for a Magellanic Penguin. Check your park map for presentation times! | 本娱乐设施正在改造，有所不便敬请谅解。参与麦哲伦企鹅游乐项目，请查阅公园地图上的表演时间。（对娱乐区域进行施工改造的说明牌） |

10

| EXCUSE OUR MESS UNDER CONSTRUCTION | 施工场所恕有不便（施工场所说明牌） |

11

| WARNING FIBER OPTICS CABLE ROUTE BURIED CABLE BEFORE DIGGING, TRENCHING OR PUSHING PIPE IN THIS VICINITY CALL THE UTILITY COOPERATING COMMITTEE AT 223-4567 OR 1-800-669-8344 | 小心纤维光缆线路这里埋设光缆在附近挖掘、挖沟或推动管道之前，电告水电协调委员会（道路下有电缆的告示） |

三十四、教堂墓地

1

**WELCOME TO THE CATHEDRAL OF SAINT PATRICK
HIS EMINENCE EDWARD CARDINAL EGAN ARCHBISHOP OF NEW YORK REV MSGR ROBERT TRITCHIE RECTOR**

欢迎来到圣·帕特里克大教堂

红衣主教爱德华阁下，纽约大主教伊根，尊敬的蒙席·罗伯特·里奇教区长。

（这是纽约市区规模非常宏大的圣·帕特里克大教堂的欢迎牌。REV MSGR 全称为Reverend Monsignor，梵蒂冈授予的头衔。纽约圣·帕特里克大教堂是纽约大主教的座堂，也是美国最大的哥特式天主教堂，可容纳2,400人。教堂外长123米，宽83米，塔尖100米，教堂内有三台管风琴，还有一些祭坛、艺术圣像和反映圣经故事的彩色玻璃窗等。）

2

For the POOR of the WORLD

请为贫困者捐款

（教堂内捐款箱上说明。在美国，教堂的运行基本依靠捐款。）

3

Catholic Student Center Chapel
1714 Rice Blvd.
Sunday Summer Mass Schedule:
10:00 AM only
Weekday Masses: 7:00PM
Wednesday

天主教学生中心教堂
莱斯大道1714号
夏季周日弥撒安排：仅上午10点
工作日弥撒：周三下午7点
（学校教堂标志牌。在美国，几乎每所大学都有一座教堂供信教学生礼拜。）

4

NOW ENROLLING 12mo. – 5yrs.
713-526-8125

现在招收12个月至5岁的孩子
（教堂门口幼儿园招生广告。美国的幼儿园很多由教堂开办。）

5

CHRIST CHURCH BURIAL
GROUND
Established 1791
Please enter on Arch Street
Open to the Public
Monday-Saturday 10:00 AM to 4:00 PM
Sunday 12:00 PM to 4:00PM
Weather Permitting
Four Group Tours
Contact Christ Church

基督教墓地
建于1791年
请从阿切大街进入
墓地对外开放
周一至周六：上午10点至下午4点
周日：中午12点至下午4点
只要天气允许，4人即可组团参观，请与基督教堂联系。
（费城内一个教堂墓地的说明牌。在这片墓地里，埋葬着7位曾经签署美国独立宣言的人物，其中最著名的是本杰明·富兰克林。）

6

HISTORIC BURYING GROUNDS INITIATIVE
GRANARY BURYING GROUND
ESTABLISHED
1660
NATIONAL REGISTER OF
HISTORIC PLACES
BEACON HILL ARCHITECTURAL DISTRICT
VISITORS PLEASE TAKE NOTICE
No gravestone rubbing.
Do not sit or lean on tombs or gravestones.
No alcoholic beverages.
No dogs allowed.
This burying ground is a place of honor and history.
The condition of the gravestones is the result of time and the effects of weathering.
Preserve this site for future generations by treating it with respect.
This site is open during daylight hours.
Park users are subject to the rules and regulations of the Parks Commission.
City of Boston, Parks and Recreation Department: 635-4505
In case of emergency, please call 911.

具有历史意义的公墓
粮仓公墓，建于1660年，全国历史名胜地
比肯山建筑区

三十四、教堂墓地

参观者请注意
请勿摩拓墓碑
请勿坐在或靠在墓冢或墓碑上
请勿饮酒
请勿携带宠物
本墓地是瞻仰荣誉和缅怀历史之场所，
墓碑的现状是年代久远风吹雨打的结果，
为了我们的后代，请尊重保护本场所。
本场所白天开放
园区使用请遵守公园委员会的规章
波士顿市公园娱乐部：635-4505
紧急情况请拨打911
（马萨诸塞州府波士顿市中心的一个公共墓地，是该市三大最古老的墓地之一，其中埋葬着三位签署独立宣言的领导人。）

新世纪美国公示语1000例

 酒店旅馆

1

With Our Compliments
If you have forgotten any essential toiletry item,
then please contact Guest Services.
We will be pleased to deliver with our compliments: shaving cream, disposable razor, comb, toothbrush or toothpaste.

顺致问候！
顾客忘记携带盥洗用具，请联系客户服务。
我们乐意敬赠剃须膏、一次性剃须刀、梳子、牙刷或牙膏。
（酒店盥洗用具提示。美国酒店一般都不会直接提供牙刷牙膏之类的洗漱用具。）

2

Please
HELP US CONSERVE ENERGY
Please turn off the lights, television and air conditioning when leaving room.
Thank you.

请协助节能
离开房间请关闭电灯、电视和空调，谢谢。
（宾馆对房客节约用电的提示。在美国，这样要求节约用电的提示牌并不多见。）

3

Crowne Plaza Cherry Hill Welcomes You!
HOTEL SAFETY: Your safety and the security of your personal property are of our utmost concern. We urge you to take advantage of the following suggestions.
FIRE SAFETY: For your safety, please familiarize yourself with the location of the hallway fire exits, alarms and extinguishers. In the unlikely event of a fire DIAL EXT. 55 to notify the operator of your location and that of the fire. If you are in your room the following should occur:
1. Take your keycard.
2. Test your door for heat before opening.
3. If the hallway is clear of smoke, exit by stairwell down to the ground level.
4. NEVER USE ELEVATORS.
Should the doorway be warm or the hallway impassible:
1. Place wet towels at the base of the door.

2. Notify the operator with name and room number.
3. Stay low to floor inhaling through wet towel.
SAFETY DEPOSIT BOXES: Please utilize our SAFETY DEPOSIT BOXES available at the front desk for money or valuables. State law limits the liability of the hotel for the loss or damage of personal property. Do not leave money or valuables in your room.
ADMITTANCE: Please identify all individuals by utilizing the door viewer before admitting anyone into your room.
KEYCARD: Please safeguard your keycard. Do not leave keycard in the room. Please do not give your keycard to others. All keycards are electronically coded; to identify room number refer to your keycard packet.
DOORS: The hotel has provided your room with a safety latch and deadbolt. We suggest that you utilize both when you are in your room. Also, be sure to engage the deadbolt and safety latch on any connecting doors.

CHECKOUT TIME IS 12:00 NOON

Please familiarize yourself with the location of your room and the fire exit stairs. In the event of an alarm, use the stairs. Elevators can be hazardous during a fire.

皇冠酒店欢迎您！

酒店安全：您的人身和财产安全是酒店最关心的，酒店敦促您采纳以下建议。

防火安全：为了您的安全，请熟悉消防通道、火灾报警器以及灭火器的位置。

万一发生火灾，请拨打55通报接线员您所处的位置和火源的位置，当然这种可能性非常小。如果您在房间里，请拿上房卡；测试房门温度再开门；走廊如无烟雾，就从楼梯下楼；切勿使用电梯。如门口热或走廊无法通行，将湿浴巾放在门下；通知接线员你的姓名和房间号码；俯身靠近地板通过湿浴巾呼吸。

保险箱：请使用前台的保险箱来保存你的现金或贵重物品。本州法律规定酒店对个人物品的丢失和损坏承担有限赔偿责任。不要将现金或贵重物品放在房间内。

进入房间：请通过猫眼确认来客后再允许进入您的房间。

门卡：请保管好门卡。勿将门卡留在房间内，勿将门卡给他人。所有门卡电子设密。确认房号，查阅门卡袋。

门：酒店已为您的房间提供了安全插销和死锁系统。酒店建议您在房间时两者同时使用，而且确保相连的房门都使用安全插销和死锁装置。

退房时间为中午12点。

请熟悉一下您房间的位置和消防楼梯。万一警报响起，请使用楼梯。火灾时使用电梯会有危险。

（美国一家酒店在门背后张贴的安全提示牌）

4

Instructions Adjust Temperature Setting

Press up ▲ or down ▼ button to set desired temperature.

Select Fan Speed

Press fan button

High—continuous high speed

Low—continuous low speed

Auto—fan turns on/off when room temperature is reached

Economy—sets to unoccupied mode

Display °F or °C

Slide °F or °C switch to display °F (English) or °C (Metric)

温度调节说明

温度设定

上下按钮设定所需温度

风扇速度选择

按下风扇钮

高速：持续高速度

低速：持续低速度

自动：达到室温，风扇自动开/关

经济模式：调整至空档

显示摄氏或华氏温度

将°F（英制）钮滑动显示°C（公制），或者将°C钮滑动显示°F。（酒店内墙壁上有关房间中央空调的说明）

5

MANAGER ON DUTY
DAVID FASLER

值班经理大卫·福斯勒
（酒店前台值班经理的告示牌）

6

**THINK GLOBALLY
ACT LOCALLY**

Did you know that linens and towels washed daily by hotels worldwide use millions of gallons of fresh water and add tons of detergents to our environment?

As part of Hyatt's ongoing commitment to improving the environment by using less energy and creating less waste, we offer a solution. During your stay, we will change bed linens and towels every three days, while still refreshing your guestroom daily. If you do not

放眼世界 从我做起

您是否知道全世界酒店每天洗涤织物和毛巾用掉几百万加仑的淡水，给环境增添成吨的洗涤剂？

凯悦酒店正在承诺节约能源，减少垃圾改善环境。我们提出方案。在您住店期间，每三天更换一次床单和毛巾，但是您的客房每天会清洁。如果您不愿意加入本计划，请联系客房服务或酒店接线员，这样您的被单和毛巾就会每天更换。很多客人有兴趣参与我们的做

wish to participate in this program, please contact guest request or the hotel operator and your linens and towels will be replaced daily.
Many of our guests have expressed interest in joining us in our efforts. We appreciate your participation. Together we can make a difference.
PRINTED ON 100% RECYCLED PAPER. LAMINATED TO REDUCE WASTE.

法，感谢您的参与，我们能够共同创造一个不同的世界。
本资料是在100%的循环纸上印刷的，且使用折叠片制作以减少垃圾。
（美国旅馆内节约水资源的宣传广告）

7

MONTAGU HOTEL
NEW ROOM RATES
Newly Renovated Rooms $42 +tax
Standard Rooms $32 + tax
Economy Rooms $25 + tax

酒店住宿对外报价说明。这是一家新装修酒店，新装修房间为42美元加税，标准房为32美元加税，经济房25美元加税。

8

CALIFORNIA PROPOSITION 65
WARNING:
THIS FACILITY CONTAINS CHEMICALS KNOWN TO THE STATE OF CALIFORNIA TO CAUSE CANCER AND BIRTH DEFECTS OR OTHER REPRODUCTIVE HARM.

加州65号建议
警告：
本设施含有本州所知的化学物质，可致癌和生育缺陷或其他生育危害。
（酒店内一房间门上告示）

9

HOTEL DEL CORONADO
<u>HAS BEEN DESIGNATED A</u>
NATIONAL
<u>HISTORIC LANDMARK</u>
THIS SITE POSSESSES

克罗纳多旅馆
已确定A级
国家历史性地标
本场所在纪念美国历史方面具有国家意义

NATIONAL SIGNIFICANCE
IN COMMEMORATING THE
HISTORY OF THE
UNITED STATES OF AMERICA
1977
NATIONAL PARK SERVICE
UNITED STATES
DEPARTMENT OF THE
INTERIOR

美国内政部国家公园服务中心
1977年立
（美国国家历史地标说明牌。这座旅馆是美国西部最早安装电灯的现代化旅馆，其中的线路就是由爱迪生布设的；罗斯福、尼克松、里根等美国总统曾经光临这里；玛丽莲梦露曾在此拍摄过电影；20世纪初爱德华八世也曾经驾临此地演绎了一场"不爱江山爱美人"的动人爱情故事。）

10

HOTEL DEL CORONADO
THIS VICTORIAN HOTEL, BUILT IN 1887, IS ONE OF AMERICA'S LARGEST WOODEN BUILDINGS. FEW SEASIDE RESORT HOTELS OF THIS SIGNIFICANT ARCHITECTURAL STYLE REMAIN IN AMERICA. THE HOTEL HAS HOSTED SEVERAL PRESIDENTS AND OTHER NATIONAL FIGURES.
CALIFORNIA REGISTERED
HISTORICAL LANDMARK NO. 844
PLAQUE PLACED BY THE STATE DEPARTMENT OF PARKS AND RECREATION IN COOPERATION WITH THE SAN DIEGO HISTORICAL SOCIETY, CORONADO HISTORICAL ASSOCIATION INC., AND SAN DIEGO CHAPTER, AMERICAN INSTITUTE OF ARCHITECTURE.
DECEMBER 17, 1970.

克罗纳多旅馆
这座维多利亚式的建筑建于1887年，是美国最大的木结构建筑之一。在美国这样沿海且具有重要建筑风格的度假旅馆已不多见；曾经有几位总统和其他国家要员在这座旅馆下榻。
本旅馆在加州登记的历史地标号码为844
1970年12月17日立
（加州圣地亚哥克罗纳多旅馆的说明牌）

OUR SERVING POLICY

We are proud to offer for sale beer and wine products to those guests who are 21 years of age or older.

We will request identification from anyone appearing 30 years of age or younger. Please be prepared to present a valid driver's license or any other valid form of identification (or Federal) as proof that you are 21 years old. One alcoholic beverage at a time will be served per guest with valid identification.

If you cannot present proof of age, we regret that we will be unable to serve. Thank you for your understanding or cooperation.

WARNING:

Drinking distilled spirits, beer, coolers, wine and other alcoholic beverages may increase cancer risk, and during pregnancy can cause birth defects.

我们的服务方针

我们非常荣幸地为21岁以上的客人提供打折啤酒和葡萄酒类。我们要求看似30岁以下人士出示身份证。请准备好出示您的有效驾照或其他有效证件（或联邦证件）以证明你已经达到21岁合法年龄。每位持有证件的客人一次提供一份含酒饮料。如果您无法证明自己的年龄，很遗憾我们不能提供服务，谢谢您的理解与合作。

警告：

饮用蒸馏酒、啤酒、清凉饮料、葡萄酒或其他含酒精饮料可能会增加您患癌症的机率，而孕妇可能会导致胎儿畸形。

（酒店服务告示牌。美国酒店门口常有人性化警示，其中最常见的就是对饮酒人的合法年龄验证；这里所提供的服务宗旨告示牌中还警示饮酒可能会导致的后果，可谓无微不至。）

新世纪美国公示语1000例

三十六

奖励通告

1

Striving for Excellence In Campus Emergency Medical Services
Rice University Emergency Medical Service is hereby recognized by the National Collegiatee Emergency Medical Services Foundation for a period of three years from 2005 to 2008 for quality in the delivery of patient care, high standards of professional education, and service to the community in fulfillment of its mission of providing Emergency Medical Services to its campus.
Presented February 26, 2005 by the National Collegiate Emergency Medical Services Foundation.

在校园医疗急救服务上追求卓越
国家大学紧急医疗服务基金会认可莱斯大学医疗急救服务机构从2005至2008年为期3年向社区提供高质量的病员护理、高标准专业教育和服务,实现其为校园提供紧急医疗服务的使命。
2005年2月26日国家大学紧急医疗服务基金会颁发。
(警察局内牌匾上有关获基金会资助的说明)

2

Striving for Excellence in Campus Emergency Medical Services
Rice University Emergency Medical Services is recognized by the National Collegiate **Emergency Medical Services Foundation** for quality and professionalism in the delivery of campus based emergency medical services for the three year period 1999–2002
Presented February 13, 1999 at Syracuse, New York

在校园医疗紧急救援服务上追求卓越
国家大学紧急医疗服务基金会认可莱斯大学医疗紧急救援服务机构从1999年至2002年为期3年向校园提供高质量和专业化紧急医疗服务。
1999年2月13日颁发。
(警察局内牌匾上有关获基金会资助的说明)

三十六、奖励通告

3

| Texas Crime Prevention Assn "Outstanding Crime Prevention Agency" of the Year **Rice University Police Department** 1998 | 莱斯大学警察局（1998）获得得克萨斯州的防止犯罪协会颁发的防止犯罪优秀机构称号（大学校园内警察局的奖状。assn等于association。） |

4

| **The Texas National Night Out (NNO)** Coordinating Committee proudly presents our **Certificate of Honor** for outstanding community participation to Rice University Campus Police for their enthusiastic support for NNO 2002 | 得克萨斯州国家夜巡协调委员会非常荣幸地将荣誉证颁发给莱斯大学校园警察，表彰其积极参与社区活动，热情支持2002年国家夜巡项目。（警察局内悬挂的荣誉证） |

5

| OUTSTANDING ENGINEERING ALUMNI (omitted) | 杰出工程领域校友（略）（校友荣誉栏中的标题。标题的下面将在工程领域做出过杰出贡献的校友名字和相片展示出来。） |

6

| **MEDAL OF HONOR** FOR ARCHITECTURAL MERIT AWARDED BY THE HOUSTON CHAPTER | 荣誉奖为建筑功绩而颁发休斯敦牧师会（荣誉奖文字说明） |

7

| The Association of Rice Alumni honors Distinguished Alumna of Rice University **Lynn Laverty Elsenhans** Bachelor of Arts, 1978 Mathematical Sciences For her achievements as an industry leader In the field of energy May 14, 2005 | 莱斯大学校友会纪念杰出的莱斯大学校友 Lynn Laverty Elsenhans （1978届文学学士）数学科学因其在能源行业领域所取得的开拓性成就而立 2005年5月14日（学生中心荣誉牌内容） |

新世纪美国公示语1000例

8

Four Diamond Award Presented to
The Tremont House-A Wyndham Historic Hotel
for providing exceptional guest
accommodations,
in the year 2006

四钻石奖章颁发给文德海姆历史旅馆，因其提供了良好的旅客住宿，2006年颁布。
（一家旅馆所获得的奖励）

9

Certificate of Recognition
On this date, May 21, 2003
The American Heart Association proudly names
Park Plaza Hospital
as an official
Get With The Guidelines-Coronary Artery Disease
Hospital
for its implementation of the
Get With The Guidelines-Coronary Artery Disease
Program

荣誉证书
美国心脏协会于2003年5月21日荣幸地命名帕克广场医院为正规的指导–治疗心血管疾病医院，因其实施指导–治疗心血管疾病项目。
（医院所获得的荣誉证书）

10

CIRCLE OF EXCELLENCE
In recognition of their demonstrated record
of excellence in patient care, customer service and
operating results,
Tenet Healthcare is proud to induct the entire staff of
PARK PLAZA HOSPITAL
into the **Circle of Excellence**
Presented 2004

荣誉勋章
为了表彰在病员护理、顾客服务和手术效果的杰出成就，特尼特护理中心非常骄傲地授予帕克广场医院的全体职员优秀集体称号，2004年颁发。
（为医院颁发的荣誉勋章证书）

11

CIRCLE OF EXCELLENCE
In recognition of demonstrated
commitment to quality, service and high
ethical standards, Tenet Healthcare is
proud to induct the entire staff of
PARK PLAZA HOSPITAL into the
Circle of Excellence
Presented 2003

荣誉勋章
为了表彰在医疗质量、医疗服务和高尚的医德标准方面的杰出成就，特尼特护理中心非常骄傲地授予帕克广场医院的全体职员优秀集体称号，2003年颁发。
（为医院颁发的集体荣誉证书）

三十七、救助

1

RICE ALLY
Providing support to gay, lesbian, bisexual and transgendered persons.

为男同性恋、女同性恋、双性恋和变性人提供帮助。
（大学学院院长家窗户上对外张贴的项目说明。RICE ALLY是休斯敦莱斯大学内设立的帮助以上人员的一个项目。）

2

Recycle Yourself
Be An
Organ Donor

循环自己
捐赠器官
（大学学院院长引导学生成为器官捐赠者的鼓动文字。在美国，很多人的汽车驾驶证上都会有DONOR的字样，以表明自己如果发生意外愿意捐赠器官。尽管在美国以这样的方式来回馈社会的器官捐赠人很多，但每天还是有十多人因无相应的器官移植而死亡。）

3

Helping Feed
The Hungry

帮助穷人填饱肚子
（募捐箱上的告示。一个名为休斯敦粮库的机构在为穷人募捐。）

4

Houston Area Women's Center Ending Domestic and Sexual Violence
BACK-TO-SCHOOL DRIVE Now through July19th

CRAYONS(16-24 PACK)	HIGHLIGHTERS
ERASERS	MANILLA PAPER
GRADING PENS/PENCILS	WHITE GLUE
WATER COLORS	GLUE STICKS

新世纪美国公示语1000例

PROTRACTOR	SCISSORS (POINTED)
COMPASS	SCISSORS (BLUNT/SEMI-BLUNT)
SUPPLY BOX	PLASTIC RULERS
3 RING BINDERS	COLORED FOLDERS W/POCKETS & BRADS
DIVIDERS	
WATER SOLUBLE MARKERS	CLEAR ZIPPERED SCHOOL POUCH (3 HOLE)
INDEX CARDS	
BACKPACKS (FOR ALL AGES)	NOTEBOOK PAPER (WIDE RULE)
	SPIRAL RING NOTEBOOKS (WIDE RULE)
	MAP PENCILS

Monetary donations of any amount for us to purchase the above items can be made by check.

Drop off Box Locations:
Allen Center
Mudd Building
Rice Memorial Center
Campus Store
Recreation Center

校园内放置的捐赠箱上的文字说明。休斯敦区妇女中心；终止家庭和性暴力；重返校园运动，从现在开始至7月19日。这一运动的目的是为了让更多的孩子重返校园，希望人们捐款捐物，其中包括彩色蜡笔（16-24支包装）、橡皮、刻度钢笔/铅笔、水彩、圆规、文具盒、3孔活页夹、索引卡片、记号笔、马尼拉纸、白胶、胶棒、（尖头）剪子、（钝头/半钝头）剪子、塑料尺子、彩色文件夹（附袋和金属架）、透明拉锁文件夹（3孔）、水溶性记号笔、索引卡片、（适宜于各年龄阶段的）肩包、笔记本活页（宽格）、螺旋装笔记本（宽格）、地图铅笔。购买以上文具的捐款，不论多少均可用支票。最后为各捐赠地点。

5

| U.S. Food Stamp—Unauthorized use punishable by law | 美国食品救济券未经认可使用会受法律制裁（美国救济券上警示） |

三十七、救助

U.S. DEPARTMENT OF ACRICULTURE

FOOD COUPON

DO NOT FOLD OR SPINDLE

NON-TRANSFERABLE

EXCEPT UNDER CONDITIONS PRESCRIBED BY THE SECRETARY OF AGRICULTURE

美国农业部食品救济券

请勿折叠或揉搓

不可转让，除非农业部长另有说明。

（美国食品救济券上部分文字说明）

新世纪美国公示语1000例

幽默告示

1

SHOPLIFTERS WILL BE BEATEN, STABBED AND STOMPED
SURVIVORS WILL BE ROSECUTED

超市防止偷窃的告示。顺手牵羊者挨揍、刀刺、践踏；幸存者被起诉。商店以幽默的语言警告有贼心者勿越雷池。

2

LAUNDRY ROOM PUSH FOR SERVICE
IF NO ONE ANSWERS, DO IT OURSELF

洗衣房告示。洗衣房，需要服务，请推门。无人应答，请自助。使用幽默语言来创造一个和谐的环境。

3

NO TRESPASSING
Violators will be shot.
Survivors will be shot again.

进入大楼的警示文字。本告示可以表示：**不准入内，违者将被摄录；幸存者将被再次摄录**。但是也可以理解成：**不准入内，违者将被击毙；幸存者将被再次击毙**。告示利用单词shoot的双重意义(摄录；击毙)来表达幽默效果，进而达到阻止入内的目的。

4

GUYS
NO SHIRT NO SERVICE
GIRLS
NO SHIRT FREE DRINKS

饭店幽默告示。**男生不穿衬衣，服务不到；女生不穿衬衣，免费畅饮**。告示的前半部分是认真的，后半部分是为了幽默。

5

Open seven days a week and weekends.

商店门前告示。**本店每周开放7天加周末**。商店老板已经忙得不知道一周有几天了。

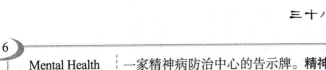

三十八、幽默告示

6

| Mental Health Prevention Center | 一家精神病防治中心的告示牌。**精神病预防中心或防止精神健康中心**。本意是要表达防止精神病发生的告示牌，但也可以理解为防止精神健康中心。 |

7

| 15 men's wool suits -$100- They won't last an hour! | 华盛顿一家衣服商店的广告。**15件男式毛衣100美元，它们不会持续1小时！** 店家本意是要说优惠活动不会超过一个小时，但是却可以让人理解为这些衣服耐穿性不会超过一个小时。 |

8

| PERSONS ARE PROHIBITED FROM PICKING FLOWERS FROM ANY BUT THEIR OWN GRAVES. | 一处墓地入口处的说明。**禁止捡拾花朵，除非从自己的坟墓上**。墓地管理处以幽默的方式劝导人们不要从墓地上捡拾花朵。 |

9

| Are you an adult that cannot read? If so, we can help. | 公用电话亭上的说明。**你是一位不识字的成人吗？如果这样的话，我们可以给你提供帮助**。打电话的人如果不识字的话，如何能够知道电话公司可以提供帮助？ |

10

| Our Motto Is to Give Our Customers the Lowest Possible Prices and Workmanship. | 一家杂货店门口的告示。**我们的宗旨就是给我们的顾客尽可能低的价格和工艺**。店家没有想到，一气连下来竟然变成了最差的工艺！ |

11

| IF YOU ARE SITTING IN AN EXIT ROW AND CAN NOT READ THIS CARD, PLEASE TELL A CREW MEMBER. | 美国西部航空公司飞机座位安全信息卡上的一个说明。**如果你坐在通道口这一排，看不见这张卡，请告诉机组人员**。既然看不见这张卡，那又怎么告诉机组人员呢！ |

12

EARS PIERCED WHILE YOU WAIT.

一家珠宝店的说明。**立等穿耳**。本来是店家要说明自己在顾客的耳朵上穿耳坠孔非常快，但是却让人产生了恐怖的感觉。

13

NOTICE
THANK YOU
FOR NOTICING THIS
NEW NOTICE
YOUR NOTICING IT
HAS BEEN NOTED
AND WILL BE REPORTED TO THE
AUTHORITIES

旅游景点幽默告示。
感谢注意新通告。
你的注意已得到关注，并将上报当局。
这类告示都是为了给游客解乏而设立的。

14

DROP YOUR PANTS HERE AND YOU WILL RECEIVE PROMPT ATTENTION

裤店内的告示。商家想表达：**裤子放在这里，我们马上就会为你服务**。但是句子也可以理解为：脱下裤子，马上就会有人注意到你。

15

Parking For Drive-Thru Service Only

快餐厅窗户上说明。**只为即买即走司机停放车辆**。既然即买即走，那还停放什么车辆呢！

三十九、其他

1

| THIS PROPERTY OWNED AND MANAGED BY **Northland** Investment Corporation | 房屋外悬挂牌，表示本房屋由北地投资公司拥有和管理。 |

2

| MASSACHUSETTS BAY LINE EXECUTIVE and ACCOUNTING OFFICE ROWES WHARF | 马萨诸塞海岸线执行官和会计师办公室（码头说明牌。ROWES WHARF（罗氏码头）是波士顿的一个码头，游船可以从这里出发沿着海岸线观光。） |

3

| **NOTICE** Issuance of hot checks or stopping payment on checks for traffic, parking fines or boot fees may result in a warrant being issued for your arrest. The outcome is depicted above. Rice University Police Department | 公 告 禁止使用无效支票或者停付支票来支付交通罚款、停车罚款或者锁定车费，否则将签发拘捕证。 详细结果请参见上图 （公告上显示一个正趴在铁窗后坐牢的人）（警察局的告示。hot checks是指各种已经失效的支票；boot fees指警察为了将违章停放车辆固定住，用一铁圈固定在车轮上而产生的费用。） |

4

| FREE BROCHURE—
PLEASE TAKE ONE | 免费小册子 ——
请自取一份
（艺术展览上免费领取小册子的说明） |

5

FILE STORAGE at the ERC

1. You can store files temporarily to the desktop folder 'SaveWorkHere' on any of the ERC's computers. However, files will be deleted on the first Monday of each month unless you have filed a specific file storage request.
2. If you are working on a long-term project and need a longer file storage period, please ask the ERC staff for file storage options.
3. If you are capturing video footage that is longer than 60 minutes, please consult the ERC staff for storage issues.

Should you have any questions, please ask ERC staff.

电子资源中心文件存储

1. 用户可在电子资源中心的任意一台计算机桌面文件夹中临时存储文件（'SaveWorkHere'），但是文件会在每个月的第一个星期一被删除，除非你提出具体的文件存储要求。
2. 如果你在研究一个长期项目并且需要一个比较长的文件存储期，请咨询电子资源中心的工作人员。
3. 如果需要获取的视频内容超过60分钟，请咨询电子资源中心的工作人员。

有问题，请咨询电子资源中心的工作人员。

（电子资源中心有关文件存储说明）

6

| PRIVATE
RESIDENCE | 私　宅
（私宅免打扰说明。一些私人住宅因为装修豪华或具有特色，经常会受到外界干扰，于是就在自家的院门上挂牌，谢绝参观。） |

7

Replacing Punch Pins

Loosen punch holding screw and remove
Insert new punch pin and hold in place with fingers
Tighten holding screw

更换订书钉

将订书器螺母松开；
插入新的订书钉并用手指压到位；
旋紧固定螺母。

（订书器说明）

三十九、其他

8

Replacing Cutting Discs
Turn punch upside down
Depress button with finger
Turn punch over and remove disc
Insert new disc and press in place

更换圆盘切刀
将订书器翻转过来；
用手指下压按钮；
将订书器翻过来取出圆盘刀；
放入新的圆盘刀再按压到位。
（订书器说明）

9

Maximum Capacity: 75 Sheets

最大装订量：75页（订书器说明）

10

PATENTED
This product is covered by at least one of the following U. S. Patents: 353,250;322,702; 322,348;304,632.
TOLL FREE: (800)368-2573

专利产品
本产品至少含有以下美国专利中的一项：353,250; 322,702; 322,348; 304,632。
免费电话(800)368-2573。
（产品专利申明）

11

We Ship Anywhere in the world.
We can Customize Art To Match Your Décor.
Anything can be Painted in Any Size.
We Display Work from over 250 Artists from all over the World.

我们可以将作品运往世界各地；
我们可以定制与你的装饰相配的艺术作品；
任何大小的东西我们都能绘制；
我们展示全世界250位艺术家的作品。
（画店告示）

12

MAGIC CHINESE BACK RUB
10 Min. $10 (Half Body)
15 Min. $15 (Half Body)
20 Min. $20 (Half Body)
30 Min. $25 (Whole Body)

华人在美国开设的按摩店价格说明。**神奇的中国式背部推拿**：根据时间长短收取不同费用，另外所揉搓的部位包括半身、全身，有的还附带足底按

1 Hour　　$50 (Whole Body　w/Reflexology)
1.5 Hour　$70 (Whole Body　w/ Reflexology)
2 Hour　　$90 (Whole Body　w/ Reflexology)
REFLEXOLOGY
15 Min.　$15
30 Min.　$30
60 Min.　$60

Gift Card Available
Open Everyday
Walk-In Welcome

Warning: The above procedure is not suited for people who has heart problem, high blood pressure, operation, or pregnant women, and others special medical conditions. If you have any of those conditions, please notify our staff before the procedure(s).

摩。另有单独的足底按摩项目，收费标准分别为15分钟15美元、30分钟30美元和60分钟60美元。这里还可以办理优惠卡，每天开放，不需预约。注意事项：以上服务项目不适宜患有心脏病、高血压、手术、怀孕以及其他特殊疾病的人。如有上述病况，按摩前需告知。美国有些店的招牌上会打出walk-in的字样，表示不需预约。在美国许多场所如医院等，没有预约，得不到即时的服务。

13

THE ROCK-RULES & REGULATIONS TO CLIMB

Everyone climbs at his or her own risk.
- We do not refund any money.
  —no exceptions—
  Our service is to put the harness, and help the climbers get to the top.
- The climbers have 2 tries to get to the top. They can choose the stations they want to climb. Once they touch the ground, they loose their tries. If the climbers do not want to try twice no one else can have his or her second try. The climbers have to stay on the climbing route of the station they choose.
- Do not hold the buzzer.

攀岩规则
攀爬风险自担。
- 不退款，无任何例外；我们协助攀爬者系好绳索，攀爬到顶。
- 攀爬者可有两次机会攀爬到顶端，也可选择攀爬的站点；一旦触地，即放弃机会；攀爬者如不想尝试两次，他人不可使用另一次；攀爬者必须沿着所选路线攀爬。
- 请勿抓住蜂鸣器不放。
- 攀爬者下落时必须蹬离墙体2英尺以上。

- On their way down the climbers have to kick off the wall no more than 2 feet away from the wall.
- When the climbers hit the ground, they have to wait to be unhooked by the person in charge, attempting to unlock the harness or release the hook by themselves could result in serious damage to the climbers.

攀爬者触地后，需要等待主管人员解开钩子；自行解开绳索或松开钩子可能会严重受伤。
（攀岩场馆外张贴的告示）

14

FOAM BEVERAGE CUPS AND THE ENVIRONMENT

- Dart foam cups have never been made using CFCs.
- Foam cups insulate better than paper cups. When you consider the fact that consumers frequently use two paper cups when drinking hot beverages like coffee, the environmental advantages of using foam cups are even more evident.
- Foam cups make up less than 1 percent, by weight and volume, of material generated and/ or disposed of in the solid waste stream.
- Foam cups use less energy and are cleaner to produce than paper cups, according to articles in Consumer's Research and Environmental Management by Dr. Martin D. Jocking, a chemistry professor at the University of Victoria in British Columbia.
- Polystyrene foam is recycled in select programs in North America. For information on foam cup recycling, please call Dart Container Corporation at 1-800-288-CARE, or visit our web site at www.dartcontainer.com.

泡沫塑料饮料杯和环境

- Dart公司泡沫塑料杯制作从未使用氯氟烃（CFC）；
- 泡沫塑料杯绝缘比纸杯好；如果考虑到消费者在饮用像咖啡一类的热饮料时使用两个纸杯，那么使用泡沫杯的环境优势就更为明显了；
- 按重量和体积，泡沫塑料杯少于固体废物产生和处理的1%；
- 根据BC省维多利亚大学化学教授马丁·D.乔金关于消费者研究和环境管理的文章，泡沫塑料杯的生产比纸杯耗能更少，更清洁；
- 聚苯乙烯泡沫在北美精选项目中回收利用，欲知泡沫杯的回收利用，请拨打 Dart Container 公司（1-800-288-CARE）或者访问网站www.dartcontainer.com。

（饮料杯包装袋上的环保说明）

15

| WEIGHT INSTRUCTIONS
Stand Still on Scale
Deposit Coin
25¢ Quarters Only | 磅秤使用说明
在磅秤上静立
投入硬币
只可使用25美分硬币
（磅秤使用说明） |

16

| WOMAN'S CITY CLUB
UNVEILED AUGUST 16, 1925
MARKER PLACED APRIL, 1962 | 女性城市俱乐部
1925年8月16日揭幕，
1962年4月设立标志牌。
（女性城市俱乐部说明牌） |

17

PACIFIC TIME ZONE

太平洋时区

（美国高速公路上时间区域标志说明。美国横跨西五区至西十区，共六个时区。每个时区对应一个标准时间，从东向西分别为东部时间(EST)(西五区时间)、中部时间(CST)(西六区时间)、山地时间(MST)(西七区时间)、太平洋时间(西部时间)(PST)(西八区时间)、阿拉斯加时间(AKST)(西九区时间)和夏威夷时间(HST)(西十区时间)，按照"东早西晚"的规律，各区之间递减一小时。美国的时区界限并不完全按照经线划分，基本上照顾各州的自然边界。）

18

Who let the Watts out?

| UNLESS ENERGY PRICES FALL DRAMATICALLY, RICE UNIVERSITY'S UTILITY EXPENDITURES COULD INCREASE BY 40 PERCENT, OR $4 | **HOW YOU CAN HELP**
Keep windows and exit doors closed.
Set your thermostat to 76 degrees |

MILLION, BEGINNING THIS SUMMER. Rice's Department of Facilities Engineering and Planning (FE&P) is working with the Office of the President and other campus leaders to develop and implement energy-use guidelines and measures to reduce consumption across campus.

But they will need your help in this effort.

when air-conditioning is needed. Never use a space healer, especially to counteract overcooling.

Report overcooling, overheating, or other energy waste to the Facilities Service Center at extension 2458 or to Housing and Dining at extension 5445 for problems in the residential colleges.

You Have the Power!

This message brought to you by FE&P. For more information about A Call to Conservation, please visit the Sustainability at Rice website at http:// sustainability. rice. edu/.

是谁让电流失？

除非能源价格大幅度下降，否则莱斯大学的用电量会在这个夏天增加40%，也就是增加4百万美元。

莱斯大学的设施工程和规划处正在和校长办公室和学校其他管理人员一起研究和实施能源利用指导方案和措施来减少全校的用电量，但这种努力需要你助力。

你能做的包括：将窗户和大门紧闭；使用空调时，将温控器调至华氏76度；切勿使用太空治疗仪，尤其是用来应对空调过冷；如果出现过凉、过热或者其他能源浪费的情况，请报告分机2458设施服务中心；所住学院问题拨打5445分机报告住房膳食科。

你有能力！

本信息由FE&P发布。需要更多有关"节能运动"的信息，请浏览莱斯大学网址：http:// sustainability. rice. edu/。

（大学校园内节约用电的告示。为了提高倡议的鼓动性，还使用了英语双关的修辞方式：你有这个能力。其中的power可以表示"能力"，也可以表示"能源"、"电力"。）

19　All posters will be recycled after 7 days　　所有海报都将在7天后再循环（告知张贴人一份海报能够保留多长时间）

新世纪美国公示语1000例

20

For rentals of **STROLLERS, WHEELCHAIRS** And **ELECTRIC CONVENIENCE VEHICLES at DISNEYLAND**
Please visit our temporary location outside of the Disneyland Main entrance near the Kennel Club.

如需在迪斯尼乐园内租用童车、轮椅以及其他电动便利车,请在养犬爱好者俱乐部附近,迪斯尼大门外的临时点联系。

(迪斯尼乐园内为方便家长带儿童游玩提供租车服务。在美国一些公园、博物馆等游乐场所,会给带孩子的家长提供租车一类的服务,而且就在入口处显眼的地方。)

21

RETURN POSTAGE GUARANTEED
RICE UNIVERSITY
6100 MAIN STREET
HOUSTON, TEXAS 77005-1892
THIS CARD IS PROPERTY OF RICE UNIVERSITY AND MUST BE RETURNED UPON REQUEST.

AUTHORIZED SIGNATURE
DO NOT WRITE YOUR PIN NUMBER ON THIS CARD

Unauthorized or fraudulent use of this card is a violation of law. If found mail to : Nevada Ebt, P.O. Box 20100, Carson city NV 89711-0100

回信邮资担保
得克萨斯州休斯敦市大街6100号
本卡为莱斯大学财产,需要时必须退回。

授权人签字(即使用卡的本人签字)

非本人或者冒用此卡是违法行为。如果捡到此卡,请邮寄以下地址(略)。
(莱斯大学校园卡正反面上的文字说明)

22

Requests for Reports

Requests for reports (Accident or Incident) will be honored:
- After five (5) business days that report was filed.
- A five dollar ($5) charge is due upon receipt.
  Check or Money Order payable to Rice University
- Only limited information except for Criminal Justice use.

三十九、其他

索取报告

事故或事件报告索取兑现将在：
- 报告入档5个工作日后；
- 5美元费用收到后，请将支票或者汇款单支付到莱斯大学；
- 所能够提供的信息有限，除非用于刑事审判。

（警察局内关于索取事故或事件报告请求的说明）

23

10¢ black & white
25¢ color
for black &white printouts,
select printer HP 4250n
for color printouts,
select printer HP 4650

CASH ONLY for printouts

Due to the high cost of ink, we must charge 10 cents for black and white printouts and 25 cents for color. Since our printers are not on the Owlnet printing network, printing cards are not applicable at the ERC. **Please pay cash at the service desk.**
Should you have any questions, please ask ERC staff.

电子资料室有关材料打印的说明。打印黑白资料10美分；彩色25美分。打印黑白资料请选择惠普4250n型打印机；打印彩色请选择惠普4650型打印机。且打印只能使用现金。由于油墨成本高，须收取10美分打印黑白材料，25美分打印彩色材料。由于打印机没有与本校打印系统联网，因此打印卡在电子资源中心无法使用，请在服务台支付现金。如果有任何问题，咨询电子资源中心工作人员。ERC等于Electronic Resources Center（电子资源中心）；Owlnet是莱斯大学的计算机系统名称。

24

SORRY NOT A WINNER!
DO YOURSELF A FAVOR, TRY AGAIN!
"Real Fact" # 444
The Statue of Liberty Wears a Size 879 Sandal.

对不起，未中奖！
帮帮自己，再试一次！
第444号"真正的事实"：
自由女神穿的拖鞋鞋号为879码。
（美国自由女神像周围一个抽奖瓶盖中的文字说明。在搞抽奖的同时还不忘宣传自己领地内的旅游知识。）

25

Lottery: It may change your life.

彩票：可能会改变你的生活
（彩票购买处提示）

26. **ATTENTION LOTTERY PLAYERS:** Help is available for you or someone you know who has a gambling problem.

彩票购买者请注意:
我们可以为您或者您认识的有赌博问题的人提供帮助。
(彩票购买处的文字提示。彩票发售处还提供心里咨询，以免发生不该发生的事情。)

27. **CLOTHING OPTIONAL BEYOND THIS POINT**

超过该点，衣着自便。
(海滨浴场告示。美国的一些海滩边常有一些标示clothing optional的游泳场所，在这里游泳者的衣着是半开放的。)

28. **ATTENTION BEYOND THIS POINT YOU MAY ENCOUNTER NUDE BATHERS**

小心!
越过此点可能遇到裸泳者
(进入裸泳沙滩前的文字提示)

29. **NUDE BEACH SWIMSUITS OPTIONAL VOYEURISM PROHIBITED! ABSOLUTELY NO PEEKING, STARING, LEERING, OR OUTRIGHT GAWKING! VIOLATORS WILL BE REMOVED FORTHWITH**

裸泳沙滩
泳衣自便
禁止观淫癖
严禁偷看、盯视、斜视或十足呆视!
违者将被清出沙滩。
(裸泳沙滩的文字提示)

30. **WHEELCHAIR RAMP**

轮椅专用坡道标识

31. **Accessible Wheelchair Ramp Is Located Behind Door**

轮椅坡道位于门后
(大楼入口处说明)

32. **RESERVED FOR WHEELCHAIR USE ONLY**

只能通行轮椅
(大楼外通道上的说明)

三十九、其他

33

Great Clips	大剪刀理发店
HAIRCUTS	理发
Adults $11	成人11美元
Kids/ Seniors $9	儿童/老人9美元
	（理发店户外告示）

34

Lens Cloths
Pre-Moistened
Net content 1 cloth
Zeiss Lens Cloths safely and quickly clean any lens, especially those with Zeiss anti-reflective multi-layer coatings. High-tech ammonia-free formula cleans effectively without leaving streaks or residue. Designed for single use.
Directions: Remove folded cloth from packet and lightly brush away dust and grit from lens surface. Unfold lens cloth and wipe surface until clean and dry.
CAUTION: KEEP OUT OF REACH OF CHILDREN.
Not for use on contact lenses. Contains Isopropyl alcohol.

镜头布（湿型），净含量1块。
蔡斯镜头布清洗镜头安全迅速，尤其适用于防反射多层膜镜头。高技术不含氨配方，能够有效清洁镜头不留印渍，一次性使用。
使用说明：将折叠镜头布从袋中取出，轻擦镜头表面灰层和颗粒，打开镜头布擦拭表面直至干净干燥。
注意事项：远离儿童放置。请勿擦拭隐形眼镜。内含异丙醇。
（蔡斯镜头纸说明文字）

35

Important Information About Procedures For Opening A New Account
To help the government fight the funding of terrorism and money laundering activities, Federal law requires all financial institutions to obtain, verify, and record information that identifies each person who opens an account.
What this means to you: When you open an account, we will ask for the following information, as appropriate—your name, address, date of birth, and other information that will allow us to identify you. We may also ask to see your driver's license or other identifying documents.

开新账户程序重要提示
为了帮助政府打击恐怖主义融资和洗钱行为，联邦政府法律要求所有金融机构索取、核实并记录新开户人的信息。
对客户就意味着：在开账户的时候，我们会要求你提供以下正确信息：姓名、地址、出生日期以及其他能够证明你身份的信息。我们也可能要求查验你的驾驶证或其他身份证件。
（银行对新开账户的说明）